PARTISAN BONDS

POLITICAL REPUTATIONS AND LEGISLATIVE ACCOUNTABILITY

Political scientists have long painted American voters' dependence on partisan cues at the ballot box as a discouraging consequence of their overall ignorance about politics. Taking on this conventional wisdom, Jeffrey D. Grynaviski advances the provocative theory that voters instead rely on these cues because party brand names provide credible information about how politicians are likely to act in office, despite the weakness of formal party organization in the United States. Among the important empirical implications of his theory, which he carefully supports with rigorous data analysis, are that voter uncertainty about a party's issue positions varies with the level of party unity it exhibits in government, that party preferences in the electorate are strongest among the most certain voters, and that party brand names have meaningful consequences for the electoral strategies of party leaders and individual candidates for office.

Jeffrey D. Grynaviski received his doctorate in political science from Duke University in 2002. Since that time he has been Assistant Professor in Political Science at the University of Chicago. He was a recipient of the prestigious George A. and Eliza Gardner Howard Foundation Fellowship for the 2006–7 academic year. His previous research has been published in a range of scholarly journals, including the *American Political Science Review*, *Journal of Politics*, *Political Analysis*, *Journal of Theoretical Politics*, *Party Politics*, and *Dubose Review*.

T0370718

POLITICAL ECONOMY OF INSTITUTIONS AND DECISIONS

Series Editors

Stephen Ansolabehere, Harvard University
Jeffry Frieden, Harvard University

Founding Editors

James E. Alt, Harvard University
Douglass C. North, Washington University of St. Louis

Other Books in the Series

Continued following Index

PARTISAN BONDS

Political Reputations and Legislative Accountability

JEFFREY D. GRYNAVISKI

The University of Chicago

CAMBRIDGE
UNIVERSITY PRESS

CAMBRIDGE UNIVERSITY PRESS
Cambridge, New York, Melbourne, Madrid, Cape Town,
Singapore, São Paulo, Delhi, Mexico City

Cambridge University Press
The Edinburgh Building, Cambridge CB2 8RU, UK

Published in the United States of America by Cambridge University Press, New York

www.cambridge.org
Information on this title: www.cambridge.org/9780521757508

First published 2010
First paperback edition 2013

A catalogue record for this publication is available from the British Library

Library of Congress Cataloguing in Publication Data

Grynaviski, Jeffrey D., 1975–
Partisan bonds : political reputations and legislative accountability /
Jeffrey D. Grynaviski.
     p.   cm.
Includes bibliographical references and index.
ISBN 978-0-521-76406-3 (hardback)
1. Political parties – United States.   2. Voting – United States.   3. United
States. Congress – Elections.   4. United States – Politics and government.
I. Title.
JK2265.G79   2010
324.973 – dc22   2009040514

ISBN 978-0-521-75750-8 Paperback

For Nicole

Contents

List of Tables

xi

Acknowledgments

Political parties are organizations created by politicians to facilitate their collection of rents from holding office, often at the expense of ordinary citizens. *Partisan Bonds* is the product of my efforts to explain why those ordinary citizens do not reject, at the polls, the politicians who belong to such an organization. I began to work on this subject when pursuing my doctorate at Duke University. While there, I benefited tremendously from the help of my teachers and classmates. My dissertation committee of John Aldrich (the chair), John Brehm, Scott de Marchi, and Mike Munger provided incredible guidance and support for my research and for my career. I am also indebted to my classmates at Duke, especially Mike Ensley, John Griffin, Renan Levine, Jenn Merolla, and Brian Newman who provided a great deal of constructive advice during the writing of my dissertation.

My work on this book continued at Chicago where I acquired numerous additional debts. Among my colleagues at Chicago, I would like to single out Chris Berry, Carles Boix, John Brehm (again), Michael Dawson, Sean Gailmard, Will Howell, Luis Medina, Jeff Milyo, Roger Myerson, Eric Oliver, Jong Hee Park, Boris Shor, Betsy Sinclair, and Duncan Snidal for their friendship and almost unrelenting criticism. Michael Dawson merits special thanks for his close reading of the entire manuscript as it neared completion.

I gained a great deal of insight from exchanges with Steve Ansolabehere, Gary Cox, Bernie Grofman, Dave Rohde, Steve Smith, and Mike Ting while the manuscript was in various stages of disrepair. I would especially like to thank Steve Ansolabehere and Dave Rohde – as I struggled to bring my book to its completion – for making demands about what I must do to ensure that the final product came close to reaching its potential and for their advice about how to get there.

Acknowledgments

I would like to thank my research assistants, including Minnie Go, Shang Ha, Kateri Somrak, and Jon Rogowski, for their help. I am grateful for the financial support provided by the Howard Foundation, which provided me with the opportunity to take a year of leave that was crucial to the success of the project, and to the Harris School of Public Policy for providing me with a home for that year. Excerpts from Chapters 3 and 4 first appeared in my paper "A Bayesian Learning Model with Applications to Party Identification." The paper is published online at http://online.sagepub.com. The final definitive version of this paper has been published in *Journal of Theoretical Politics*, vol. 18, 2006, by Sage Publications Ltd., All rights reserved. I would also like to thank Eric Crahan and his colleagues at Cambridge University Press for their encouragement, patience, and professionalism.

Most of all, I would like to thank my family. For too long, my mood at home has been affected by how I felt about my progress on this book. I am thankful for my children who lifted my spirits when I was discouraged and for their patience when my writing kept me away from them. I promise that next Saturday will be a "stay-home day" for Daddy too. I am also thankful to my wife, Nicole. She has stuck with me every step of the way, from the day I first sat down to work on my dissertation proposal to the penning of these acknowledgments. I don't know how she put up with me during the years in between, but I am deeply grateful that she did. I am so lucky to have her by my side.

I

Introduction

The success of representative democracy as a political system arguably hinges on the ability of the electorate to replace elected officials who fail to act in the public interest with others who will. This sort of democratic accountability requires (1) that ordinary citizens be able to pin credit or blame on the correct set of incumbent officials for their policy choices and (2) that citizens must reasonably believe that challengers will perform better in office. Neither of these conditions is trivial to satisfy. Identifying whom to hold responsible for government performance is virtually impossible, because passing laws is a team effort where individual contributions are often unobservable and disagreement among legislators makes it inappropriate to hold the entire chamber accountable. Meanwhile, challengers, by virtue of being out of office, have a difficult time providing credible signals about how they would act if they were in an incumbent's shoes, especially in light of the fact that voters know that office-motivated candidates have incentives to say whatever it takes to win elections.

Classic scholarship identifies political parties as offering a possible solution to both of these problems (Lowell 1913; Schattschneider 1942). Woodrow Wilson (1900), for one, argues that in cabinet governments (i.e., the Westminster system), parties act as unified teams because party leaders have the ability to dissolve the government and to expel defectors from the party (see also Huber 1996; Diermeier and Feddersen 1998). In this way, the majority party assumes collective responsibility for the organization and operation of government, thereby allowing voters to hold its members accountable, as a group, for their performance in office (Palmer 1995). Meanwhile, the minority party, waiting in the wings, informs voters about how it would act if in government through its pattern of support and opposition to the majority party's program. Because it has the same capacity to whip its members as the majority in the event of its election, the minority party's reputation provides the electorate with credible information about how challengers tied to the party would act in office (Downs 1957).

Many of these same studies also argue that in the American system of Congressional government, political parties cannot provide for the exercise of collective responsibility (cf. Ranney 1954). The committee system, which allows powerful chairmen accountable only to their own districts to dominate the legislative process, prevents the great number of citizens from holding elected officials accountable for the choice of public policies that may affect them (Wilson 1900). Meanwhile, sitting members of Congress (MCs) have the freedom to put together legislative records that differentiate themselves from the party and to campaign on the basis of private brand names that appeal to local constituents, thereby depriving voters of any motivation for holding individual politicians responsible for their party's performance in office (Burns 1949).

Over the past two decades, scholars have examined how political parties have adapted to the United States' constitutional structures so as to provide for reasonable levels of accountability in Congressional government. In particular, considerable progress has been made in understanding how Congressional parties overcome the collective action problems inherent in the team production of public policy (Aldrich 1995; Cox and McCubbins 1993, 2005). However, to date, even the best answers to the question of how parties provide credible information about the attributes of opposition candidates and incumbents with poorly developed private brand names still rely on the assumption, more appropriate to understanding party competition in the Westminster system than in the United States, that voters have a close knowledge of the parties' whip systems and the penalties that party organizations impose on their members for failing to toe the party line (Ashworth and Bueno de Mesquita 2008; Snyder and Ting 2002, 2003). The purpose of this book is to provide the reader with a better understanding of how parties in the United States perform this function necessary for accountable governance based on a realistic assessment of public knowledge.

My argument is that American political parties perform the role of a surety (i.e., a third-party guarantor, such as a bail bondsman) who offers a credible signal to voters about the performance of its candidates in office when individual candidates cannot. A party performs this function by developing a reputation as being an organization whose members, although not fully committed to a specific platform, support a broader set of principles about the range of acceptable public policies. Political parties value this reputation, in turn, because it helps their candidates to win elections. Thus, party nominations are akin to the issuance of performance bonds, in the sense that the organization places its ability to continue to benefit from its reputation in jeopardy in the event that too many party members fail to live up to constituents' expectations. Voters who recognize that the national parties value their reputations therefore find party affiliations to be credible signals of a candidate's likely contribution to public policy, thereby allowing the national parties to promote accountable governance despite the weakness of formal party organizations in the United States. In this way, political parties make representative democracy viable in the United States despite a Constitutional design that otherwise renders responsible governance impossible.

The argument that party affiliations provide credible information to voters about a politician's influence on legislative outcome draws from and contributes to three important literatures in political science. First, it has implications for research on why voters draw upon party images when conducting candidate evaluations. Previous research on the subject, drawing primarily from concepts in social cognitive psychology (see Fiske and Taylor 1991), explains voters' reliance on party brand names as a rational response to the cost of gathering and processing relevant information specific to each candidate they confront at the ballot box (Downs 1957; Feldman and Conover 1983). One important theme in this literature is that large numbers of people hold stereotypical images about the policies supported by Democratic and Republican party candidates that they draw upon to develop theories about a politician's issue positions or personal characteristics, in much the same way that consumers hold stereotypical images about the types of goods and services they associate with a firm's brand name (Conover and Feldman 1989; Desart 1995; Hamill and Blake 1985; Hayes 2005; Popkin 1991; Trilling 1976). Another theme in this literature is that to maintain cognitive efficiency, many people continue to rely on these stereotypes even when candidate-specific information is made available (such as during a high-salience Presidential election campaign or in a controlled laboratory setting) and that information contradicts the preexisting stereotype (Conover and Feldman 1989; Rahn 1993). The conclusion drawn from the literature regarding the former finding is that the quality of voters' decisions is, in many cases, made worse by their use of party brand names because people trust these stereotypes rather than the more accurate and available (and contradictory) candidate-specific information (Bartels 1996; Lau and Redlawsk 2001).

This book adds to the literature on why voters value candidate partisanship as a decision-making cue by noting that it is the credibility of the information conveyed that explains why people use brand names when trying to minimize the cost of collecting and processing information. Thus, this book provides an explanation for why voters are more dependent on party affiliations than on other easily available cues such as race (Reeves 1997) or gender (McDermott 1997) when conducting candidate evaluations. The reason offered is that voters prefer to use credible information when they cast their votes and that they believe that a candidate's party affiliation provides more credible information about her characteristics than, say, ethnicity or gender. Along these same lines, this book explains why it may be rational for people to ignore or forget relevant candidate-specific information that is given to them. The basic idea is that if voters believe that it is in a candidate's best interest to mislead them about how she will act in the event of her election, then it is foolish for them to take a campaign promise to be a credible commitment to a future course of action. Thus, in the absence of some sort of credible signal from a candidate about how she will act, it is rational for voters to use information from the party rather than an individual candidate's campaign promises.

PARTISAN ELECTORAL TIDES AND
COLLECTIVE ACCOUNTABILITY

Second, the arguments in this book provide a rationale for why, given the candidate-centered nature of American elections, there exist national partisan electoral tides, as documented by researchers such as Stokes (1965), Claggett, Flanigan, and Zingale (1984), and Cox and McCubbins (1993). Previous explanations for why the electoral fortunes of a party's members tend to rise and fall in unison have identified macro-level variables, such as national economic conditions and Presidential approval, to be key predictors (e.g., Tufte 1978; Jacobson 2004).

National partisan tides are somewhat difficult to reconcile with the classic theory of candidate-centered elections, because it would seem that incumbent politicians on both sides of the aisle would routinely be in

4

trouble, especially when times are bad. Electoral challengers could always claim that they would have behaved exactly the same way as the incumbent on issues that were appealing to local voters, but that they would have voted differently on issues where the incumbent cast votes that were less popular back home. Because the challenger can point to previous votes as evidence about how the incumbent will act on these more controversial issues, the incumbent lacks the flexibility to precisely match her campaign promises with district preferences, and challengers have great advantages at the polls (Enelow and Munger 1993). As a result, one would expect anti-incumbent tides (or at least regular challenger successes coming from both sides of the aisle) rather than partisan tides that improve the electoral fortunes of one party and worsen those of its opponent. For example, in the 2006 Congressional elections, it is striking that Republicans who voted with President Bush in support of his Iraq policies faced electoral retaliation at the polls, whereas the seats of House Democrats who supported his policies remained safe.

One part of the explanation for partisan tides in a system of candidate-centered elections, which this book shares with the extant literature, is that the electorate has a shared sense nationwide as to whether times are good or bad and which party's policies are responsible for these outcomes (cf. Erikson, Mackuen, and Stimson 2002). The original contribution of this book is to explain why attribution of responsibility is partisan in nature, given that it is often true that politicians on both side of the aisle may have supported these policies.

Its argument is that challengers' campaign promises are taken to be credible only if those promises are consistent with their party's reputation. Thus, if times are good, ruling-party members should have safe seats in the general election: members who vote with their party, because they get to take credit for their actions, and members who vote with the opposition, because opposition-party challengers will have difficulty offering credible commitments to support popular ruling-party policies. In contrast, opposition-party members will be vulnerable to ruling-party challengers in the general election if times are good: opposition members who vote with their party on controversial issues will be vulnerable because they opposed the policies that were well received by the public, and ruling-party challengers could campaign on the basis of partisan appeals; opposition members who voted with the ruling party might also be vulnerable because ruling-party challengers would be expected ex ante to support the same desirable policies. A symmetric set of ideas applies to the case when times are bad, where voters are pushed to vote against ruling-party members and to support opposition-party candidates. Thus, an important consequence of challengers' reliance on party brand names is that they cannot credibly commit themselves to act contrary to party principles, which means that elections can perform the role of a referendum on the ruling party's policies despite the candidate-centered nature of political organization in the United States.

INCENTIVES FOR PARTY ORGANIZATION

Third, this book speaks to the literature concerning the incentives that politicians have to create a party control apparatus in the United States. The standard view is that the incentives to create a party hierarchy with the power to discipline group members are extremely weak (cf. Krehbiel 1998; Mayhew 1974a). To begin, the Constitution provides no institutional powers (especially the ability to dissolve the government) that party leaders might use to enforce party discipline. In fact, the great historian Richard Hofstadter (1969) characterizes the United States as having "A Constitution Against Parties," a claim strongly supported by the writings of the Founders themselves (cf. Federalist 10, Federalist 51). Instead of establishing party hierarchies in Congress, the Constitution gives all MCs equal power. Furthermore, rather than providing incentives for MCs to cede some of their independence to a *Legislative Leviathan*, the Founders believed that by assigning each MC a constituency with distinct interests, legislators would oppose the creation of hierarchies that could force themselves to cast hard votes contrary to their parochial concerns.

Based on previous scholarship and the new insights provided by this book, there are three sets of incentives for the creation of partisan institutions to regulate party elites' behavior, with the strength of the party control apparatus in Washington varying over time as party members weigh its benefits against its costs. One such motivation is to ensure that members of Congress are able to realize gains from legislative bargaining. The central concern in this line of research is that because of the heterogeneity of legislators' preferences in government, MCs must trade their votes in favor of policies that are of little benefit to themselves or their constituents for the votes of other members on policies beneficial to themselves. Legislators hoping to realize the gains from trade associated with this kind of logroll benefit from the creation of partisan institutions that help to enforce these sorts of agreements (Aldrich 1995; Rohde 1991; Schwartz 1977).

A second incentive for the creation of a party hierarchy in government is to solve the collective dilemma created by the presence of a shared party label (Aldrich 1995; Cox and McCubbins 1993, 2005; Evans 2001; Grynaviski 2006; Lipinski 2005; Snyder and Ting 2002). Cox and McCubbins (1993) argue that this shared brand name is subject to a "commons problem": each party member represents a district that prefers that their representative deliver a certain set of local goods and services (e.g., roads, farm subsidies) that are not of national benefit, but if each politician delivers to her district the optimal set of policies locally, then the party will develop a reputation for spending and taxing too much. This book argues that party brand names are subject to another kind of commons problem in that if party members come into excessive conflict over public policy choices, they create uncertainty about the attributes of party members. With a risk-averse electorate, this greater uncertainty harms candidates who depend on the party's brand name to win elections. Politicians therefore benefit from the creation of institutions to protect their shared brand name.

A third incentive for politicians to agree to the development of a party hierarchy is to solve the adverse selection problem that politicians wish to address when they seek office. The problem of adverse selection that politicians confront is that they possess private information that is not known to the voter about their own issue preferences and the legislation they expect to advance once in office. Building on the basic intuitions of Downs (1957) and elaborated by Snyder and Ting (2002), this book argues that party brand names provide a possible remedy to this problem: if voters believe that the national party suffers a penalty if it is linked to too many politicians who prove to be out of step with the organization ideologically, and the party has a reputation for electing politicians only on the political left or right, giving rise to the appearance that it can regulate member behavior, then voters may rationally infer that a candidate's party affiliation is a credible signal of her political attributes. Politicians early in their careers therefore value institutions that protect party brand names, because this solution to the adverse selection problem improves their own electoral prospects. More established party members also value institutions to solve the adverse selection problem, because they value majority-party status, which requires the current majority party to replenish the ranks of retiring politicians with electable replacements, and the minority party to field credible challengers. Fortunately for American voters, the solution parties provide to the adverse selection problem improves voters' ability to hold elected officials accountable for their performance in office.

All models of party government share in common the perspective that the national electorate's choice of a ruling party has consequences for the policies adopted by the government. If a liberal party captures control of government, the policies it adopts will be to the left of center. Conversely, if a conservative party captures control of government, the policies it adopts will be to the right of center.

An adequate theory of party government that helps to make sense of the American political system must address two sets of questions. First, it must explain why ordinary citizens routinely vote for the candidates of one of the two major political parties. If those votes translate into policy outcomes to the left or right of the political center, as models of party government require, then voters at the political center, and everyone on the losing side of the policy space, are made worse off by its actions. These groups together constitute a majority and have the power to vote against the majority party's candidates in retaliation against its failure to respect the wishes of the political center, thereby denying the organization procedural control over the legislature. Yet, they do not. An adequate theory of party government must explain why.

Second, it must explain why it makes sense for voters to infer that the election of members of a liberal party will contribute to the passage of policies to the left of center and that the election of members of a conservative party will contribute to the passage of policies to the right of center. In providing such an explanation, the challenge is to demonstrate that a ruling party might be able to deliver on its policy commitments even though its members, once in office, have the constitutional authority to cast votes in opposition to their party's program. This applies especially to the contemporary American political system, where party leaders do not have control over the slating of candidates for office and, therefore, the career prospects of their back-benchers.

Chapter 2 sketches an answer to both of these questions. It begins by arguing that the electorate accedes to the majority party's exertions on behalf of noncentrist public policies because of the benefits that it receives from a system of party government. It argues that in a political system without parties, a number of seats in the legislature will be captured by politicians who place ideological considerations above their prospects for reelection, with the result being that the government adopts policies at odds with the preferences of the political center. So long as the ruling party can credibly promise that the election of its candidates to national office will result in something less extreme than that observed in a political system without parties, voters prefer a system of party government to the alternative.

Having established a rationale for party government, the chapter proceeds to explain how voters and politicians might receive the benefits of a system of party government in the absence of "responsible" parties. The argument, which is developed in the second half of Chapter 2, is that a political party performs this function by acting as a surety, or a third-party guarantor, on behalf of its candidates, similar to the way that a firm might enter into a brand licensing agreement when it introduces a new product. The basic idea is that someone selecting among experience goods knows that if they choose a product or candidate that is unsatisfactory, the brand name of the firm or party loses value even though the parent organization is not in direct control of the attributes of the object of choice. Thus, decision makers who believe that a parent organization values its brand name should also infer that it takes steps to monitor the quality of its affiliates, even though they do not actually observe this monitoring.

Applied to the study of politics, it is argued that a political party develops a reputation for being linked to a set of candidates whose behavior in office falls within some range (e.g., Democrats tend to be to the left of the political center, Republicans to the right); that the party values this reputation because it decreases the costs of winning office for its members; and that the smaller the perceived variance in party members' positions is, the greater the benefit to the party. Consequently, it is rational for voters to infer that if a politician captures office and then acts contrary to her party's reputation, she imposes a cost on that organization. Because voters know that parties want to avoid suffering these costs, they infer that party organizations create norms and procedures to ensure some level of party loyalty, making it rational for the electorate to treat a candidate's party affiliation as a credible signal about the range of policies that a politician might support in office. So long as the party is able to maintain reasonably high levels of party unity in Washington, voters do not need to know the details of the control apparatus that party leaders wield to protect their reputation.

This theory explaining why ordinary citizens might infer that votes for candidates belonging to a party might translate into policy outcomes rests on the claim that when parties in government are more unified, they develop a reputation that they value. Chapter 3 of the manuscript develops and tests a model of how parties form these reputations. Building on classic models of rational voter learning (e.g., Achen 1992; Fiorina 1981), it argues that voters form beliefs about whether they prefer Democrats or Republicans on average based on their observations of the two parties over the course of their lifetimes. It departs from the classic approach – which treats learning as myopically focused on voter efforts to discern whether Democratic or Republican policies yield better outcomes – by arguing that when voters observe members of Congress over time, they are also trying to ascertain whether party labels provide credible information about the issue positions of a "typical" Democrat or Republican. Consequently, the basis of voter learning is a sample of information about the issue positions of individual party members that is collected over the course of a person's lifetime. Based on the information from this sample, voters form beliefs about how liberal or conservative a party's members are on average and the level of ideological agreement within the organization.

There are two original implications of the learning model that must be satisfied for voters to trust party labels as a signaling device. First, beliefs about parties must be sensitive to the level of party unity in government, because voters use this information to discern whether parties possess the organizational capacity and/or the incentives to regulate the actions of party members in government. Second, because voters are unable to observe the institutions of partisan control employed in the United States, their beliefs about parties must take into account past behavior, so that people may be able to assess a party's commitments to a particular set of principles over the long term. Without drawing upon this history, voters who observe high levels of party unity today may be uncertain whether it is a consequence of short-run forces that give rise to high levels of agreement with the party on the issues of the day, or a long-run commitment by the party to protecting its brand name. Conversely, voters who observe high levels of internal party disagreement on some issue that is not a core partisan commitment may mistakenly infer that a party does not value its brand name without looking at the range of other issues where the organization has maintained high levels of party unity over the long term. A testable implication of this latter claim is that there will be observable differences in voter beliefs about parties across generations.

The second half of the chapter tests the empirical implications of the learning model. To that end, a half-century of individual-level survey data is used to rigorously demonstrate that people's beliefs about the scope of conflict between Democrats and Republicans and their uncertainty about the parties' issue positions vary systematically with changing levels of inter-party conflict and intra-party unity in government. It is also shown that there are predictable differences across generations in people's beliefs about the two parties based on the actions of the parties in government over the course of their lifetimes. For example, young people who came of age during the contemporary period of party polarization see the greatest differences between the two parties, whereas during the 1960s and 1970s young people who came of age during the period of party decline saw the least differences. The most important novel points for the purposes of this book are that party reputations are influenced by the level of party unity in government and that if party unity breaks down, then voters will remember that failure.

Chapter 4 contends that higher levels of voter certainty instilled by party unity create electoral rewards for the national parties. This argument is motivated by the assumption that party evaluations are based on the utility that a person expects to receive from the election of a candidate belonging to that party. It follows from this assumption that, if voters are risk-averse and their uncertainty about a party member's issue positions is a function of the actual level of intra-party conflict over the course of the voters' lifetimes, then they will have more favorable evaluations of more unified parties.

To support this claim, individual-level survey data are used to demonstrate that individuals with the most crystallized views about a party evaluate it more favorably; longitudinal data are used to demonstrate that, in the aggregate, the strength of party preferences varies systematically with the level of party unity; and these time-series data are broken down by birth cohort to demonstrate that the strength of party attachments varies by generation in a manner consistent with voters granting or withholding support based on a lifetime of evidence about a party's ability to maintain discipline in government. Thus, this chapter demonstrates that a party benefits from being unified in government because it increases the number of strong partisans, and that if party unity breaks down, then it forfeits those benefits for quite some time.

Chapter 5 squares my theory with the American system of candidate-centered elections, with a special focus on why it is compatible with politicians' political ambitions to agree to the establishment of institutions to promote party unity. First, I address the argument that candidates contest elections based on personal reputations, not party labels. In response, it is argued that in order for politicians to use a private brand name as a credible signal of their future behavior in office, voters must believe that a candidate has a reputation that she values. This requires that citizens can recall a politician's name and that they know something about her record in office. The chapter reviews a great deal of evidence demonstrating that in Congressional elections neither of these conditions is satisfied for a great number of ordinary Americans – even in an era of candidate-centered elections, the overwhelming share of voters must rely on party labels at the ballot box because they know little about individual candidates.

Second, I address the argument that parties cannot develop a reputation for being unified around a certain set of issues because members of Congress cast votes in order to develop a private brand name that appeals to those voters who do pay attention to the goings-on in Washington. The response begins by teasing out the electoral incentives that MCs have to vote contrary to the party. It is argued that strong electoral incentives for voting contrary to the party line exist only when an important group of constituents have preferences at odds with the party; that these constituents are not marginal nationally, so that legislators are not compelled out of electoral concerns to vote against their party on lopsided votes; and that these issues actually have to come to the floor for a vote. Working from the Cox-McCubbins model of majority party agenda control, it is demonstrated formally that on those issues that majority party leaders allow to reach the floor for a vote, only (the usually small number of) "centrist" politicians on that issue (i.e., left-of-center Republicans and right-of-center Democrats) might feel electoral pressures to vote contrary to the party line. Extending this logic over the course of an entire session of Congress, it is argued that the incentive for investment in private candidate brand names that differentiate a politician from her party is greatest for centrist incumbents who have a record of voting contrary to their party's line (with the opposition party) and weakest for more ideologically extreme representatives (who vote against their party only on lopsided votes). To substantiate this claim, it is shown empirically that centrist incumbents are more likely to make contact with constituents – a behavior that is consistent with the actions of someone trying to cultivate a private brand name. It is also shown that these efforts to develop a stronger private brand name are successful for centrist incumbents in that a larger number of their constituents are able to recall their name, especially in elections not contested by a quality challenger. The take-home point from this section is that given the way that agenda control is exercised in Congress, it is the exception rather than the rule that MCs feel sufficiently strong electoral pressures to cast votes to differentiate themselves from their party and then engage in costly efforts to inform the public about those differences. Chapter 5 concludes with a discussion of how the arguments in this chapter shed light on the periods of party decline and renewal in American politics during the second half of the twentieth century.

Having made the case in previous chapters that the national parties benefit from party unity and that in most circumstances it is incentive compatible for party members to cooperate with their co-partisans, a series of case studies is provided in Chapter 6 that illustrate the political implications of party brand names. The first case study is of the first mass parties in New York during the early nineteenth century. It documents how party brand names were developed and maintained by the period's newly emergent class of professional middle-class politicians to signal their commitment to a common set of ideological convictions. By contrasting the first mass parties' emphasis on loyalty to the organization and protection of the group's reputation with the transient factions organized around charismatic leaders that the mass party replaced, this case study provides a nice illustration of how aspiring politicians might benefit from their association with a unified party when competing against a better-established incumbent.

The second case study is of the electoral strategies of the opposition party in Congress over the past twenty years, with a particular focus on the Republicans in 1994 and the Democrats in 2006 – the two examples in the last-half century when an out-party managed to capture a legislative majority in national elections. These case studies document that key features of the Republican Party's strategy in the late 1980s and early 1990s and of the Democratic Party's strategy in the early 2000s to retake the House was to act in the manner of a responsible opposition party of the sort advocated by Woodrow Wilson, Lawrence Lowell, and E. E. Schattschneider a century ago. Accordingly, both parties placed heavy emphasis on being unified in opposition to the ruling party's policy agenda and, in the run-up to the Congressional election, publicly offered a Congressional party platform that communicated their willingness to stake their organization's reputation for being unified on a common issue agenda on the performance of their party's challengers in the event of their election. It is argued that the parties' electoral strategies in these years definitively show that party leaders believe it is incentive-compatible to act in the manner of a responsible opposition party that uses a unified partisan message to elect new members to Congress.

The third case study is of the Democratic Party and its handling of the emergence of its conservative Southern wing during the 1930s, with an eye toward reconciling the breakdown in Democratic Party unity in government with the surety model of party government. The case study shows that Southern Democrats' move to the political right was a rational response to the growing conservatism of the South; that Franklin Roosevelt tried to purge conservative Southern Democrats from the party in 1938 in a manner consistent with a party leader trying to protect his organization's liberal reputation; and that after the failure of FDR's purge signaled to the national party the South's preference for more conservative legislators, the Democrats adopted institutional reforms (the Hatch Act; the Legislative Reorganization Act of 1946) that gave Southern Democrats the ability to better develop private brand names because the party needed to retain those seats to maintain its majority status. In short, it is argued that the party's response to the rise of the Southern Democrats is exactly what would be expected from an organization hoping to maintain its majority.

Chapter 7 concludes the book with a brief recap of its main arguments, its implications, and directions for future research.

2

Theory

The United States Constitution never mentions a political party. Seemingly few constitutions for representative democracies do (except, perhaps, to ensure that it is illegal to prevent their formation). Yet, parties organize both elections and legislatures in every political system that conducts free and fair elections on a large scale.

The standard explanation for the ubiquity of parties in representative democracies is that they are political organizations that provide solutions to a host of problems confronting politicians (cf. Aldrich 1995). For example, parties provide a potential solution to problems of social choice in legislatures (Schwartz 1977); parties provide economies of scale in the organization of election campaigns (Osborne and Tourky 2007); and parties provide office-seekers with brand names that reduce voters' uncertainty about candidates' issue positions and ideology (Cox and McCubbins 1993; Snyder and Ting 2002). Politicians, recognizing these and other potential benefits to themselves, therefore incur the costs of developing and maintaining partisan institutions.

The argument for why politicians might create political parties is compelling, but it does not address an essential ancillary question: namely, how is it possible for a political party to ever capture a majority of seats in a national legislature if it performs the functions that party theorists claim that it performs. The root of the problem is that if party theorists are correct, then politicians create parties to (1) distort election outcomes in favor of a political coalition with a particular set of ideological convictions and/or (2) influence the legislative process so as to achieve non-median or non-centrist policy outcomes. However, if the election of a majority party yields an outcome that is different from that favored by voters at the center of the national electorate, then it would seem that those voters (and everyone on the losing side of the policy space) have every incentive to vote against candidates belonging to that party (cf. Krehbiel 1993). Given the incentives of voters in a majority of districts to vote against the candidates of a presumptive ruling party, there is good reason to question why politicians would incur the costs of creating these institutions.

This chapter builds on the insights of the citizen-candidate model of political elite motivation (e.g., Besley and Coate 1997; Osborne and Slivinski 1996) to explain why a system of party government emerges in virtually all representative democracies. The premise of the argument is that the actors who are willing to pay the costs of running for election are, for the most part, those individuals who have policy preferences that are extreme relative to ordinary citizens. Some of these individuals may, because they intend to run for reelection or place some normative value on being an effective delegate, place their constituents' interests ahead of their own in the event of their election. Others, on the other hand, may be citizen-candidates who pursue their own ideological concerns in the legislature. Because it is difficult for voters to know ex ante which type of candidates are contesting elections in their district, the legislature is inevitably filled with some number of citizen-candidates, with policy veering toward the side of the policy space with the most such legislators. Politicians on the losing side of the policy space therefore have incentives to form an opposition party in order to secure more seats in future elections, which sparks counter-organization. Voters accept parties that promise non-centrist outcomes so long as their policy commitments are more moderate than the outcomes voters anticipate if too many citizen-candidates unrestrained by party leaders capture office. Having identified the rationale for party government, the chapter then provides an explanation for how, by operating on the surety model, the benefits of party government might be realized in the United States despite the apparent weakness of partisan institutions in this country compared to that observed elsewhere in the world.

THE ARGUMENT AGAINST PARTIES

Before presenting this book's rationale for voter acceptance of parties, it is useful to first clarify why one might think that voters would be inclined to reject any party that distorts policy outcomes. The argument against parties, which is somewhat of a folk wisdom shared in seminars and workshops related to Congressional parties (an argument that is often attributed to Keith Krehbiel, with its roots in David Mayhew's view of Congressional organization), proceeds by considering who benefits from the creation of political parties with the ability to coerce their members in government into adhering to a national party program. If it is the case that ordinary citizens tend to prefer to vote for candidates who are not affiliated with a national party program, then the folk wisdom suggests that it is quite unlikely that politicians would favor the creation of a party control apparatus able to coerce themselves into voting in accord with that program (and against constituent interests). To the extent that political parties and the control apparatuses of these organizations are the endogenous creation of politicians, and these politicians prefer not to create institutions of party influence, it seems reasonable to conclude that these institutions would not be created at all.

To demonstrate that voters and politicians alike might prefer that institutions of party influence not exist, the folk wisdom offers a simple but powerful model of the political process. It proceeds from the assumptions that there are a large number of electoral districts, each of which elects a single member to the national legislature by plurality rule. Voters in each electoral district have ideal points along a liberal-conservative ideological spectrum that determine their preferences over a range of public policies. Voter utility declines the further a public policy is from their ideal point. Candidates are purely office-motivated and contest elections based on announcements of a platform describing how they intend to conduct themselves in office. Voters and candidates know one another's preference functions. In each electoral district, there is duopolistic competition in the sense that only two candidates are allowed to contest the election.

Following the election, the folk wisdom assumes that the winner from each local district becomes a member of the national legislature. In each session of that legislature, nature introduces some issue for the government to consider and the reversion policy that would be implemented if the government failed to pass new legislation. If some legislator chooses to do so, she would be given the opportunity to introduce a bill on that issue. Legislators are then given an opportunity to freely introduce germane amendments to the legislation. Each amendment is pitted against the previous version of the bill in a series of majority-rule votes. Finally, the bill as amended is pitted in a pairwise vote determined by majority rule against the reversion bill. This process is consistent with what Cox and McCubbins (2005) refer to as the floor agenda model of the legislative process (see Chapter 5 of this book for a more in-depth analysis).

The process then repeats itself, except now incumbents run for reelection against office-motivated challengers from the rival local duopoly.

Given this basic set-up, it is possible to make a set of predictions about the legislature's choice of public policies in a world where parties do nothing more than field candidates for election. To begin, following the logic of the median voter theorem, in each electoral district both candidates announce as their policy platform the ideal point of the median voter in their district (and voters, recognizing that their representative wants to be reelected, believe that these promises are credible commitments on the politicians' parts). The winner of each election is, in effect, the result of a coin toss by a district's median voter. After the election, the winners of the "coin tosses" from all of the districts arrive in the national legislature. When it comes time to make policy decisions, every legislator acts as if she were the agent of the median voter in her electoral district, knowing that she will have to stand for reelection shortly. The median voter in the legislature is, therefore, the legislator representing the district whose ideal point is the median of all of the district medians. Thus, in a world without party influence, the national government adopts as law the policy positions favored by the median voter in the median district nationally.

Now, the folk wisdom identifies the legislature's choice of public policies in a world where the incumbent politicians in the legislature decide to form political parties on the basis of ideological divisions. To that end, it supposes that the median legislator and everyone to her left in the chamber come together to create the "Left" Party and everyone to her right come together to create the "Right" Party, and that these parties ally with the local duopolists in districts where they are the out-party. It supposes further that these parties commit their members to a national platform (or, equivalently, that they came together to support a set of non-centrist policies in the legislature and, when they run for reelection, the public casts votes based on their party's record) such that the nominees of all of the local Left Parties commit to one platform to the left of the national median, and that the nominees of all of the local Right Parties commit to another platform to the right of the national median. When the election is held, in each district the nominee of the party closer to the median voter wins office and, when it comes time to legislate, the median voter in the legislature is a member of the party winning a majority of the seats.

Finally, the folk wisdom asks us to evaluate who benefits and who loses from the introduction of political parties. When we compare the two stylized models just presented, it is clear that the commitment of

candidates to non-centrist national platforms has important implications
for all of the actors in the model. First, the national median no longer
realizes her ideal policy outcome. Second, and somewhat distressingly
from a normative perspective, in a clear majority of districts, a majority of voters prefer that parties do not exist at all. These voters would
prefer to live in the world where parties were just labels attached to the
local electoral duopolists who did little more than field office-motivated
candidates. Third, an office-motivated candidate in the out-party in these
unhappy districts would prefer to run without being committed to a
national party platform. Because voters and candidates both prefer that
a system of party government not exist, the folk wisdom concludes that
there is little reason to believe that one would ever come about.

One obvious response to the folk wisdom is that it proceeds from the
unrealistic assumption that the policy space is one-dimensional. Building
on the work of McKelvey (1976, 1979) and Schofield (1978), if a policy
space is multi-dimensional, then there is no equilibrium platform (e.g., the
median voter's ideal point), nor is there an equilibrium policy proposal
in the legislature. One might therefore imagine a group of politicians
coming together to form a political party (complete with institutions
of party influence) in order to secure policy outcomes near their ideal
point, especially if they had reasonably homogenous policy preferences
or represented similarly minded districts (e.g., Aldrich and Rohde 1994).

Although it is correct to argue that an equilibrium policy outcome does
not ordinarily exist if the policy space is multi-dimensional, social choice
theorists have demonstrated that if the number of voters is large and
ideal points are distributed in a reasonably symmetric way, then there are
relatively small subsets of the policy space such as the so-called "yolk"
(McKelvey 1986) or the "heart" (Schofield 1985) at the center of voters'
ideal points toward which public policies tend to gravitate with reasonable amendment procedures and sophisticated voting (e.g., Ferejohn,
et al., 1984). If voters observe public policies routinely being adopted
that are distant from the yolk, say, one would expect their reaction to be
exactly the same as in the folk wisdom – voters with ideal points near
the yolk, and those on the losing side of the policy space, would all vote
against incumbents who supported a set of rules that enabled the passage
of the non-centrist policies. Anticipating that response, a politician who
is worried about her career would refuse to join a political party.

In sum, given that voters in many places prefer an office-motivated
candidate to someone committed to their national party platform, and

candidates prefer to win elections by rejecting national party platforms in favor of adopting the ideal point of the median voter in their district, the folk wisdom concludes that it is hard to imagine that national parties, organized as ideological policy-making teams, are sustainable in equilibrium. Thus, there is little reason to believe *theoretically* that political parties have significance beyond fielding candidates and performing the other sundry functions necessary to organize elections. (Although it may seem far-fetched to see parties as irrelevant institutions in the United States in the early twenty-first century, that was the *dominant* view of political observers a generation ago.)

THE EVIDENCE AGAINST THE FOLK WISDOM

The folk wisdom, while offering a potentially compelling argument against the creation of a system of party government, is not well supported by evidence.

Party Elite Polarization

One problematic feature of the folk wisdom is that it implies that political parties are just empty labels assigned to candidates who adopted campaign platforms that maximized their appeal to local constituents. The local constituents, in turn, basically flip a coin when choosing between the two candidates competing locally – with the winner of the coin toss appearing in the national legislature. Consequently, partisanship would not appear to be a very good predictor of a legislator's voting behavior.

Empirically, the claim that a legislator's party affiliation is a poor predictor of her voting behavior is false. To demonstrate this, it is helpful to use Poole and Rosenthal's first dimension DW-Nominate Scores for Democrats and Republicans in the U.S. House, where the DW-Nominate Scores provide estimates of individual legislators' ideological location along a left-right continuum, as inferred from their roll call votes. Figure 2.1 provides kernel density plots of Democratic and Republican DW-Nominate scores for the 109th Congress. It reveals that there is no overlap whatsoever in the preferences of Democrats and Republicans in the House from 2005 to 2007. Given that every Republican has a more conservative voting record than the most conservative Democrat in that Congress, legislators' party affiliations are clearly quite good predictors of their voting records in recent Congresses.

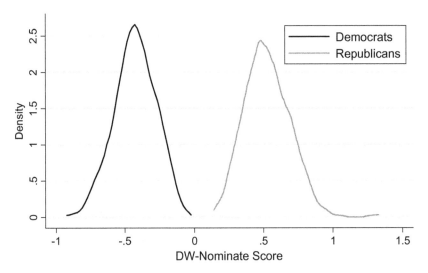

Figure 2.1. Kernel density plots of Democratic and Republican DW-Nominate scores, 109th Congress. *Source:* voteview.com.

Partisan Sorting on District Ideology

A defender of the folk wisdom might respond to the evidence of party elite polarization that House members elected from left-leaning districts just self-identify as Democrats and legislators elected from right-leaning districts as Republicans. Legislators' voting records may, therefore, be predictive of their party affiliations, but the label remains an empty one – it has no actual influence on their conduct in office. This seems an odd claim because it seems like it would only be true if legislators chose their party affiliations after their election to the national legislature – otherwise, by the folk wisdom's logic, we should observe Democrats winning their coin flips in conservative districts and Republicans winning their coin flips in liberal districts appearing in the legislature. Bracketing that problematic feature of the response's logic (not to mention the fact that Congressional elections are often lopsided at the district level and not determined by a "coin toss"), it is still possible to demonstrate that partisan sorting based on district ideology is not sufficient to explain party elite polarization.

To see this, note that the folk wisdom proceeds from the assumption that office-motivated legislators assiduously adhere to the interests of their constituents without regard to their party affiliation. This implies that the distribution of Congressional districts' preferences should look

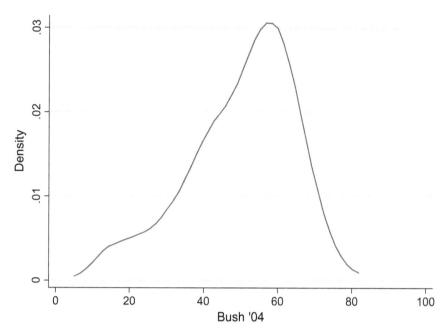

Figure 2.2. Kernel density plot of votes for Bush in 2004 by Congressional district. *Source:* swingstateproject.com/diary/4161/.

a lot like the distribution of legislators' DW-Nominate Scores. In light of the evidence presented previously, this suggests that the preferences of Congressional districts should also follow a bi-modal distribution. However, as an empirical matter it does not appear that Congressional districts are polarized ideologically in the same way as the United States Congress. To illustrate this, I use the percentage of the vote within a Congressional district for the Republican Party's Presidential candidate, a standard measure of Congressional district ideology, where the greater the percentage of the vote for the Republican Party's Presidential candidate, the more conservative the district. To maximize the comparison with the 109th Congress, data are taken from the Presidential election of 2004 between George Bush and John Kerry, which was held in concert with the elections for the 109th Congress. The kernel density plot of the Presidential election returns by district reported in Figure 2.2 reveals a clearly unimodal distribution of voter preferences at the level of the Congressional district. Based on the figure, it is quite difficult to conclude that the large numbers of ideologically extreme MCs are assiduously adhering to the wishes of their constituents – a result inconsistent with the perfect sorting of Democrats and Republicans into distinct ideological camps.

District-by-District Divergence

An alternative line of response to the evidence of party elite polarization might be that the folk wisdom, as portrayed earlier, rests heavily on the median voter carrying the day in Congressional elections. It is well known in the formal theoretic literature, however, that the median voter theorem is a knife-edged result. Grofman's (2004; see also Aldrich and Grynaviski forthcoming) survey of the literature on spatial models of elections demonstrates that there are no fewer than a dozen assumptions in the simple spatial model of electoral competition that, if relaxed, create the possibility that a pair of rational candidates motivated, at least in part, by electoral considerations will take positions on opposite sides of the median voter in their electoral district. If one were to simply call the candidate who diverged to the left the Democratic Party candidate and the candidate who diverged to the right the Republican Party candidate, then one could imagine an argument being advanced that liberal legislators would sort into the Democratic Party and conservative legislators would sort into the Republican Party.

The problem with this argument is that it still implies much more overlap in the distribution of Democratic and Republican preferences than is observed in Congress. The crux of the matter is that when an election is held, Democratic Party candidates who win election in liberal districts will be quite liberal and Republican Party candidates who win election in conservative districts will be quite conservative – so they will be well sorted along party lines; however, they win these elections, in effect, by a coin toss. Meanwhile, Democratic Party candidates who win the electoral coin toss in conservative districts will not necessarily be liberal (some will even be to the right of the national median) and Republican Party candidates who win the electoral coin toss in liberal districts will not be conservative (some will even be to the left of the national median). The result of legislative elections under these assumptions is significant overlap in the political ideologies of legislators from the two parties.

Evidence of Party Influence in Congress

A final piece of evidence inconsistent with the folk wisdom is provided by a series of studies demonstrating that politicians' party affiliations have a meaningful effect on their voting behavior in a manner that gives the appearance that they are succumbing to partisan pressures. Snyder and Groseclose (2000), for example, proceed from the assumption that if party pressures exist, they would be most likely to be revealed on contested measures where party whips actively strive to change legislators' votes. Snyder and Groseclose therefore use scaling techniques to estimate legislator preferences on measures that are not closely contested and use these preferences together with a legislator's party affiliation to make predictions of their voting behavior on more closely contested votes. They find that in these contested votes, a legislator's party affiliation is a significant predictor of her behavior controlling for her preferences, which is consistent with an independent effect of partisanship. In subsequent work, they confirm this finding using measures of legislator preferences gleaned from surveys conducted by the researchers at Project Vote Smart to compare the effect of partisan forces on contested and non-contested votes and again find a more pronounced effect of party influence on the contested measures (Snyder and Groseclose 2001; see also Ansolabehere, Snyder, and Stewart 2001).

Taking a somewhat different tack, McCarty, Poole, and Rosenthal (2001) argue that if party pressures affect voting behavior, then, holding legislator preferences constant, Republicans will be more predisposed to vote for conservative policies and Democrats will be more predisposed to support liberal policies. In other words, party pressures induce Democrats and Republicans into seeing the same policy as located at different points along an ideological continuum. Based on the results of their statistical analyses of legislator voting behavior, they find that party pressures lead roughly 10 percent of MCs to change their roll call on an average vote.

A final piece of evidence supporting the presence of party effects on voting behavior is provided by studies of individuals who switched parties while in office. These studies consistently demonstrate that changes in party affiliations have a very substantial effect on estimates of legislator preferences based on their voting behavior (Clinton et al. 2004; McCarty, et al. 2001; Nokken 2000; Nokken and Poole 2004).

WHY VOTERS VALUE FORMAL PARTY ORGANIZATION

The purpose of this part of the chapter is to provide a theoretical rationale for why voters might place sufficient value on party government that they tolerate the election of candidates who support their party's pursuit of non-centrist public policies.

The Adverse Selection Problem

The impetus for voter acceptance of national parties with the ability to implement non-centrist policy programs is the problem of adverse selection. This is a concern that emerges in a wide variety of contexts and occurs when two or more actors hoping to engage in some kind of transaction have asymmetric information about the quality of the goods being exchanged, often to the detriment of both parties. The consequences of adverse selection may be most familiar in markets for experience goods, which are products whose attributes (other than their price) are known to the seller of the good, but which cannot be fully discerned by the buyer prior to their purchase. Thus, experience goods describe a broad category of products ranging from automobiles, where consumers do not know ex ante whether they are buying a lemon, to cans of green beans, where it is not known what, exactly, is in that can they are pulling off the supermarket shelves.

Experience goods are problematic for market exchange because of buyer uncertainty about whether they are purchasing a high- or a low-quality product. In the face of this uncertainty, the buyer is naturally unwilling to pay the seller market value for a high-quality product because there is some chance that their purchase will ultimately prove to be of low quality. The seller of high-quality products, in turn, is unwilling to sell their product because they will not receive fair market value (and they will not want to warrant their product because such a guarantee may encourage buyer misuse). As a result, only low-quality products are exchanged even though buyers are willing to pay fair market value for high-quality goods and sellers are willing to sell at that price (Akerlof 1970).

Politicians as Experience Goods

The concept of adverse selection informs the study of elections because politicians are experience goods in the sense that voters do not know prior to an election how someone will act in public office. Candidates may claim that they intend to do this or that, but voters have no reason ex ante to believe the statements of someone who wants to get elected, especially in light of the fact that most politicians are typically recruited from the pool of political activists who have political views that seem extreme relative to those of ordinary citizens.[1] Further, in the absence of some incentive to behave similarly moving forward, there is little reason to even use a candidate's record of legislative accomplishments as evidence of their future behavior (e.g., Alesina 1988; Harrington 1992).[2] After all, politicians may decide to seek higher office, retire in the near future, and so forth, which may affect how they would respond to similar issues moving forward.

This description of politicians may sound quite cynical, but there is good reason to believe that voters find politicians' campaign promises to be for naught. First, a great deal of evidence points to the fact that campaign promises are only imperfectly kept. The most on-point evidence is provided by a series of studies which demonstrate that although many candidate pledges are reflected in official behavior, some campaign promises are left unfulfilled. For example, Fishel (1985) reports that Presidents only attempt to keep about 60 percent of their campaign promises, Ringquist and Dasse (2004) report that House members' voting behavior reflected their campaign promises on environmental legislation only around 70 percent of the time, and Ringquist and Neshkova (2006) find that members of the Senate kept their promises on this issue less than 60 percent of the time. These studies complement a substantial body of research which demonstrates that incumbent politicians are susceptible to the influences of their own preferences, lobbyists, party leaders, and political action committees (e.g., Arnold 1990; Kingdon 1981).

Second, Snyder and Ting (2002) find that in their last year of service prior to retirement, legislators significantly change their voting behavior in Congress, presumably because they no longer feel compelled by electoral pressures to vote their constituencies' interests and therefore vote in line with their own preferences.

Third, even if it were true that politicians do not mislead the public in their campaign statements, large numbers of Americans believe that they do. According to one study, more than 70 percent of respondents agreed with the statement that "to win elections, most members of Congress make campaign promises they have no intention of fulfilling

---

[1] Davis and Ferrantino (1996) discuss the incentives that politicians have to lie when personal reputations cannot be transferred to other actors.
[2] Keefer (2007) argues that an important factor retarding economic development in emerging democracies is the inability of politicians to solve these kinds of commitment problems.

(Ladd 1990)." Similarly, in an internet-based survey of adults under age 25, I find that 66 percent of respondents agreed with this statement and only 12 percent disagreed. These findings are consistent with Gallup Poll data from the mid-1970s through the present which consistently show that fewer than 20 percent of Americans rate the honesty and ethical standards of Congressmen as either high or very high (Cooper 1999, p. 198). Thus, voters see politicians as a type of experience good whose actions cannot be accurately forecast prior to their election.

The Implications of the Adverse Selection Problem in Elections for Voters' Relationship with Politicians

That politicians are a kind of experience good has some fundamental similarities to that associated with market exchange. Politicians have every incentive to make campaign promises that are especially appealing to their constituents in the same way that a used-car salesman might swear to some lucky buyer that the Ford Pinto on her lot is not a lemon. Politicians have the incentive to make these campaign promises even if they intend to act in government in a manner that is consistent with their own ideological commitments, rather than actually pursuing district interests. Furthermore, voters know that candidates who intend to act contrary to the wishes of their constituents in the event of their victory are unlikely to reveal those intentions over the course of an election campaign. In the absence of some kind of mechanism to credibly signal candidates' policy commitments, voters therefore have no way of discriminating "high-quality" office-motivated types of politicians who will pursue constituent interests from "low-quality" ideology-motivated politicians who will act in accord with their conscience regardless of district preferences.

Despite the similarity in the nature of uncertainty in market exchange and in elections, the consequences of adverse selection are quite different in these two settings. First, adverse selection does not distort the composition of the choice set confronting decision makers in elections in the same way that it distorts the choice set in markets. As previously noted, sellers of high-quality goods leave the marketplace because consumers are unwilling to pay full price for their product because of uncertainty about its attributes. High-quality politicians, on the other hand, have little incentive to leave the market because the value of office (i.e., the price paid for their services) does not change when low-quality politicians are also contesting elections.

Second, the welfare implications for consumers who choose a lemon are quite different from those for voters who choose a committed ideologue. Consumers who purchase a product incur the full incidence of their choice in the sense that if they choose a low-quality product and pay high prices, then they are going to own a lemon and be that much poorer. As a result, they demand some kind of credible signal from the seller that the product is of the quality she claims. In elections, on the other hand, citizens are insured against the consequences of casting votes for a low-quality politician. One form of this insurance is that no one vote is likely to be pivotal in any election, so the cost of making a bad decision is virtually nil. Another form of this insurance is that even if a person cast the tie-breaking vote in a legislative election, in the worst-case scenario her decision would only shift policy one legislator away from her ideal point. Consequently, a liberal citizen, say, might cast the tie-breaking vote for an ultra-right-wing ideologue, but public policy would only shift slightly to the right.

In thinking about the welfare implications of the adverse selection problem in elections, on the one hand, there is something reassuring about the observation that it is almost impossible for a citizen to cast a vote that would cause serious harm to her own welfare (or to society writ large). On the other hand, there is something quite disheartening about the fact that voters have little reason to become informed about the ideological commitments of the politicians who are campaigning in their district.

Incentives for Investments in Brand Names

A common solution to the adverse selection problem in market exchange is for the sellers of experience goods to cultivate brand names (Klein and Leffler 1981; Shapiro 1983). Numerous scholars have suggested that candidates affiliate with a political party that provides them with a kind of brand name that reduces voters' uncertainty about their political convictions in order to increase their electoral appeal (e.g., Aldrich 1995; Snyder and Ting 2002; Kiewiet and McCubbins 1991; Cox and McCubbins 1993, 2005; Ashworth and Bueno de Mesquita 2008) in the same way that a local restaurant might pay a franchise fee in order to increase traffic to its location due to its brand name. However, it is straightforward to show that simply introducing the assumptions (1) that voters are risk-averse decision makers who gain utility from the legislature's policy choices (based on spatial proximity), (2) that voters are uncertain about the policy positions of candidates who do not belong to a national party, and (3) that parties reduce voter uncertainty about the preferences of the politicians running locally is not sufficient to motivate candidates to form national parties.

To see that a party system may not be sustainable given these assumptions, it is instructive to extend the folk wisdom's model of the political system with influential parties to the case where voters are uncertain about candidate preferences and candidates are given the opportunity to join a national party. Thus, assume that the Left Party has a brand name that signals to voters that candidates carrying its label are to the left of the national median and the Right Party has a reputation for fielding candidates to the right of the national median. To simplify the discussion, assume that the two parties are equidistant from the median voter in the median district nationally. Assume further that candidates from the local Left Party duopolies are given the opportunity to commit to their party's national platform and the candidates from the local Right Party's duopolies are given the opportunity to commit to their party's national platform. Again, to keep things as simple as possible (and, it would seem, giving the argument for why politicians would make costly investments in a party brand), assume that if the candidates make these commitments, then risk-averse voters believe that there is no probability that they will stray from their platform in office. If a candidate from a local duopoly fails to commit to a national platform (call these candidates "unaffiliated"), then voters from their district assign some probability distribution to the set of policies she may pursue in office. Finally, assume that beliefs about the distribution that voters assign to unaffiliated candidates' policy positions are common knowledge.

Given this set-up, if all of the local candidates choose to affiliate with their national party, then the median voter in the median district nationally will be indifferent between the two parties. She flips a coin to decide which local candidate she sends to the national legislature, the median voter in every district to her left chooses the Left Party's candidate, and the median voter in every district to her right chooses the Right Party's candidate. The party of the candidate who wins the coin toss in the median district nationally captures majority control of the legislature and implements its platform. The results are exactly the same as in the folk wisdom with influential parties.

The question that follows is whether the introduction of voter uncertainty about the platform decisions of the candidates from the local duopolies is sufficient to induce politicians to commit to the platform of their national party. For a large number of candidates, the answer appears to be an emphatic no. For every Right Party candidate to the left of the national median and every Left Party candidate to the right of the national median, it is obvious that committing to the national platform does not make them better off, because they expect to lose the election. One might argue that they would join the national party anyway if they expected to lose the election if voters preferred the sure bet on the candidate committed to the other party's platform to the risky bet on the unaffiliated candidate. However, this argument ultimately depends on the median voter locally believing either (1) that the expected value of the unaffiliated candidate's ideology is more distant from her ideal point than the platform of the party that she prefers or (2) that she has tremendous uncertainty in her estimate of the candidate's ideology and is risk-averse.

One might argue that these conditions are satisfied in most real-world cases so that candidates who are electorally disadvantaged by their party's national platform are indifferent between affiliation and not. On the other hand, it is easy to construct examples where neither of these conditions is satisfied. One obvious example occurs when preferences cluster by geography (so that preferences within electoral districts are homogenous and preferences across districts are heterogeneous) and candidates are believed to be random draws from the local population. In this circumstance, politicians from both parties will ordinarily prefer to run as a "random draw" from their district over running as someone ideologically committed to a national party program. This occurs because, in most cases, the median voter in each district locally prefers taking a chance on a fellow resident of her community (whose residents have homogenous preferences) chosen at random to the sure bet of either party's platform. The exception to the rule are candidates who belong to a party whose platform is quite proximate to the ideal point of the median voter in their district who benefit from the small reduction in voter uncertainty provided by the party label; however, even in these exceptional cases, only one of the two candidates receive a benefit from party ties, the other prefers to opt-out of the party system. Thus, with this kind of geographic sorting and candidate-selection mechanism, national parties are not sustainable in equilibrium because candidates prefer to opt out of the national party in a clear majority of districts.

Because the foregoing example demonstrates that voter uncertainty and risk appetites are not sufficient to maintain incentives for national parties in all cases, it is instructive to focus attention on cases where one might believe that voter uncertainty and risk aversion would advantage party members over unaffiliated candidates. Specifically, assume that voters believe that local candidates are random draws from the national electorate, in which case voters have tremendous uncertainty about the political ideology of the candidate. Even with this assumption, it is straightforward to show that politicians in a majority of districts (from both parties) weakly prefer to run as unaffiliated candidates.

To see this, note that it has already been established that Right Party candidates in districts to the left of the median district nationally and Left Party candidates in districts to the right of the median district nationally weakly prefer to campaign as unaffiliated candidates. So, in every district except the median district nationally, there is a candidate from one of the two local duopolies who believes that she would be no worse off without committing to a national party platform. It turns out that the candidates of both local duopolies in the median district nationally also prefer to run as unaffiliated candidates because the median voter in that district prefers the lottery to the certain bet on one of the major party platforms.

That the national median weakly prefers the unaffiliated candidate in her district regardless of her beliefs about how that candidate might act in office seems counter-intuitive, but consider the consequences to the median voter of her choice given the different possible outcomes that might be realized from the election of the lottery candidate. Assuming the affiliated candidate is from the Left Party (with a symmetric set of results if the affiliated candidate is from the Right Party), there are three cases to consider: the case where the unaffiliated candidate is weakly to the left of the Left Party platform, the case where she is between the two parties' platforms, and the case where she is to the right of the Right Party's platform. If the unaffiliated candidate is to the left of the Left Party's platform, then her vote does not affect the policy position of the median legislator, so she is indifferent about whether she prefers the affiliated or the unaffiliated candidate. If the unaffiliated candidate is between the two parties' platforms, then the unaffiliated candidate becomes the median voter in the legislature. Because the median voter in this district strictly prefers anything between the two parties' platforms, she prefers the unaffiliated candidate to the affiliated candidate. Finally, if the unaffiliated candidate is to the right of the Right Party's platform, then policy outcomes are again unaffected by the choice of either the affiliated or the unaffiliated candidate, so the median voter in the median district nationally is again indifferent between her two choices. Thus, although there may be extreme variance in the policy preferences of the unaffiliated candidate, there is no risk of a worse outcome for the median voter than the platform of one of the major parties.

Given that the median voter in the median district nationally prefers unaffiliated candidates to affiliated candidates, politicians in those districts strictly prefer not to be tied to their national party's platform. Even being generous in the assumptions made about voter preferences and the extent of voter uncertainty about candidates' intentions once in office, there is still little reason to believe – on theoretical grounds – that candidates join political parties to reduce voter uncertainty about their policy commitments.

The Implication of the Adverse Selection Problem for National Policy Making

The error in concluding that the adverse selection problem in elections is not a concern is that it only addresses the welfare consequences for voters from the election of "low-quality" candidates from their own district. Legislative elections involve a large number of electoral districts, each of which confronts the possibility of electing an ideologically extreme politician. Concerns about what is happening in other districts dramatically modify the conclusions that one draws about why voters (especially, centrist voters) might value political parties able to commit their members to a national program and why politicians would, therefore, want to join a party.

To understand how the adverse selection problem modifies the conclusions one draws about the desirability of political parties, consider once again the folk wisdom's model of the political system without influential parties. Suppose, however, that voters assume that some share p of politicians will vote their conscience if elected to the legislature. The remaining $(1 - p)$ politicians are office-motivated types who are assumed to vote in accord with the preferences of the median voter in their district. To capture the essence of the adverse selection problem in elections, assume too that voters do not know ex ante the candidates' type: that is, voters do not know whether candidates are a conscience type or an office-motivated type. Finally, suppose that all politicians enter politics because they have extreme policy preferences relative to the electorate and that voters *know* the ideal points of the two candidates running for office – call those points L and R (and that L is to the left of R).[3]

Absent some kind of device by which candidates credibly commit themselves to being office-motivated types (or to some policy platform), voters in each district are confronted with a choice between the candidate who prefers L and the candidate who prefers R. Because voters are uncertain if these candidate are office-motivated or conscience types, they evaluate them on the basis of their expected policy positions. For the candidate who prefers L, voters calculate that her expected policy position is $pL + (1 - p)$ (the ideal point of the median voter in this district). For the candidate who prefers R, voters calculate her expected policy position to be $pR + (1 - p)$ (the ideal point of the median voter in this district). Given this set-up, there is a cut-point midway between L and R such that all voters (including the median voter) to the left of $(L + R)/2$ prefer L and all voters to the right of $(L + R)/2$ prefer R. Thus, the candidate who prefers L will win the election in every district where the median voter is to the left of $(L + R)/2$ (capturing the votes of the median voter and everyone to her left) and the candidate who prefers R will win election in every district whose median voter is to the right of $(L + R)/2$ (capturing the votes of the median voter and everyone to her right).

In expectation, when the victors arrive in the legislature, a proportion p of legislators have ideal points at either L or R and a proportion $(1 - p)$ of legislators vote as if they had ideal points equal to that of the median voter in their district (for brevity's sake, for office-motivated legislators, their ideal points will be described as being the ideal point of the median voter in their district). In the special case where $p = 0$, all legislators act on behalf of their constituents and the government adopts as policy the ideal point of the median voter in the median district (as in the folk wisdom's model of the political system without influential parties). In the special case where $p = 1$, all legislators are ideologues and the government adopts as policy L if the candidates who prefer L are the majority party and R otherwise. (From the perspective of the median

---

[3] The formal intuitions presented in the chapter depict all districts as being strictly between L and R. The conclusions should not change, however, as long as L is to the left of the point labeled M*. Similar results would be realized if one were to assign a probability distribution to candidate ideology, with liberal candidates being random draws from the left side of the policy space with expected value L and conservative candidates being random draws from the right side of the policy space with expected value R.

voter in the median district, having a legislature full of conscience-type candidates therefore gives rise to consequences that are worse than in a model with party influence, because the parties would likely moderate their policy positions so as to appeal to a greater number of voters, whereas ideologically inclined candidates lack these incentives.)

To characterize the policy choices (and implications for voter welfare) for the remaining cases where $0 < p < 1$ is challenging to do in the most general form because the results depend greatly on the nature of the distribution of the ideal points of the median voter in each district nationally. Rather than presenting a lot of math, it is more useful to consider a pair of cases where the distribution of district medians is bell-shaped, in a manner that is consistent with the evidence from Presidential election returns presented previously.

CASE I

To establish a baseline, consider first the case where the national electorate is not polarized and the median voter in the median district nationally is indifferent between L and R. This case is represented in panels A and B of Figure 2.3 by the lightly shaded bell-shaped distribution of district medians where the median voter nationally has an ideal point at $(L + R)/2$. Based on the results of the electoral stage of the model just developed, all districts to the left of the median voter nationally elect candidates who prefer L, all districts to the right of the median voter nationally elect candidates who prefer R, and the median voter nationally flips a coin to determine whether the L or R candidate wins election from her district. In expectation, a proportion p of legislators will be conscience types who are unwilling to compromise their personal political convictions for the welfare of their district. In expectation, there are equal numbers of victors preferring L and R and equal numbers of L and R conscience types in office. For the cases where $p = 0.10$ and $p = 0.50$, the resulting expected distribution of legislator "ideal points" (i.e., the ideal point of the legislator if they are conscience types or the ideal point of the median voter in the district they represent if they are office-motivated types) is depicted with the more darkly shaded distributions in Figure 2.3.

The figure reveals a number of interesting consequences from the introduction of conscience types into the legislature. First, because most legislators represent centrist districts (and politicians from centrist districts are assumed to be as likely as politicians from extreme districts to be conscience types), a great number of conscience types are elected from

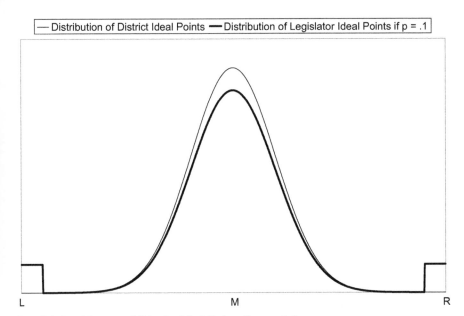

Panel A. Legislator and District Ideal Points for p = 0.1

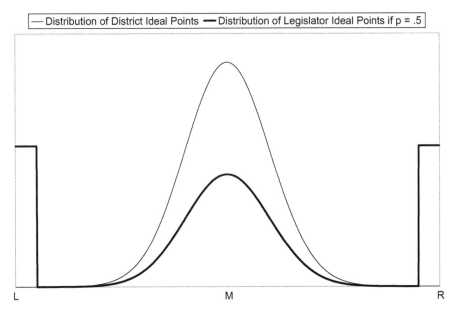

Panel B. Legislator and District Ideal Points for p = 0.5

Figure 2.3. The adverse selection problem when the national median is indifferent between L and R.

the political center. Comparatively few conscience types are elected from the more ideologically extreme districts. This point is illustrated by the difference in the heights of the distribution of district medians and legislator ideal points. Second, comparing the case where p = 0.10 with the case where p = 0.50 reveals that as p gets larger, the political center becomes increasingly empty (and emptier at a faster rate than the ideological poles) as the legislature becomes more polarized. Third (in expectation), the identity of the median voter in the legislature remains the legislator representing the median voter in the median district.

CASE 2

It is straightforward to show that the seemingly desirable outcome in Case 1 is a knife-edged result deriving from the assumption that the median voter in the median district nationally is strictly indifferent between L and R. To illustrate the nature of the problem, consider the case where the median district nationally prefers L to R. This distribution is portrayed in panels A and B of Figure 2.4 by the lightly shaded bell-shaped distribution centered to the left of the midpoint between L and R. Now when the election is held, all districts to the left of the cut-point $C = (L + R)/2$ are represented by the candidates who prefer L and all districts to the right of that cut-point prefer the candidate who prefers R. Furthermore, in expectation, there are equal numbers of conscience types elected on either side of the median voter nationally; however, now there are greater numbers of candidates in office who prefer L to R. Because ideology is not correlated with being a conscience type, this implies that in expectation there will be a greater number of conscience-type L legislators than conscience-type R legislators.

The election of more conscience-type Ls than conscience-type Rs proves to be bad news for the median voter in the median district nationally. To understand why, it is helpful to reference panel A for p = 0.10 and B for p = 0.50, which compare the darkly shaded distributions of legislator ideal points with the lightly shaded distributions of district ideal points. As in Case 1, most of the conscience types are being elected from the center of the political spectrum, which makes the legislature more polarized than the electorate, and as p gets bigger the extent of the polarization grows. Unlike Case 1, however, the election of conscience types changes the identity of the median voter. This occurs because every conscience-type legislator elected from districts whose median voter has

Theory

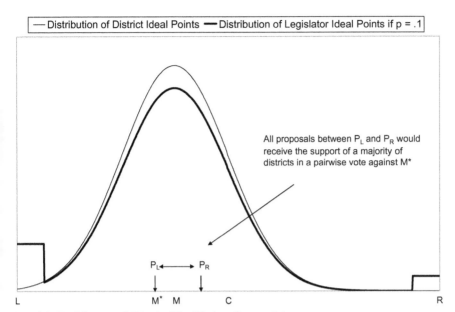

Panel A. Legislator and District Ideal Points for p = 0.1

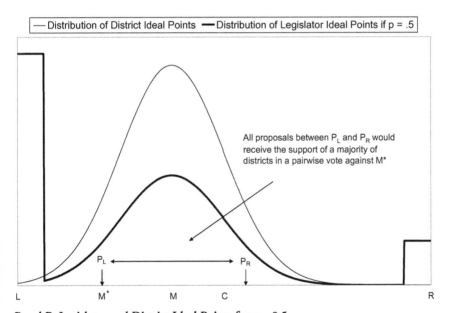

Panel B. Legislator and District Ideal Points for p = 0.5.

Figure 2.4. The adverse selection problem when the national median prefers L.

an ideal point between M and the cut-point C shifts the ideal point of the median legislator by one actor toward L. Furthermore, for each conscience-type legislator between M and C, there is the probability p of an additional shift of the ideal point of the median legislator by one actor toward L. (And, for each of these additional shifts to the right, there is the further probability p of yet another shift to the right, and so forth.) The points labeled M* represent the district that, in expectation, is represented by the median voter in the legislature.

Looking across the various cases that have been considered, a few points stand out. First, comparing the locations of the median voter for $p = 0.10$ with the results for $p = 0.50$ illustrates that as the probability of electing a conscience type increases, the distance between the spatial location of the median legislator and the median voter in the median district nationally grows. In fact, for the case where $p = 0.50$, the location of the median legislator is really quite distant from that favored by the median district. Second, comparing Case 1 with Case 2 demonstrates, somewhat perversely, that this result depends on the median district nationally having a preference for either L or R – holding constant the number of voters at the center of the electorate, this means that as an L-leaning median district comes to favor L more (or, symmetrically, an R-leaning median district comes to favor R more), the distance between M and M* increases. Third, the median voter in the median district and everyone to her right (that is, a clear majority of districts) prefer any policy proposal between $P_L = M^*$ and $P_R = M + |M - M^*|$ to M*. Strategic voting is unlikely to remedy this concern because of the challenge of coordinating which districts should cast votes against their sincere preference for an L- or R-party candidate.

The Rationale for Party Government

The analysis of the adverse selection problem in legislative elections demonstrates that the folk wisdom proceeds from a false premise. Namely, it presumes that without party government, the median voter in the median district nationally would get her way. By introducing uncertainty about whether candidates campaigning in each electoral district might be ideologues committed to a set of public policies that are more extreme than that desired by voters in each locality, it is clear that the national legislature could adopt public policies that are seemingly quite distant from that preferred by voters at the political center.

Given that there is little reason ex ante to expect centrist policy outputs by the legislature in a political system without parties, it is possible to provide a rationale for party formation that is consistent with the interests of both voters and politicians. To see this, consider the fate of the politicians who prefer R in the preceding examples. This group of politicians loses elections in a majority of districts and observes policy shifted away from their ideal point because of the adverse selection problem. Working as individual actors, they know that there is relatively little that might be done to address the problem. They also know that a majority of districts prefer that policy be shifted away from M* toward R – in fact, any policy in the range between P_L and P_R would receive the support of voters in a majority of districts. It seems logical for this group of candidates to mutually agree to form a national party and to pledge themselves to support some platform between P_L and P_R so that they could secure a national majority. Furthermore, given that the candidates preferring R have secured an electoral advantage from forming a party, it is easy to imagine the candidates preferring L to follow suit – promising a platform less extreme than M*. So long as both parties could credibly commit their members to supporting a program no more extreme than M*, it would seem that a political system with two influential parties might be sustainable in equilibrium because it would be welfare-enhancing for a majority of voters (or, at least, a majority of voters in a majority of districts).

NECESSARY CONDITIONS FOR PARTY GOVERNMENT

Thus far, this chapter has established that it can be welfare enhancing for many candidates and citizens (formally, at least a majority of voters in a majority of districts) to have some form of party government. Given that it is in these actors' mutual interest and (working as a group) capacity to achieve this outcome, it would seem trivial to conclude that party government is inevitable. However, party government faces a number of challenges where individually rational behavior by the beneficiaries of the partisan organization of government jeopardizes the ability of the group to realize the benefits to their welfare.

The Need for a Party Control Apparatus

The first, and perhaps most obvious, of these hurdles is that the ruling party must have the ability to implement its program. That is, the ruling party must be able to ensure that a majority of legislators (who do not, necessarily, need to be members of that party) will support its policy commitments.[4] If it is unable to meet this commitment, then either voters will choose to vote for the opposition party, which would be bad for ruling party members in terms of career and ideological concerns, or they will reject national parties entirely.

However, the members of the ruling party face a kind of collective dilemma because, on any given issue, some members of the organization may have incentives to cast votes contrary to their party program. In the simple framework developed earlier, office-motivated types may be sorely tempted to vote contrary to the party program when their districts prefer the alternative, and conscience types may have a hard time bringing themselves to vote with their party on issues when their ideology places them at odds with their party program. Relaxing the assumptions of the set-up just discussed, there is also the possibility that a politician may have campaigned as a member of one party even though she is more sympathetic to the other party's program (in the manner, for example, of the conservative Southern Democrats of the mid-twentieth century), in which case both district preferences and political ideology would weigh against cooperation with the party.

The Need for Institutions to Regulate Candidate Entry

A second obstacle to party government stems from a heretofore unrecognized collective dilemma created by ordinary citizens' desire to benefit from their uncertainty about candidates' ideological commitments. The nature of the problem is that voters in a majority of districts would prefer to elect a national party committed to a program between P_L and P_R rather than face the outcomes that they would endure without national parties. (In fact, a majority of districts may favor both parties' programs over the outcomes they would endure in a political system without national parties.) However, at the ballot box, individual voters do not get to choose between a political system with parties or a political system without parties – they only get to choose which candidate to vote for. There is a collective dilemma because, as argued previously, voters in many districts (including the all-important centrist districts) favor unaffiliated candidates to major-party candidates, even in the face of great uncertainty

---

[4] Most importantly, the ruling party needs to ensure that it does not pass policies more extreme than P_L and P_R.

about the unaffiliated candidates' political beliefs. If unaffiliated candidates were to run for office in those districts, it would therefore be in those districts' short-run self-interest to vote for those individuals. The result would be that candidates everywhere would choose to run without party affiliation so that parties able to commit their members to a national program would not exist.

The Need for Credible Commitments by Parties to Their Programs

A third challenge to party government is that voters must believe that the ruling party will pursue its national program if given the opportunity. To the extent that a party addresses the aforementioned challenges (so that the leadership of the majority party has been equipped by its members with the resources needed to discipline group members), this really can be reduced to a question of whether the party's leadership has appropriate incentives to whip its members in ways that result in the implementation of the group's platform.

There are two main obstacles to this kind of action. First, the leader of the majority party must not have coercive powers that allow her to realize her own most favored policies (and the incentives to pursue those ends) at the expense of the interests of her co-partisans or those of the voters who supported her party. If voters believe that she will exploit her powers in pursuit of policies that are too extreme, then they will not vote for her party's candidates. Similarly, if her co-partisans believe that she will exploit her powers in ways inconsistent with their interests (e.g., acting in a manner that results in their loss of majority status) and for some reason cannot remove her, her back-benchers will deny her the party control apparatus she needs to enforce party discipline.

Second, the leader of the ruling party must not be in jeopardy of losing her position (or, her party control apparatus) if she acts to advance her party's program. If she believes her back-benchers will depose her because they are intolerant of the party whip and she values her position of leadership within the legislature, then she is unlikely to use her party control apparatus. Building on that notion, voters who believe that party leaders will not exercise their coercive powers will not see national parties as a solution to their collective dilemma. The incentives for coordination at the electoral level on major party candidates will therefore break down, candidates will prefer in many cases to run without party affiliations, and the potential benefits of party government are forfeit.

THE SURETY MODEL OF PARTY GOVERNMENT

The argument of this book is that the United States Congress operates on a surety model of party government that consists of the following components. There are two political parties competing for control over a national legislature. The leadership of each party has its own beliefs about the public's preferences and a program of government policies that it believes will fulfill those preferences. Through election campaigns, the leadership of each party announces its program (or, because of its past record, voters infer what that program is likely to be), and voters believe that if it receives an electoral majority, it will pursue its program and will not allow policies more extreme than its program to be adopted. In each electoral district, citizens vote for the candidate they believe is most likely to contribute to the passage of policies that they favor, taking into account their beliefs about the types of policies a particular ruling party will pursue, local politicians' commitment to their party's policies (i.e., are they ideologues or office-motivated types), and the preferences of other members of their district (since those would strongly influence the behavior of office-motivated candidates). After the votes are cast, the party winning elections in a majority of electoral districts determines how much control over the legislative agenda to grant their party leaders. Given the agenda-setting powers granted by their back-benchers, majority-party leaders try to implement a set of public policies as close to their party program as possible given the preferences of the other members of the legislature.

The surety model departs from classic accounts of party government in that it does not depend on party responsibility. Responsible parties operate on the premise that party leaders are able to bark orders to their back-benchers in the same way that employers are able to demand obedience from their employees. The surety model, on the other hand, operates on the premise that party leaders are "hired" by their back-benchers to serve as a third-party guarantor of the performance in office of the candidates who carry their party's label.[5] The nature of the guarantee is not that the party ensures that an individual legislator adheres to her own campaign promises or the party's program per se: rather, the guarantee is that even if a legislator intended to pursue an extreme set of party

[5] The view that party leaders are "hired" by their back-benchers is also very much the view of the theories of conditional party government and procedural cartel theory. Also as in these theories, I believe that if party leaders use their control apparatus in a manner that is inconsistent with the organization's collective interests, they may be "fired" by their back-benchers.

positions if given the chance, her district would be spared the adverse consequences because her party's control over the legislative agenda would prevent those policies from ever being considered.

The Party Control Apparatus

In the U.S. Congress, the majority party is able to honor its guarantee to the public through a combination of two channels. First, through the influence of the party leadership–dominated Rules Committee, the majority party is able to control what matters get voted on in Congress. In particular, the Rules Committee has the power to create special rules that govern what amendments may be introduced before the Committee of the Whole (Bach and Smith 1989). Of particular import, given the rationale for the creation of parties articulated earlier, is the fact that the rules may be designed such that ideologues (and members of the minority party) are not given the opportunity to introduce viable amendments to legislation whose passage would be inconsistent with the interests of the majority party.

In addition to its influence over the process of marking up legislation in the Committee of the Whole, the majority-party leadership is also able to influence what bills are even considered on the floor of Congress. According to House Rules, the Speaker is given the power to schedule when legislation is taken up. This power is important because it means that she can determine Congress' priorities: a measure that she assigns a low priority may, therefore, never be put forward for a vote. By exercising this power, she is able to prevent legislation from being introduced whose passage may be favored by the minority party (that could pass, for example, with the support of office-motivated politicians in the majority party whose districts favor the measure) or by ideologues hoping to secure an extreme policy outcome (that could pass, for example, if there were a large number of majority party members who personally favored an extreme measure) to the detriment of their party (Cox and McCubbins 2005; Sinclair 2006). (Chapter 5 discusses how the admixture of legislator ideology, constituent interests, and legislative rules interact in more detail).

A second, complementary power is the majority-party leadership's control of the drafting of the legislation they put forward for a floor vote. One part of this power derives from the party leadership's influence on the assignment of its members to the Congressional committees who ordinarily draft legislation, especially its influence in the post-reform House over the choice of committee chairmen. This influence is important because it (1) allows party leaders to assign legislators to committees where the members' interests are aligned with that of the party and (2) allows party leaders to reward/punish their caucuses' members for adherence to the party's program. Another part of this power derives from the majority-party leadership's ability to simply rewrite legislation that it does not like after it has been discharged from committee and before it is put forward for consideration on the floor (Rohde 1991; Sinclair 2006).

The party leadership's ability to control the legislative agenda allows it to honor its commitments to the public under the surety model and to pursue a particular policy program in two regards. First, it provides the party leadership with a de facto veto over any legislation that it believes to be either too extreme or inconsistent with its own values. Second, the leadership's exercise of agenda control forces individual legislators to cast a simple yes or no vote on each measure. An MC representing a centrist district may, therefore, vote in support of a non-centrist policy without fear of electoral retaliation so long as the policy is better than the alternative.

The Enforcement of a Procedural Cartel. Ultimately, the party leadership can only exercise its agenda-setting power to control the legislative process when its members vote with their party on the rules governing the amendment process (even when they might not vote in support of the legislation). This need would appear to be especially critical for MCs whose districts prefer that a bill fail. To a large extent, these actors would seem to be shielded from electoral retaliation for voting with their party for a rule if they subsequently voted against the bill – given the negative vote on final passage, it would be hard for a reelection challenger to use the vote on the special rule against the incumbent. However, the question remains why they would vote in support of a rule that enabled the passage of legislation that they voted against.

There are at least three factors that might encourage legislators to support what Cox and McCubbins (2005) describe as the majority party's procedural cartel. First, they may value the party's ability to serve as a surety. In particular, when the party serves as a surety, it may improve individual incumbents' reelection prospects and their party's ability to retain majority status in future elections. An incumbent legislator may therefore vote against her own interests on some rule with the expectation that her co-partisans would act the same way on legislation they might

44

not personally favor, so that they may all continue to benefit from the surety relationship among politicians, party leaders, and the electorate.

Second, a member of the majority party may personally support a piece of legislation even though her constituents oppose the measure. In fact, her vote in favor of the rules may be necessary to pass the legislation because, for example, there may be members of the minority party in the same boat (that is, they personally oppose the legislation and would vote against the rule, but would vote yes on final passage because of electoral considerations). Therefore, the majority-party member votes with her party on the rule and subsequently votes against the party on final passage in order to advance policies she favors and her district opposes.

Third, the party may provide side payments to its back-benchers to encourage them to support the rules, especially in cases where they are personally opposed to the legislation. For example, numerous observers of the legislative process have documented that one factor influencing committee assignments – something of considerable import to professional politicians – is whether party leaders believe that a back-bencher is sufficiently loyal to the party (e.g., Masters 1961; Sinclair 2006). Systematic evidence for this claim is provided by a series of studies on committee transfers. Rohde and Shepsle (1973) report that Democratic party loyalists were more likely to receive a new committee assignment if that they had requested a transfer – a phenomenon they observed even during the period when other Congressional observers saw Congressional parties as especially weak (e.g., Mayhew 1974a). Similarly, Smith and Ray (1983) find that when the Democratic caucus holds its elections to Congressional committees (whose outcomes are often foreordained by the party's Steering Committee), party loyalty scores are significant predictors of who wins a committee assignment. Cox and McCubbins (1993) note that among both Democratic and Republican MCs, party loyalty scores are important predictors of whether a legislator receives a transfer to a seat on one of the highly coveted control committees (i.e., Appropriations, Rules, Ways and Means, and Budget).[6]

There is also evidence suggesting that party leaders provide rewards to politicians who later become party loyalists, either to raise the status within the party of those actors they expect to be loyal to the leadership

---

[6] Cox and McCubbins (1993) also find that party loyalty is negatively related to being denied a transfer request and positively related to being "drafted" to transfer without a formal request.

or to build up a reservoir of good will that they can tap into to garner support on hard votes in the future. To that end, Cox and McCubbins (1993) observe that among freshman MCs seeking their initial committee assignments, individuals who ultimately proved to be party loyalists were more likely to get the committee they placed at the top of their request list. They also find that when Congressional party leaders make assignments of seniority among members of the same freshman class, future party loyalty is positively related to initial seniority status. Similarly, Leyden and Borelli (1994) find that although campaign funds tend to be targeted to vulnerable incumbents and are not a reward for party loyalty, those individuals who receive much-needed funds in hard-fought reelection contests become substantially more loyal partisans after the fact.

One final observation in closing this section is that the observed effects of efforts to encourage party discipline are likely to understate the "true" total effect of partisan institutions because of their influence on politicians' entry decisions. When politicians choose which party to affiliate with, it seems likely that they will take into account the payoff that they will receive from winning elections. If it is the case that the national parties are more welcoming of MCs willing to cooperate with the organization and that they provide these individuals with the most desirable committee assignments and other perks while marginalizing legislators who are out of step with the party, then politicians are most likely to join the party where they generally agree with incumbent members of the organization. Thus, candidates' anticipation of party pressures in the legislature may be sufficient to ensure reasonably high levels of partisan preference homogeneity in government even if the national organization is not especially active in the recruitment and nomination of candidates to office (Snyder and Ting 2002).

Entry Deterrence and the Electorate's Collective Dilemma

The argument for why the electorate would accept a system of party government is that if the national parties organized the legislature, they could secure less extreme policy outcomes than what voters expect to observe if the government were ruled by ideologically motivated legislators not bound to a party program. As argued earlier, this requires that voters nationally commit to voting only for major-party candidates. One might expect voters to therefore form a kind of tacit agreement among themselves, promising not to vote for an independent or third-party candidate. However, voters face a commitment problem in that in many districts there are short-term incentives to defect from the national agree-ment to vote for only major-party candidates. If it were believed that districts would succumb to that temptation, then candidates everywhere would refuse to run as affiliates of one of the national parties. A necessary condition for party government is therefore that politicians must believe that other districts' commitment to the national agreement is credible.

Repeat Play. A critical element of the solution to voters' commitment problem is simply that legislative elections occur repeatedly over time. The repetition of elections proves important because it is often possible to induce individuals who have incentives to defect from an agreement to cooperate if they are subject to retaliation in the future (e.g., Axelrod 1984). By this logic, voters who might be tempted to capture short-term gains by voting for an independent or third-party candidate would be deterred from doing so if they believe that in future elections voters elsewhere would also vote for an independent or third-party candidate – the result of their defection is that they risk a return to a world without parties.

Electoral Rules as a Barrier to Entry. It is well known that repeat play is no guarantee that voters nationally will cooperate. The folk theorem indicates that almost anything is possible in repeated interactions. Fortu-nately for voters in the United States, two additional factors encourage them to act in ways that allow them to overcome their collective dilemma.

One supplement to repeat play that encourages voters to coordinate on two parties in the United States is the rules used in legislative elections. In this country, legislative elections are conducted in single-member electoral districts with elections determined by plurality or majority rule. Follow-ing Duverger's (1954) logic, these so-called first-past-the-post electoral systems encourage a tendency toward two-party competition.

There is no reason, simply by Duverger's logic, to conclude that a candidate allied with the national parties would be one of the two con-testants in any given district. However, incumbent political parties have a first-mover advantage in announcing their national programs that may allow them to deter third-party candidates from entering in first-past-the-post electoral systems. The rationale, first articulated by Palfrey (1984), is that if the two parties adopt appropriate platforms on either side of the median voter in an electoral district, then there does not exist a platform that a third party could adopt that would allow it to secure a plurality of the vote. That being said, Palfrey limited his argument to party platform

choices within a single electoral district, and a national platform that
deters entry in a legislative district with one set of preferences may not
deter entry in another district with a different set of preferences.

To see how Palfrey's intuitions might play out in legislative elections
with national parties, note first that the entry of a third party to the left
of the Left Party's platform or the right of the Right Party's platform
is largely irrelevant to the legislature's policy choices. In cases like these,
voters in non-centrist districts might sincerely prefer the third party's program; however, the election of a third-party candidate from their district
would not change the spatial location of the median voter in the legislature, so ideologically extreme voters would be indifferent between the
third-party candidate and their preferred major-party candidate. Further,
with sincere voting, the entry of the third party could, perversely, lead
to the election of the national party least preferred by those individuals
who cast votes for the third party because the third party and its near-
est national party would split the votes on their side of the ideological
spectrum.

A third party that entered at the center of the political spectrum (perhaps adopting the ideal point of the median voter in the median district
as her platform) would be potentially more successful in districts at the
center of the ideological continuum because voters might be able to gain
from her election. In fact, a major-party candidate who defected from her
party to join the third party would be certain to win the election if the
third party was closer to the ideal point of the median voter in such a district if her party did not field a replacement. However, if the party of the
defector fielded a replacement candidate, the third-party candidate might
nevertheless have difficulty securing the required share of the votes needed
to win election. The problem that the centrist third-party candidate faces
is that the Left Party monopolizes the votes to her left and the Right Party
monopolizes the votes to her right, and both the Left and Right Parties
get votes from centrist voters with ideal points between their platform
and that of the third party. To secure victory therefore requires that there
be a very dense clustering of voters around the third-party's platform,
which may be possible in some districts, but which is not a general rule.
(It is not possible to simply invoke the possibility of gains from strategic
voting to create incentives for voters to reject a major-party candidate,
unless there is some way for voters to coordinate on the third party.)

National Parties Benefit from Scale Economies. The other key barrier to
entry by independent and third-party candidates in the United States is

the sheer cost of organizing an election campaign. Although the models developed previously give the appearance that parties contest elections simply by announcing where along a left-right ideological continuum a candidate might reside, it is obvious that there is much more involved in running for office in real-world contests. Politicians must devise some way of informing large numbers of voters about their policy positions, turning out their supporters, and so forth.

An association with a major political party reduces these costs in a number of important regards. First, political parties have brand names that communicate credible information about how votes for a particular candidate will translate into public policy decisions. This provides a candidate campaigning as a party member an important advantage because ordinary citizens can look to her party affiliation as a signal about the positions she is expected to take on various issues once in government. Now, I argued earlier that this advantage is not sufficient to induce voters in centrist districts to support major-party candidates. However, it is clear that party brand names nevertheless encourage voters to coordinate on major-party candidates in several ways. To begin, voters in liberal districts and voters in conservative districts prefer candidates belonging, respectively, to liberal and conservative parties to an independent or third-party candidate who may claim to have views consistent with those of her district, but who cannot convey that information credibly. Furthermore, the argument that centrist districts would prefer an unaffiliated candidate to a major-party candidate was predicated on there not being many circumstances where they would be made worse off by the election of the unaffiliated candidate; however, the strength of the incentive to vote for an unaffiliated candidate varies positively with the probability that centrist districts will prefer that candidate to a major-party candidate. If voters do not assign a high probability to a candidate's being a centrist because she lacks a brand name that credibly conveys that information, then their incentives to defect from the national electorate's agreement are quite weak.

Second, incumbent parties already have a campaign infrastructure in place. Organizing election campaigns is a time-consuming and costly affair. Major-party candidates in the United States therefore benefit from the fact that their parties provide support in the form of financial support (both direct contributions and putting their candidates in touch with other donors), advice about what issues (if any) to emphasize in their district, guidance about how to frame issues during the campaign so as to maximize their appeal, and, perhaps most importantly, a group of political activists in their district who are willing to put up yard signs, canvass their neighborhoods and distribute campaign literature, make phone calls on candidates' behalf, bring friends and family to the polls, and so on. Independent and third-party candidates, in contrast, must build their own campaign operation – often from scratch. This places them at a competitive disadvantage. It also creates powerful incentives for talented politicians to join one of the major parties rather than to set out on their own.

Third, and perhaps most importantly, major party candidates have tremendous advantages just in terms of getting on the ballot. Historically, this was accomplished by the party strip ballots of the nineteenth century, where third-party candidates would have to incur the cost of printing their own ballots (e.g., Rusk 1970). More recently, this has been accomplished by restrictive ballot access laws, where it seems that the major parties have colluded to protect the members of both organizations from third-party challenges by preventing the entry from these groups (e.g., Issacharoff and Pildes 1998).

Credible Commitments

The surety model of party government depends on voters believing that party leaders will follow through on their commitment to pursue their party's program. This requires that two conditions be satisfied. First, voters must believe that party leaders do not fear being deposed by their back-benchers if they use the resources at their disposal to implement their party's program. Second, voters must believe that there are negative consequences for party leaders if they fail to fulfill their promises to the electorate in the same way that a bail bondsman forfeits the bond she posts in the event that a criminal suspect fails to appear for trial.

The Importance of Party Unity. A recurring theme of this book is that voters have confidence that party leaders will perform the functions of a surety when they observe sufficiently high levels of party unity in government. This is clearly important for the question of whether voters believe that party back-benchers will depose leaders who try to follow their party's program. Simply put, if voters observe members of a political party work together as policy-making teams, then they have confidence either (1) that party members have reasonably homogenous preferences and are happy to go along with the wishes of party leaders or (2) that party leaders have an incentive system in place which is such that they can whip members into toeing the party line without fear of backlash.

Brand Names. Party unity is also important to establish the "bond" that parties post for the candidates carrying their label. Needless to say, parties do not issue a performance bond that is similar to a traditional surety company's guarantee of a cash payment to the principal if the agent fails to meet expectations. Instead, parties stake their reputations on the performance of the candidates who carry the party label. Useful comparisons in industrial organizations might include a franchise, where a parent firm markets the right to use its reputation to local retail outlets, or a brand licensing arrangement, where a company leases the right to use its brand name to a firm in a related industry to produce something akin to a brand extension. The fundamental similarity among these three very different organizational forms is that the parent organization is, essentially, pledging that people who have favorable evaluations of its "brand" will also have a favorable evaluation of the products offered by an independent actor – the candidate, the local outlet, or the company paying a licensing fee – who uses its brand name.

It is reasonable for people to interpret pledges by franchises, political parties, and the like as a credible signal of candidate or product quality if they believe that the parent organization suffers long-term consequences if it makes a sufficient number of bad pledges. Thus, the reputation of McDonald's suffers if too many of its local stores offer cold French fries and poor customer service. Similarly, the reputation of a party suffers if it throws its support to too many candidates at odds with their organization on key issues. In both cases, the brand name no longer reduces the public's uncertainty about product or candidate quality, and "brand equity" is lost, with people now more open to sampling new "products" rather than remaining loyal to an existing brand. The effects of greater uncertainty about product or candidate attributes would be amplified by the loss of credibility. A high failure rate would lead people to infer that either the parent organization does not value its reputation sufficiently to incur the costs of policing the behavior of its affiliates, or something has occurred that prevents the organization from performing its function as a surety. Thus, not only would a party's endorsement of candidates who frequently vote contrary to the party line increase voter uncertainty about the organization, it would also encourage people to look for more credible cues than a candidate's party affiliation when deciding how to vote.

In short, a high rate of defection within a party jeopardizes partisan brand loyalties. To the extent that party members value their brand loyalists because they promote their personal political ambitions and help parties capture legislative majorities, partisan endorsements could be treated as credible signals of a candidate's behavior once in office.

The Benefits of Partisan Brand Names. The argument just developed suggests that if a party values its brand name because it brings the organization electoral rewards, then it is reasonable for voters to see party nominations as credible signals of a candidate's attributes. I believe that the primary benefit that a party receives from its brand name is that it helps it to cultivate a group of strong partisans in the electorate who contribute to the electoral success of incumbent party members and to the organization's prospects for capturing legislative majorities. Elsewhere in the book I discuss how the public forms strong partisan attachments, and other research provides better theoretical foundations for why strong partisans act in the ways described later (cf. Campbell et al. 1960). The purpose of this section is simply to document with evidence up to the modern period a variety of ways that the presence of strong partisans in a district improves party members' electoral prospects.

The most obvious benefit of brand loyalists in the electorate is that they are the individuals least likely to defect to the other party come Election Day (e.g., Campbell et al. 1960; Bartels 2000). This is important because these individuals deliver votes, but also because they allow candidates to focus their persuasive appeals to individuals who are on the fence.

In addition to their loyalty at the polls, strong partisans aid incumbents by lowering the costs of campaigning in noteworthy ways. One advantage of strong partisans is that they are considerably more likely to turn out to vote (e.g., Campbell et al. 1960). Evidence to this effect is provided in Figure 2.5, which plots the percentage difference in the self-reported voter participation rates between individuals who describe themselves as strong partisans and those who do not in Presidential election years from 1952 through 2004 (Source: American National Election Study).[7] The

---

[7] Admittedly, self-reports of voter turnout are biased upward, presumably because people want to give the socially desirable response that they voted. For this to be a major concern for my argument, however, it would have to be true (1) that strong partisans are more likely to mislead interviewers than other Americans and (2) that the rate of lying among strong partisans has increased over time. I believe that an argument could be made that strong partisans experience greater social desirability

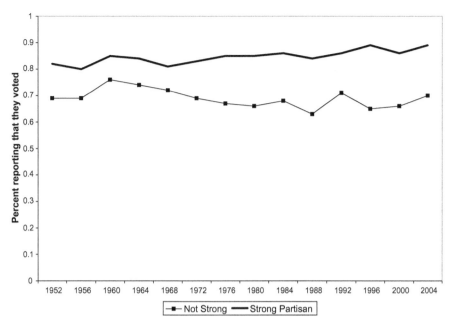

Figure 2.5. Self-reported voter turnout of strong partisans relative to other respondents. *Source:* American National Election Study Cumulative Data File, 1952–2004.

figure shows that strong partisans have turned out to vote at a rate at least 10 percent higher than the rest of the public in every Presidential election since the first Eisenhower-Stevenson contest in 1952 and that this difference has grown markedly over time.

The high turnout rate among strong partisans could point to one of two different phenomena, both of which would be of benefit to the party. It could be that strong partisans naturally turn out at higher rates because they feel more passionately about the outcome than other citizens, and their participation would allow candidates to target resources to something other than their mobilization. Alternatively, it may be that the turnout rate among strong partisans is greater because these are the individuals most likely to be targeted by local political operatives for mobilization, because it is safe to say that they will not vote for the challenger. In any event, as long as parties prefer to have a group of

effects (although I do not find it plausible that strong partisans are less likely to turn out to vote than weak partisans and independents), but it seems implausible to me that these effects would have grown consistently stronger over time.

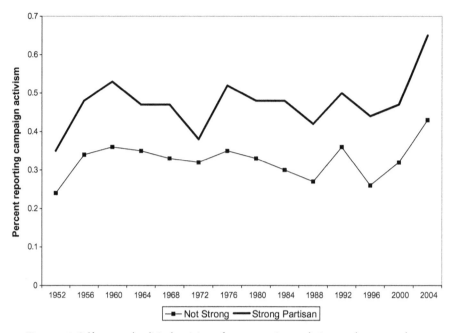

Figure 2.6. Self-reported political activism of strong partisans relative to other respondents. *Source:* ANES Cumulative Data File, 1952–2004.

committed partisans locally because they turn out to vote more readily, or because if turned out by the party they are more loyal, the presence of strong partisans is an electoral asset. Notably, the growing difference in the participation rate of strong partisans over the past fifty years suggests that the value to the party of possessing brand loyalists has grown over time.

A further advantage of strong partisans is that they are more likely to become campaign activists who contribute their own time and money to their party's electoral fortunes. In fact, the effect of party spirit on political activism is noticeably stronger than that observed for turnout. Figure 2.6 illustrates the difference in self-reports of campaign participation between strong partisans and other people in Presidential election years since 1952 (source ANES). The possible types of contributions include things like trying to influence others' votes, attending political meetings, working for a party or candidate, wearing a candidate button or displaying a sign in a yard, and donating money. Figure 2.7 portrays only the difference in the rate of giving money – an activity that some might think is more valuable to the candidate and more costly to the ordinary person than

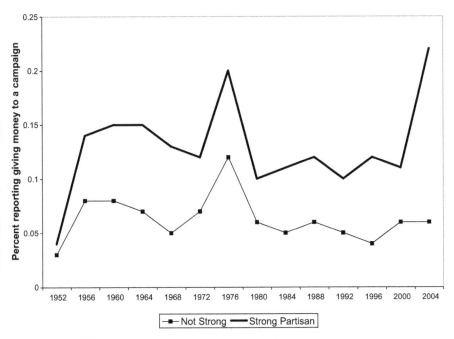

Figure 2.7. Self-reported campaign giving of strong partisans relative to other respondents. *Source:* ANES Cumulative Data File, 1952–2004.

wearing a button or attending a campaign rally. The figures reveal that over the past half-century, strong partisans have been between 35 percent and 70 percent more likely to contribute to a campaign (in some form other than voting) than other Americans and are somewhere between 30 percent and almost 300 percent more likely to give money to a candidate or party. Thus, parties value brand loyalists because these individuals provide the pool of individuals who are most willing to contribute to the organization's electoral fortunes. Echoing the pattern observed with respect to voter turnout, it is again noteworthy that strong partisans have become more valuable to parties over time as their rate of campaign participation has risen markedly relative to that observed among the general public.

CONCLUSION

Classic accounts describe a system of party government as consisting of the following components (cf. Ranney 1954). There are two ideologically cohesive and disciplined political parties competing for control over a national legislature. Each party has its own beliefs about the public's preferences and a program of government policies that it believes will fulfill those preferences. Through election campaigns, each party announces its program and then seeks to convince the public that its program will better meet their needs. In every electoral district, the people vote for the candidate who belongs to the party that they most prefer. The party whose candidates win in a majority of electoral districts gains full control of the government and implements its policy platform. Voters learn what kinds of outcomes (as opposed to promises) to expect from governance by the ruling party, and the process then repeats itself.

Many political scientists of the early twentieth century argued that party government is beneficial to the operation of a large industrial society. Their argument was predicated on the assumption that the organization of such a society requires the creation and maintenance of such complex policy instruments that direct popular control of the government is not feasible. At the same time, they understood that autocracy, for all the usual reasons, is not an enviable alternative. They saw a system of party government as providing an admirable middle ground in that it provides ordinary people with the ability to influence, in broad terms, the direction of government through their choice of which party to support, without requiring each voter to become a specialist in the details of national policy (American Political Science Association Committee on Political Parties 1950).

Political scientists have long held the view that a system of party government requires "responsibility" in the sense that the elected officials (and the nominees) belonging to a party organization maintain a high degree of internal cohesion. Responsibility is often seen as necessary for party government, in part, because the majority party must marshal the support of its members to push the program it promised to the electorate through the legislature (Wilson 1900). Responsibility is also seen as important to realizing the benefits of party government because politicians who are given the opportunity to differentiate themselves from the other members of their party are likely to do so in order to increase their appeal to constituents in their district (Schattschneider 1942). The result is that candidates everywhere will take policy positions that maximize their appeal to local constituents such that it no longer makes sense for voters to treat the national party as a collective agent.

Political scientists have also long held the view that the United States does not (and many have argued cannot) have a system of party government. The chief obstacle to party government is that there is little motivation for politicians to create responsible parties. In particular, the American system of electing legislators from single-member electoral districts creates seemingly powerful incentives for candidates to declare their party affiliation to be merely a label that conveys no information about their political views and to try to create personal reputations perfectly catering to local tastes. To the extent that a party control apparatus must be agreed to by members of the party organization, it therefore seems that politicians motivated by the desire to win elective office would resist the creation of institutions that might be used to coerce themselves into voting against the interests of their constituents (Mayhew 1974a; Krehbiel 1993). Because party government requires cohesive responsible parties, such a system is unlikely to emerge in the United States.

This chapter argued that a system of party government is consistent with the interests of politicians and voters in the United States. The building block of the argument was the observation that most candidates for public office have relatively extreme policy views and that at least some of these candidates would pursue these interests if elected even if doing so was harmful to the interests of their constituents. One consequence of having politicians motivated by policy considerations is that legislators tend to sort on the basis of political ideology into those who support the policies enacted by the government and those who do not, even when parties do not exist. This pattern of support and opposition to the government's policies encourages both groups to form parties to advance their shared interests (i.e., capture majority control of government). Voters may come to value the form of party government that results because the less ideologically driven candidates in the ruling party rein in their ideologues so as to protect their seats and majority status from the looming threat of an opposition-party takeover.

This chapter also introduced the surety model to explain how the United States is able to realize many of the benefits of a system of party government without responsible parties. The theoretical argument is summarized in Figure 2.8. The first part of the story concerning what goes on in Washington, which will be familiar to students of legislative politics, is that a party's members have a shared interest in winning majority control of Congress. To facilitate this end, they develop institutions that provide party leaders with the ability and incentives to promote legislation that is viewed favorably by large numbers of voters so that the organization develops a reputation for delivering good outcomes to a certain

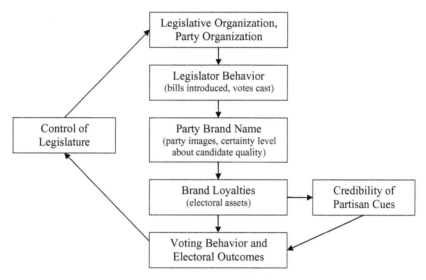

Figure 2.8. Overview of the theory.

segment of the population (cf. Aldrich 1995; Cox and McCubbins 1993, 2005).

The second part of the story, which is the central theme of this book, concerns why someone might find party labels to provide credible predictors of how vote choices for individual politicians in November might translate into policy outcomes given that the national party has little say in who gets to run. The argument is that in the same way that voters look to the past issue positions of the national parties to make inferences about how the party is likely to act in the future, they also look to the level of intra-party conflict in government to infer whether a party has institutions in place to enforce party discipline and otherwise implement its program. On the one hand, if party unity is low, then voters have little reason to trust that party labels will be useful guides to their voting behavior. On the other hand, if party unity is sufficiently high that people may infer that institutions to promote party discipline exist, then that increases certainty that support for a party's candidates translates into support for the party's program, which increases the likelihood that ordinary citizens will become brand loyalists who incur private costs of participating on the party's behalf. Furthermore, to the extent that parties believe that brand loyalists are a valuable electoral asset that will be forfeit if party unity breaks down, and ordinary citizens believe that parties believe that brand loyalists are a valuable electoral asset (and so on), it is rational for people to infer that party members in government will continue to incur the private cost of maintaining high levels of party discipline in the future. As a result, parties with a reputation for maintaining high levels of party unity in government are also able to use their labels as credible signals about the attributes of its candidates.

3

Voter Learning about Parties

The classic account of how voters use party labels to reduce their uncertainty at the polls is provided by Anthony Downs in *An Economic Theory of Democracy*. A fundamental assumption motivating Downs's work is that citizens wish to invest an optimal amount of personal resources into the acquisition of political information that they may then use to guide their political behavior. In the language of neoclassical economics, voters should therefore seek information up to the level where its marginal cost equals its marginal benefit. Because people receive virtually no private return from casting an informed ballot, this means that voters should incur virtually no costs in information search.

According to Downs, it is fortunate for democracies everywhere that office-motivated politicians have incentives to solve this problem by providing information to voters during the course of election campaigns and that party brand names provide a particularly useful vehicle for conveying that information. He argues that the actions that parties take when in government, and the consequences of those actions for the average person, provide voters with readily available information (i.e., who is in power and whether times are good) to evaluate the performance of the incumbent party. If times are good, voters are likely to believe the incumbent party's promise to continue these policies, knowing that the incumbent party will want to build a reputation for delivering a certain set of outcomes to the electorate. If times are bad, then opposition parties have strong incentives to communicate to the public the connection between the incumbent's behavior and national outcomes and to offer an alternative vision for the direction of government.

Downs's ideas have proven incredibly influential, but their applicability to the study of American political parties is suspect because of the way that he models how voters *learn* which party they prefer to hold office.

Compared to political systems in other parts of the world, the United States has notoriously fractured national parties, with individual politicians often taking policy positions that place them at odds with other members of their party. As a result, it is a mistake to treat American political parties analytically as if they are a single actor and, perhaps more importantly, to assume that voters treat parties as if they are a perfectly unified organization whose performance in office can be rewarded or punished.[1] In fact, it is the possibility that internal party fissures might emerge that raises the question as to why voters might find party labels to be credible predictors of candidate quality in the first place.

The purpose of this chapter is to develop and test a model of how people form beliefs about political parties given the presence of internal party conflicts. Understanding this process is essential to understanding how people employ partisan brand names to inform their political behavior

VOTER LEARNING AND PARTISANSHIP

Although I disagree in some fundamental ways with how previous researchers have conceptualized voter learning about parties, my methodological approach to modeling this process shares a great deal with the work of previous researchers who have modeled how Downs's rational voters learn about political parties. In the first incarnation of a formal model of voter learning about parties, Fiorina (1981) describes the learning process as voters maintaining a "running tally" of the relative performance of the two parties in office over the course of their lifetimes. Thus, one might imagine voters maintaining a mental ledger of the parties' performance in office – good outcomes under a Democratic administration or bad outcomes under a Republican administration are positive entries in the ledger, while bad outcomes under a Democratic administration or good outcomes under a Republican administration are negative entries. People's beliefs about parties are the sum of these ledger entries, perhaps with some discounting of times long ago, that reveals to the voter which party to support.

In subsequent scholarship, researchers amended Fiorina's model by applying concepts from probability theory to model the learning process

---

[1] Downs (1957) recognized a similar problem in his discussion of multiparty political systems with coalition governments where the attribution of credit and blame is difficult among coalition members.

of a "rational" voter who combines information that she has received over the course of a lifetime when assessing her party preferences. Using the mathematical logic of Bayesian learning, Achen (1992) argues that beliefs about how a party performs are based on a lifetime of experiences with Democrats and Republicans in office, with current events given no more weight than the experiences of early adulthood. As a result, as people get older, their beliefs about the relative performance of the two parties become more stable. The logic underlying this result is that with greater experience, the information received during the most recent election cycle will be dwarfed by the set of experiences that they accumulated earlier in their lifetimes. Achen describes this process as "rational learning" because it gives an unbiased (in the statistical sense) forecast of future party performance, writing: "only the true mean benefit is of interest to the voter. She wishes to forecast future benefits so that she can vote intelligently.... Hence to predict benefits to come, she can do no better than to forecast the mean" (Achen 1992, p. 199).

A third approach taken by scholars is to point to dramatic fluctuations in public opinion data concerning people's preferences for retaining the incumbent political party, data which suggests that the American public is much more sensitive to short-run information than Achen allows. Gerber and Green (1999; Green, Palmquist, and Schickler 2002) argue in their response to Achen's work that rational voters should discount the past because more recent observations provide a better sense of which party would perform better given current circumstances. To advance this claim, they too develop a formal rational learning model grounded in probability theory and prove formally that if voters "know" how much variation exists in party performance over time, then rational voters will discount previous experience as a function of variance in party performance: greater over time variation causes them to increase the weight they give to the most recent events.

A MODEL OF VOTER LEARNING

To develop a model of voter learning about parties, it is necessary to amend previous approaches in three important ways. First, previous models in political science have treated the object of voter learning to be "net party benefits," which represents the difference in the quality of Democratic and Republican performance in office. My approach is to treat each party as a distinct object of voter learning. One benefit of this tact is that it may matter to voters (and our understanding of voters) whether they like both parties, dislike both parties, or have split opinions in that they like one party and dislike another. This distinction is important because it is possible, for example, that in terms of net party benefits the following two cases are equivalent: (1) a person could have strong positive opinions about Democratic policies and neutral opinions about Republican policies and (2) a person could have neutral opinions about Democratic policies and strongly negative opinions about Republican policies. It seems likely that in the former case a person would think of themselves as having a strong preference for the Democrats because of their positive evaluation of that party, whereas in the latter case a person might feel alienated by the party system and think of themselves as a political Independent. Because a model of learning about net party benefits obscures this distinction, it is important to treat the two parties as distinct objects of voter interest.

Second, previous learning models have aggregated all aspects of governance into a single measure of preference; however, it seems likely that people's images about political parties are more nuanced than a simple pro or con assessment of party performance over time. For example, voters may hold beliefs about whether a party is liberal or conservative, about its positions on particular issue areas, or about which social groups a party's issue positions might benefit. This difference is important because it means that public opinion about which party's candidates they hope to win the next election may change with the country's circumstances even though their party images, as well as their general predisposition for Democrats or Republicans, may remain stable over time. For example, during a recession, voters may believe that the Democrats will do a better job of funding social welfare programs that ease the economic hardships of those thrown out of work. On the other hand, during a foreign policy crisis, voters may believe that the Republicans will do a better job of handling things.

Third, and most importantly, previous work assumes the expected value (i.e., the mean) of net party benefits is an unknown quantity that is the object of voter learning, while it assumes the variance of net party benefits is "known" (i.e., not an object of learning). It is useful to relax the latter assumption for two reasons. To begin, it seems implausible to assume that the American people know the variance of the distribution of "net party benefits" but not the mean, and this assumption drives the results in earlier studies. In Achen's work, this assumption strongly influences the result that people's evaluations of party performance become inexorably more stable over time because it, in effect, prevents people from "scratching their heads" when confronted with new information that strongly contradicts their prior beliefs. For Gerber and Green, the "known" variance in net party benefits determines the rate at which people discount the past when making predictions about party performance. If this known variance is high, then voters should discount everything but their most recent political experiences because current events provide the best predictor of outcomes in the immediate future; if this quantity is low, then rational voters incorporate experiences from earlier days to make party assessments. In both cases, the assumptions that the researcher makes about the variance term greatly effect the results.

The other concern with this assumption is more foundational for understanding parties as extended brands in that in this framework voters' beliefs about parties are derived from their observations of individual party members over time, not just their assessments of outcomes when a particular party is in control of government. As a result, a voter who observes the actions of a national party will form some estimate of the policy position of the average Democrat or Republican in office. Furthermore, they will generate an estimate of the variance in Democratic or Republican Party members' issue positions. The latter point is essential to understanding the process of partisan branding, because a rational voter observing internal party divisions will be unlikely to associate the national party with a particular set of political ideals and may be more reluctant to draw upon partisan cues to inform her vote choices come Election Day. It is therefore assumed that voters draw upon their political observations over time to learn about both the mean and variance in the issue positions of party members.

The Formal Model

For the purposes of this book, rational learning is represented as a Bayesian updating model in which voters make inferences about a party's ideology or issue positions based on their political observations.[2] Stated

---

[2] There is dispute about people's capacity to employ Bayes' Rule. The problem is that people often use heuristic devices that simplify the task of making probabilistic judgments rather than obeying the axioms of probability theory (e.g., Tversky and Kahneman 1974, 1983). Speaking in broad terms, the finding in the literature is that these heuristics generally perform well, but that in some situations they cause people to make systematic errors in uncertainty assessment and choice. While understanding these systematic errors may ultimately prove useful in understanding candidate and party evaluations, the empirical leverage provided by my model for the typical voter is clearly demonstrated in this and later chapters.

in formal terms, this model is based on a few simple definitions and assumptions. First, assume that an individual's beliefs about the distribution of party members' positions along a liberal or conservative ideological continuum (which are represented by points along the real line) is determined by their observations of party members over time. Let y_j denotes the jth candidate observation associated with a political party and $j \in \{1, \ldots, n\}$.

Second, assume that each observation is a random draw from a distribution of party members with unknown mean μ and unknown variance σ^2. For simplicity the normal distribution is used. Thus, $y_j \sim_{iid} N(\mu, \sigma^2)$ for all j.

Third, assume that an individual's prior belief about the mean and variance in the party's positions is represented by a normal-inverse-chi-squared distribution ($N - \chi^{-2}$). The normal-inverse-chi-squared distribution is convenient because it is the conjugate prior distribution for μ and σ^2 if the data are normally distributed. Thus, prior beliefs about μ and σ^2 are given by:

$$\mu, \sigma^2 \sim N - \chi^{-2}(\mu_0, k_0, v_0, \sigma_0^2), \; k_0, v_0, \sigma_0^2 > 0$$
(parameterized as in Gelman, Carlin, Stern, and Rubin 1995).

The interpretation of the prior parameters $\mu_0, k_0, v_0, \sigma_0^2$ is easiest if one decomposes the joint distribution of μ and σ^2 into $p(\mu, \sigma^2) = p(\mu \,|\, \sigma^2)p(\sigma^2)$. In this case, $\mu \,|\, \sigma^2 \sim N(\mu_0, \sigma^2/k_0)$ and $\sigma^2 \sim \chi^{-2}(v_0, \sigma_0^2)$. So, μ_0 represents the prior beliefs about the party's average issue position and σ^2/k_0 the amount of prior uncertainty around that location. Whereas σ^2/k_0 indicates the prior uncertainty about the mean, σ^2 provides information about uncertainty in y_j. The prior information about σ^2 is given by σ_0^2 and v_0, which denote, respectively, the prior scale and degrees of freedom such that the expected prior uncertainty about the party's location is $E[\sigma_0^2] = \sigma_0^2[v_0/(v_0 - 2)]$. Overall, this probability model is flexible enough that it could provide a reasonable approximation for many individuals' prior beliefs. The main restriction is that beliefs must be unimodal and symmetric about μ.

Fourth, assume that people obey the standard axioms of probability theory including Bayes' Rule. Individuals observe y_j – the individual messages about the party – and use these additional data to update their beliefs about μ and σ^2.

The assumptions are simply a statement that individuals pursue a Bayesian learning process and provide the distributional assumptions of the model. Given these definitions, it is straightforward to identify an individual's beliefs about a party's issue positions following a set of political observations.

Proposition One: Following n observations, the joint posterior distribution of μ and σ^2 is:

$$\mu, \sigma^2 | y \sim N - \chi^{-2}(\mu_n, k_n, v_n, \sigma_n^2),$$

where $\mu_n = (k_0/(k_0 + n))\mu_0 + (n/(k_0 + n))\bar{y}_n$

$k_n = k_0 + n$

$v_n = v_0 + n$

$\sigma_n^2 = \{v_0\sigma_0^2 + (n-1)s_n^2 + [(k_0 n/(k_0 + n))(\bar{y}_n - \mu_0)^2]\}/v_n$

$s_n^2 = \sum(y_i - \bar{y}_n)^2/(n-1)$

$\bar{y}_n = \sum y_i/n$

The marginal posterior distribution of μ is:

$$\mu | y \sim t_{v_n}\left(\mu_n, \sigma_n^2/k_n\right)$$
$$\text{Therefore, } E_n[\mu] = \mu_n$$

The marginal posterior distribution of σ^2 is:

$$\sigma^2 | y \sim \chi^{-2}\left(v_n, \sigma_n^2\right)$$

Therefore, $E_n[\sigma^2] = (\sigma_n^2 v_n)/(v_n - 2)$ (Gelman et al. 1995, pp. 72–3).

The key elements of the proposition for present purposes are $E_n[\mu]$ and $E_n[\sigma^2]$, which are the expected values for the average party message and the variance in those messages. The interpretation and implications of these two expressions will be considered in turn.

Implications of Bayesian Learning about the Mean

The result for the average party message, $E_n[\mu]$, states that beliefs about the position of the average party member will be based on a weighted average of prior beliefs μ_0 and the sample mean $\bar{y}_n$ of the observed candidate messages, where the weights are given respectively by the amount of prior information k_0 and the number of new messages n.[3] As a result,

---

[3] With the exception that I am modeling issue positions rather than net party benefits, this result is similar to that of Achen (1992).

when confronted with information contrary to their prior beliefs, a person will update their view of the party's ideology to make their posterior beliefs more consistent with the new data. For example, someone who observes that incumbent politicians within a party today are pursuing a political agenda further to the political left than her prior beliefs would have led her to believe will come to see the average party member as being more liberal. Conversely, someone who observes incumbent politicians in the party pursuing a political agenda further to the political right than her prior beliefs would have led her to believe will come to see the average member of the organization as being more conservative. The rate of change in a person's beliefs depends on the volume of information received: beliefs will change more as the amount of information collected during an election cycle that contradicts prior beliefs increases. Similarly, beliefs will change more if someone's prior beliefs were weaker. Thus, beliefs will change most among politically inexperienced people actively following the current campaign.

The most important implication of this result is that as the national parties polarize, voters should come to see bigger differences between the Democratic and Republican Parties.[4] The one subtlety about this result concerns the relative weight that people are said to give to new information about the party and a person's prior beliefs. According to my model, people place equal weight on every piece of data that they receive about the political world. This claim may seem surprising because

---

[4] It would seem that there would be little dispute over such a simple proposition, but similar arguments by political scientists have been met with considerable controversy. One point of disagreement involves the observation that supporters of the Democratic and Republican Parties appear to have different beliefs about objects in their political environment (e.g., Campbell, et al. 1960; Zaller 1992). This observation proves important in the assessment of learning models because individuals who obey a Bayesian learning process and who are exposed to the same set of information should inexorably come to see the world in the same way even if they begin with different sets of prior beliefs (Bartels 2002). I think that in many cases, differences in the opinions of Democratic and Republican identifiers are easily explained by the fact that these two groups frequently have different preferences and therefore do not evaluate political outcomes in the same way (see also Gerber and Green 1999). Thus, supporters of the Democratic Party perceive the Democrats to handle the economy better because they favor its emphasis on low levels of unemployment, whereas Republicans tend to prioritize low inflation. Even on objective questions that do not require voters to take their personal issue preferences into account, people could have dissimilar beliefs about a party simply because they have received different messages from political elites. For example, liberal and conservative voters could see the same party in a different manner just because of differences in content of the news coverage that they prefer.

it would seem that the most recent information would loom largest in the individual's mind: wouldn't a rational voter place a premium on current information in the manner suggested by Gerber and Green (1999; see also Fiorina 1981; Green et al. 2002)?[5] I would argue that the answer to this question is "no:" a rational person who relies on party brand names to make inferences about candidate positions would not discount the past any more than a rational consumer would quickly forgive a firm that introduced a low-quality product extension. This is because party brand names do more than just communicate information to voters about a candidate's policy positions; they also convey information about a party's commitment to a particular set of policy positions. If it is the case that a party has tolerated substantial dissension in the past, then a voter observing those conflicts would not believe that the party values its brand name enough to perform its function as a political surety. Thus, a rational voter would value information about past performance even if a party's previous activities seem less relevant today.

Implications of Bayesian Learning about the Variance

The second part of Proposition One describes how voter uncertainty, represented by the term $E_n[\sigma^2]$, responds to new information about the party. The proposition states that new information can be placed into two general (but not mutually exclusive) categories that influence how party messages influence people's level of uncertainty. The first category of new information is conflicting messages about the party within a single period: high levels of intra-party ideological conflict within an electoral cycle increase uncertainty, whereas low levels of intra-party conflict decrease

[5] Gerber and Green (1998) offer some empirical support for their perspective, but their evidence does not address my theory (nor, presumably, that of Achen, whose work they were critiquing) because the survey instruments that they use to test the learning model are not an accurate measurement of the theoretical concept implied by the model developed here. To assess people's responsiveness to new information, they use responses to questions such as "Looking ahead for the next few years, which political party do you think will do a better job of keeping the country prosperous – the Republican Party or the Democratic Party?" (Gerber and Green (1998, p. 799). Answers to questions like this are not statements about party preference in general, but are conditional on things like which party is currently in power and its current performance of government. For example, during the 1990s, many Republicans may have stated that the Democrats would be better for the economy over the next few years' boom because they thought Clinton would continue to be effective in office, but that does not that mean that they believed that Democrats, in general, would be better for the economy.

uncertainty. With respect to the level of ideological conflict within a single period, both age and political information play a similar role to that in learning about the average party position. Thus, politically attentive people will respond more quickly to changes in the level of ideological conflict within parties. Additionally, recent information about the level of ideological conflict within a single period will have a larger impact on younger individuals than on older people. This is because younger people have less knowledge than older people about the parties incorporated in their prior beliefs that might dampen the influence of current events.

The second category is new information that conflicts with prior beliefs about the party's average policy position. If a party is consistent in its messages over time, then new information confirms prior beliefs and decreases uncertainty; but if the party is erratic and constantly changes its platforms, then new information may increase uncertainty so that the party label conveys no useful information that could inform voter choice. Notably, the role of political attentiveness and especially age as moderating factors for this type of new political information operates in a different manner than described previously. In this case, when information coming from political elites contradicts prior beliefs about the party, then it is the oldest people with the strongest prior beliefs whose uncertainty is most affected: it is the set of individuals with the greatest accumulated knowledge whose beliefs would be most shaken by the introduction of contradictory information about the parties. For example, if all of a sudden Republicans unified around a liberal program of massive federal expenditures to help the poor, then young people who were not exposed to the idea that Republicans oppose big government would be reasonably certain that Republicans are liberal. Older people, however, who lived through an era when Republicans were conservative, would have their beliefs about the ideology of the Republican Party thrown into doubt by its move to the left. Interestingly, the effect of political attentiveness will be quite different for young and old people in this scenario. This is because people with weak priors will generally be unaware of the fact that the parties are changing, so more current information will not change beliefs much. On the other hand, those with strong priors who are attuned to current events will receive clear messages about the extent of partisan change and will therefore have their beliefs thrown into greatest doubt. Importantly, because this kind of fundamental transformation in a party's issue positions would require a major change in the behavior of incumbents and these kinds of changes in behavior are damaging to incumbents as "experience goods" this behavior is "off the equilibrium path" in the sense that this kind of dramatic shift on an issue that party members previously agreed about is unlikely to be observed.[6] As a result, a test for this effect is not attempted in the analyses reported here.

Discussion

For the most part, the empirical implications of the learning model jibe nicely with an important body of research attempting to identify the effects of elite conflict on voters' perceptions of politicians and parties. The major theoretical claim made in this work is that before the public is able to perceive an issue as important, nevertheless for it to be able to discern the differences between Democrats and Republicans on that issue, it is necessary for political elites to come into conflict. As V. O. Key famously put it:

[V]oters are not fools. To be sure, many individual voters act in odd ways indeed; yet in the large the electorate behaves about as rationally and responsibly as we should expect, given the clarity of the alternatives presented to it and the character of the information available to it. (Key 1966, p. 7)

Accordingly, scholars over the years have found that voter beliefs about parties have responded to the presence or absence of conflict between the national parties on a host of topics ranging from political ideology (Hetherington 2001), to race (Carmines and Stimson 1989), to foreign policy (Page and Shapiro 1992).

Although there are important similarities, the theoretical implications of my Bayesian learning model depart from previous accounts in two important ways. First, previous work has generally claimed that older people are more informed about politics in general and better able to perceive differences between the two parties because they have a greater store of experiences to draw upon (e.g., Delli Karpini and Keeter 1996). In contrast, my model predicts that although these kinds of life-cycle effects may exist, they will be conditional upon the behavior of parties

---

[6] Support for the claim that parties view large-scale fundamental changes in their core issues to be harmful is provided by evidence taken from Democratic and Republican Party platforms over the course of American history. Gerring (1998) shows that the Democrats and Republicans have scarcely changed their issue positions in the years since World War II. I see variation over time in the mean ideological locations of the two parties to reflect changes in the willingness of Republicans to support tradition-ally Democratic issues (e.g., support for Social Security) or of Democrats to support traditionally Republican issues (e.g., large investments in military capability), rather than a large change in philosophy.

over the course of a person's entire lifetime. For example, a young adult who came of age during the contemporary period of party polarization may see larger party differences than their parents whose first political experiences came during the period of party decline even though the young person has been exposed to relatively little information.

Second, previous work does not distinguish the effects of conflict between the parties from conflict within the parties on the clarity with which people perceive differences between Democrats and Republicans. To a certain extent, this failing makes sense because these variables will often be highly correlated; however, it is certainly possible to have high levels of inter-party conflict and low levels of intra-party unity or vice versa. This distinction is represented graphically in Figure 3.1, which depicts the distribution of the two parties' issue positions along a left-right continuum in two hypothetical examples. In panel A, there are noticeable differences between the center of the two parties, but there is also considerable overlap between the distributions of legislators in the two parties. In this case, voters who observe a sample of Democratic and Republican positions should be quite uncertain about the positions of the parties on the issues of the day. In contrast, panel B portrays a situation where the center of both parties is at precisely the same location as described in panel A, but the variance in the distribution of both parties' membership is substantially less and there is little overlap between the policy positions of Democrats and Republicans. Voters observing a sample of Democratic and Republican positions in this latter case should be quite certain about the differences between the two parties, and this greater clarity is a result of higher levels of party unity in government, not greater extremism. Party labels are only useful to voters as predictors of legislator behavior if there are differences between the average Democrat and the average Republican and voters believe that the average Democrat and Republican are representative of other politicians carrying their label.

TESTING THE LEARNING MODEL

A test of the learning model confronts a number of major hurdles. First, the theory predicts that voter learning about parties will occur quite slowly for the great bulk of the population who have already been exposed to considerable political information. Consequently, a test of the learning model requires the use of data about both party elite behavior and public opinion that is consistent across a large swath of American history. Second, high-profile legislative action in particular policy domains occurs

Panel A. Uncertain Voter

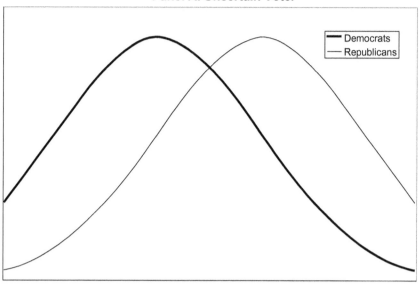

Panel B. Certain Voter

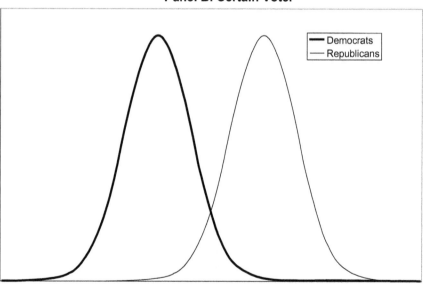

Figure 3.1. Illustrations of certain and uncertain voters.

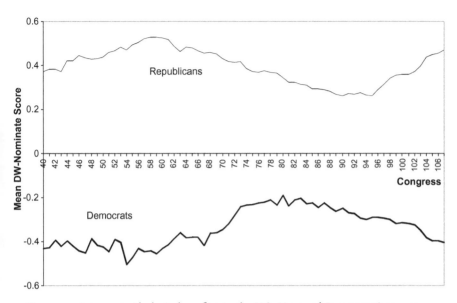

Figure 3.2. Inter-party ideological conflict in the U.S. House of Representatives, 1921–2006. *Source:* Keith Poole and Howard Rosenthal (voteview.com).

very rarely, so it is not practical to use changes over time in the voting coalitions surrounding a specific issue as a predictor of changing opinions about Democratic and Republican Party images. Third, people's attentiveness to the actions of government is likely to be limited to debates over policy most relevant to themselves. To the extent that each voter cares about a distinct set of issues, it is unlikely that we will see large aggregate changes in public opinion about the parties in any one policy domain.

To overcome these hurdles, changes in the overall level of inter-party ideological conflict and intra-party unity over the past century are used as predictors of voter beliefs about parties. The idea of the test is that during the first half of the twentieth century, there existed well-defined differences between Democrats and Republicans nationally, characterized by clear ideological conflicts and high levels of party unity in government. Beginning in the early 1960s, the level of ideological conflict between the Democrats and Republicans began to decline while levels of intra-party within both parties also waned. Then, in the mid-1970s, party conflict was reinvigorated, with growing distinctions between national Democrats and Republicans and increasing levels of unity within both organizations. The long-term trends in the level of conflict between the national Democrats and Republicans and within each party are portrayed in Figures 3.2 and 3.3. Figure 3.2 presents the difference in the average ideological

73

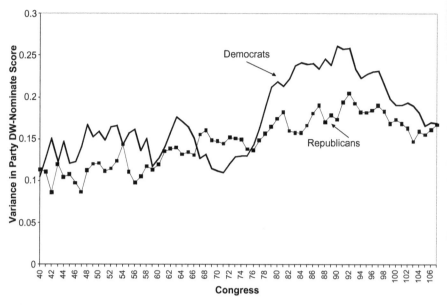

Figure 3.3. Intra-party ideological conflict in the U.S. House of Representatives, 1921–2006. *Source:* Keith Poole and Howard Rosenthal (voteview.com).

location of the Democratic and Republican members of Congress from 1921 through 2006, where legislator ideologies are measures using Poole and Rosenthal's (1997) DW-Nominate scores.[7] Figure 3.3 describes the variance in the ideological locations of Democratic and Republican MCs during the same swath of time.

If it is true that voters are generally aware of the actions of the national parties in government, then these long-term trends in inter- and intra-party ideological conflict in government can be applied to the Bayesian learning model to make predictions about voter beliefs about Democrats and Republicans. Focusing attention first on the model's implications for voter beliefs about the average party position, it is possible to generate three hypotheses.

First, it is hypothesized that voters' beliefs about the scope of inter-party conflict should decline over the period from World War II through the mid-1970s, and then rebound with the resurgence of inter-party conflict in Washington.

---

[7] The value of this measure compared to an alternative measure based on, say, interest group ratings is that the DW-Nominate scores are based on legislators' voting history over their entire tenure in Congress, so that comparisons of the ideological composition of Congress *over time* are possible (Poole and Rosenthal 1997).

Second, the learning models predicts that individuals with the highest levels of political interest will see the greatest differences between the two parties and that their beliefs about the scope of party conflict will be most sensitive to short-run changes in the level of inter-party conflict in Washington. Thus, it is hypothesized that the effect of political knowledge will be greatest during the late 1970s and early 1980s and again during the mid-1990s when the rate of change in the extent of inter-party conflict was greatest.

Third, the learning model predicts that the effects of current information flows will be moderated by people's prior experiences with Democrats and Republicans. Drawing upon the evidence about the actual level of inter-party ideological conflict during the twentieth century, it is therefore possible to generate hypotheses about how people at different stages of the life cycle will react to new information flows at different points in American history. For the early years of the study, it is hypothesized that older voters will perceive greater differences between Republicans and Democrats because many of their political experiences occurred during an era when ideological conflict was great relative to that experienced by individuals who came of age during the 1960s and 1970s. Over time, however, age should have a decreasing influence on the clarity with which people report substantial inter-party differences. This is due to two factors. To begin, over time, individuals who were older in the early years of the ANES died, so there were relatively few people with much political experience prior to the period of party decline. The older people of the 1980s and 1990s had once been the young people of the 1960s and 1970s. Thus, in the same way that individuals who were older in the 1960s were resistant to information about party decline, the opposite should have been true in later years, with older people now resistant to new information about party resurgence. Meanwhile, the younger people in the later portion of the sample would only have experienced high levels of inter-party conflict, so they should be more accepting of that information. In fact, because only older people have observed periods with low levels of inter-party conflict, one might even expect the relationship between age and perceptual clarity to have changed signs, with younger people now reporting clearer differences between Democrats and Republicans despite their political inexperience and their socialization by parents who once thought that inter-party conflict was not very important.

Applying the longitudinal data on intra-party conflict to the learning model generates a similar set of hypotheses about voter certainty about parties. First, it is hypothesized that the average level of voter certainty about Democrats and Republicans should decline during the period from World War II through the early 1970s and then rebound with changes in the level of party unity in Washington.

Second, it is hypothesized that more politically aware people should generally be more certain about the parties' positions on the issues of the day and be more sensitive to changes in the level of intra-party unity; however, these sensitivity effects may be ameliorated among sophisticates who are also more aware of changes in the average party position that co-vary with changes in party unity.

Third, because voters combine information over the course of a lifetime, it is hypothesized that data on partisan certainty will exhibit substantial cohort effects. Following a similar logic to that developed earlier with respect to perceptions of inter-party differences (and speaking in general terms at first about both parties), it is hypothesized that during the 1960s and 1970s age will be positively related to partisan certainty, since older voters in the sample would have lived through a period when Democrats and Republicans were largely unified on the key issues of the day, whereas younger people would have been most familiar with the tumult that wracked American parties at mid-century. Over time, however, the effects of age is expected to have declined as voters who were politically aware during the period of high levels of party unity through the New Deal passed away, and those who remained in the sample were increasingly dependent on information about the parties during the period of decline. It is also hypothesized that age will be negatively related to partisan certainty in the most recent years, because younger voters today have had political experiences only during the contemporary period when Democrats and Republicans are highly unified on the issues of the day. Because the Democratic movement toward greater party unity has been reasonably steady since the early 1970s, it is anticipated that the trend in the age groups who perceive the greatest partisan certainty will be steadily downward for that party; however, because Republican party unity peaked in the mid-1990s and has begun to decrease slightly since that time, the age of people with the greatest certainty about the Republican Party will be slightly greater in the 2000s than in the early 1990s.

Data

To test these hypotheses, the historical data reported in Figures 3.2 and 3.3 about the level of inter-party conflict and intra-party unity are pooled

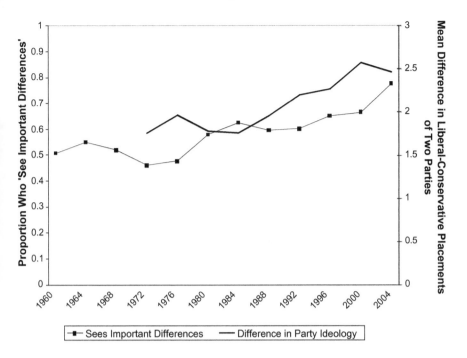

Figure 3.4. Public perceptions of inter-party differences. *Source:* ANES Cumulative Data File, 1952–2004.

with survey data from the American National Election Studies conducted during the years from 1952 through the present. To measure voter perceptions of party differences between Democrats and Republicans, two questions that have been routinely asked by ANES interviewers over the past three decades or more are used. The first question, whose use dates to 1960,[8] asks voters: "Do you think there are any important differences in what the Republicans and Democrats stand for?" Figure 3.4 plots the proportion of respondents to the ANES in Presidential election years who reported that they did see important differences between Democrats and Republicans from 1960 through 2004. Nicely, the figure reveals that voter perceptions of party differences dipped during the latter part of the period of party decline and rebounded in subsequent years, in the manner anticipated by the first research hypothesis concerning inter-party conflict.

---

[8] This question was not asked in 1962, 1970, 1974, 1978, 1982, and 2002.

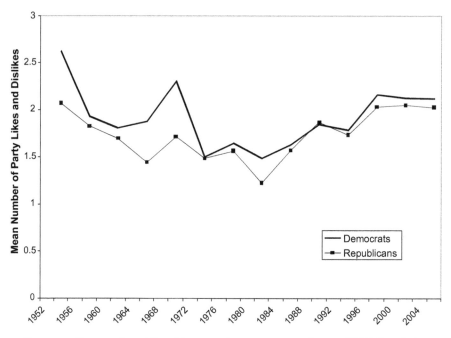

Figure 3.5. Democratic and Republican certainty, 1952–2004. *Source:* ANES Cumulative Data File, 1952–2004.

The second measure of voter perceptions of party differences is based on respondents' placements of Democrats and Republicans on liberal-conservative ideology scales. People are asked: "We hear a lot of talk these days about liberals and conservatives. I'm going to show you a seven-point scale on which the political views that people might hold are arranged from extremely liberal to extremely conservative. Where would you place the Democratic [Republican] party? 1. Extremely liberal; 2. Liberal; 3. Slightly liberal; 4. Moderate, middle of the road; 5. Slightly conservative; 6. Conservative; 7. Extremely conservative." The *Perceived Distance* between the two parties can be measured on a scale from −6 to 6 by the difference in respondent placements of the parties on these scales, thereby providing a more fine-grained measure of the extent of party differences than the dichotomous *Sees Differences* measure. Figure 3.4 plots the over-time trend in the average *Perceived Distance* between the parties for the years from 1972 through 2004. Consistent with the trend observed for the *Sees Differences* measure, Figure 3.5 reveals that voters on average perceive substantially more ideological conflict between Democrats and Republicans today than a generation ago.

Unfortunately, there is not a direct measure of voters' beliefs about the variance in party positions over time. To test for the effects of *Intra-Party Conflict* on voter uncertainty, I therefore focus on an observable implication of internal party conflict at the respondent level based on research in social psychology about how people are affected by consistent or inconsistent experiences with an object in their environment. The measure of *Democratic* and *Republican Certainty* is simply the total number of responses that people give to open-ended questions where they are asked to list the reasons that they like or dislike a political party.[9] The motivation for the measure is that psychologists believe that when people are asked these kinds of open-ended questions, the answers they give are the most salient and accessible images they hold of that object in memory and that these kinds of salient and accessible images will form only if a person has had a consistent set of experiences that communicate the association between the object and the image (Fiske and Taylor 1991).[10] If party unity is high, voters will receive consistent exposure to party members' positions on key issues, the social groups the party's issue positions are targeted to help, and the rhetoric the party uses to justify its issue positions; voters will form more salient and accessible party images along these dimensions as a result. If party unity is low, voters will be confronted with conflicting information about the parties' issue positions, and so forth, and they will therefore be less likely to form salient and accessible party images. Although this measure may not be a perfect measure of uncertainty, it is a familiar measure of how salient partisanship is to voters (e.g., Hetherington 2001; Trilling 1976; Wattenberg 1982, 1994), and it is sufficient for the broader purposes of

---

[9] Specifically, respondents are asked a series of questions beginning: "I'd like to ask you what you think are the good and bad points about the two national parties. Is there anything that you like about the Democratic Party? If the respondent answers yes, they are then asked: "What is that?" "Anything else [that you like]?" "What is that?" The process is repeated, with the respondent given the opportunity to list up to five things that they like about the Democratic Party. The respondent is then asked: "Is there anything in particular that you don't like about the Democratic Party?" A similar set of follow-up questions is asked and then the process is repeated for the Republican Party.

[10] Pope and Woon (2008) show that survey respondents' beliefs about the level of intra-party agreement in legislative voting are closely correlated with the actual level of agreement.

this book to show that party salience is affected by the level of party unity in government and that this had consequences for voter evaluations of parties and candidates, even if you disagree that this measures uncertainty per se.[11]

Figure 3.5 plots the average level of *Democratic* and *Republican Certainty* by election year for the period from 1960 through 2004. As anticipated by the learning model, this figure reveals that the level of *Partisan Certainty* for both Democrats and Republicans trended with the actual levels of intra-party conflict described earlier. Thus, *Partisan Certainty* declined from 1960 through the mid-1970s. Once the actual levels of party unity reversed course, the level of *Partisan Certainty* followed suit and has generally been on the upswing since that time. For the population as a whole, it appears that the prediction of the learning model that the uncertainty of people's partisan evaluations is related to the actual level of intra-party conflict is supported by the data.

The key independent variables for the multivariate analyses are the level of *Inter-Party Conflict* measured by the distance between the Democratic and Republican Parties' mean DW-Nominate scores and Democratic and Republican *Intra-Party Unity* measured by the variance in the parties' respective DW-Nominate scores. In addition, the hypotheses drawn from the learning model suggest that prior political experiences and political interest may moderate the effects of party elite behavior on voter beliefs. To operationalize the effects of prior political experiences on voters' current beliefs about parties, a relationship that the theoretical model suggests may be non-linear, *Age* and *Age*^{2} are used as predictors of *Important Differences*, *Perceived Distance*, and *Democratic* and *Republican Certainty*. As will become clearer later, the coefficients for *Age* and *Age*^{2} can be used to document changes in the age groups who report seeing the clearest differences between the two parties. The hypothesis is that for early years in the sample, the data should exhibit traditional "life-cycle" effects, with older people reporting the greatest values of the dependent variable; however, over time, these life-cycle effects should

[11] An alternative explanation for change in *Partisan Certainty* is that the set of considerations that people bring to bear when evaluating parties has varied over time – perhaps people cared about more issues in the late 1990s and early 2000s than they did in the late 1960s and early 1970s. Although that explanation makes sense logically, it is hard to imagine that in the midst of the civil rights movement, school desegregation, the Vietnam War, widespread rioting in American cities, the Cold War, rising inflation and unemployment, and so on, the public cared about more issues than they during the Clinton years when *Partisan Certainty* was at comparatively higher levels.

vanish, with increasingly younger people having more crystallized beliefs as the party system polarizes. To operationalize the effects of *Political Knowledge*, ANES interviewers' assessment of a respondents' informedness about politics and public affairs is used because it is the best available measure that allows for a comparison of the behavior of politically knowledgeable individuals today with those thirty years ago.[12] Individuals judged to have high levels of information about politics are scored as ones on *Political Knowledge* and zero otherwise.

Although these considerations are outside the model, it also seems prudent to take into account variation across individuals due to personal circumstances that could influence whether differences between the two parties on the issues of the day appear large or small. Demographic variables are included as proxies for differences in political preferences. The intuition behind the use of demographic variables is that party polarization may occur on issues that are important to some social groups but not to others, so that people react to the same level of polarization in uneven ways. Accordingly, dummy variables for *Black*, *Female,* and *South* (named groups are coded as ones) are included to allow for differences in party beliefs according to race, gender, and region. *Income* is included as a control because it is expected that high-income people who have more at stake in absolute terms due to redistributive policies will be more aware of differences between the two parties.[13] A dummy variable, *Retired*, is included, for individuals who are 65 years or older, because the survey responses of these older individuals exhibits substantially greater instability year-to-year than younger groups (Gerber and Green 1999). Furthermore, one factor that becomes apparent from the data (and from anecdotal reports from ANES interviewers) is that there are a number of people who simply refuse to give responses to open-ended questions

---

[12] Zaller (1992) argues that the interviewer assessments perform about as well as 10 to 15 direct knowledge questions and reports that in earlier studies he found no evidence that interviewers were biased in their assessments in terms of a respondent's race, gender, and so forth. Zaller's recommended alternative is to use respondents' ability to place Democrats to the left of Republicans on issue scales, but that would be redundant with the dependent variable in my analysis. To increase my confidence in inter-coder reliability of this variable and to facilitate the data analysis that follows, *Political Knowledge* is coded as a one if a respondent is considered to have a very high or fairly high level of information about politics and a zero otherwise.

[13] Income is measured along a five-point scale. $1 = 0$ to 16 percentile, $2 = 17$ to 33 percentile, $3 = 34$ to 67 percentile, $4 = 68$ to 95 percentile, and $5 = 90$ to 100 percentile.

to save time. For models of *Democratic* and *Republican Certainty*, the dummy variable *No Answers* is included, which takes the value one if a person refuses to provide any responses to open-ended questions about the other party. Finally, to include as many years of data as possible, data from both Presidential and Congressional election years are included; however, because of differences in the intensity of campaigns in years without Presidential elections, the contextual variable *Off-year elections* (equals one if it is not a Presidential election year) is also included as a statistical control.[14]

Methodology

Traditionally, scholars have used one of two distinct methods to test for the effects of party elite behavior on public opinion, neither of which is appropriate for this study. One of these methods has been a pure time-series model examining variation in the behavior of the average individual at different moments in history as a function of national events (e.g., Carmines and Stimson 1989); the other is a pooled cross-section model that considers how over-time change influences the behavior of individual members of the population (e.g., Hetherington 2001). The pure time-series approach is not suitable for the current project because the object of interest is variation within individuals due to their prior political experiences and their political knowledge within a single election year, not just the behavior of the aggregate population. The standard pooled cross-section approach does allow for individual-level variation in independent variables; however, in prior work I have shown that the Type-One error rate of party polarization on voter perceptions of party differences is ten times what one would expect from random chance because errors in the multivariate model tend to cluster by year, which creates a very serious problem with serial correlation.[15]

To test the learning model, a two-stage estimation procedure is used that addresses the need for individual-level variation within years while also identifying good estimates of the effect of over-time changes in party

---

[14] Including demographic controls may also prove important because there appears to be an empirical regularity demonstrating that whites and men are more likely to use extreme values on seven-point issue variables than blacks and women, which may represent a psychological predisposition toward extremism or moderation for these different groups (Mondak and Anderson 2004).

[15] The high Type-One error rate holds even when using estimators that correct for standard errors for sample clusters.

elite behavior on public opinion.[16] In the first stage, separate models are estimated for each year to determine the effect of only the individual-level variables on perceptions of inter-party differences and partisan certainty. Ordinary least squares is used to estimate the first-stage model for *Perceived Distance* and *Democratic and Republican Certainty*, and logistic regression is used for *Important Differences*. In the second stage, over-time changes in the coefficient estimates from the first-stage model are then treated as the dependent variables influenced by contextual factors such as *Inter-Party Conflict* to see if their behavior accords with the hypotheses generated by the learning model.

To understand the process, it is best to introduce the relationship between the first- and second-stage models by an example. For the *Perceived Distance* model, the first-stage regression is *Perceived Distance$_{it}$* = $b_{0,t} + b_{1,t}$ *Political Knowledge$_{it}$* + $b_{2,t}$ *Age$_{it}$* + $b_{3,t}$ *Age$^2_{it}$* + *Other Individual-Level Variables$_{it}$*. In the second stage, the year-specific intercept term $b_{0,t}$ provides a measure of the average level of *Perceived Distance* in year t controlling for individual-level variables. It is therefore possible to estimate the linear model: $b_{0,t} = a_0 + a_1$*Inter-Party Conflict$_t$* + a_2*Off-Year Election$_t$* to estimate the effect of these contextual variables on *Perceived Distance* via the intercept of the first-stage regressions. If the research hypothesis is correct, then a_1 should have a significant positive coefficient. Similarly, it is possible to add the year-specific intercept with the coefficient for other dummy variables, such as that for *Political Knowledge*, and use the resulting statistic $b_{0,t} + b_{1,t}$ as a measure of the average level of *Perceived Distance* in year t for high-knowledge individuals controlling for other factors. It is then possible to estimate the linear model: $b_{0,t} + b_{1,t} = a_0 + a_1$*Inter-Party Conflict$_t$* + a_2*Off-Year Election$_t$* to estimate the effect of contextual variables on just high-knowledge people. If, as hypothesized, high-knowledge people are more sensitive to *Inter-Party Conflict*, then the coefficient a_1 in this second-stage model should be larger (in absolute magnitude) than that where just $b_{o,t}$ is the dependent variable. Similar tests can be conducted to see if, for example, women or African-Americans have responded differently to party elite polarization than other segments of the population.

Finally, to assess the hypothesized over-time changes in the effects of political experience on individuals' beliefs about parties, the joint effect of *Age* and *Age^2* on *Perceived Distance* is considered. Based on some simple

[16] Achen (2005) recommends this kind of simple two-step estimator even when the first stage model is non-linear, such as a logistic regression.

Table 3.1. *Second-Stage Model for Perceptions of Inter-party Differences*

Dep. Var. Indep. Var.	Perceived Distance (Intercept-Only)	Important Differences (Intercept-Only)
Inter-Party Conflict	6.57**	3.73**
	(1.12)	(1.60)
Off-Year Election	0.01	−0.18
	(0.22)	(0.32)
Constant	−4.15**	−3.43**
	(0.77)	(1.16)
R^2	0.74	0.37
n	16	15

Cell values are OLS regression coefficients (robust standard error estimates).
** Indicates statistically significant at $p < .05$ (two-tailed).

back-of-the-envelope calculations, the estimated age of a person with the greatest *Perceived Distance* is $- b_{2,t}/2b_{3,t}$ if $b_{3,t} < 0$.[17] However, if $b_{3,t} > 0$, then the expression $b_{2,t}$ Age $+ b_{3,t}$ Age^2 does not have a maximum value. In this case, I assume that the age of the person perceiving the greatest differences between the two parties is either 18 (the minimum voting age) or 65 (the age just before the retirement variable interferes with the interpretation of the age coefficients). This quantity is chosen to be 18 if $b_{2,t}18 + b_{3,t}18 > b_{2,t}65 + b_{3,t}65$ because this implies that, controlling for all the other variables in the model, an 18-year-old sees greater differences between the two parties than a 65-year-old. Conversely, the maximum is chosen to be 65 if $b_{2,t}18 + b_{3,t}18 < b_{2,t}65 + b_{3,t}65$. If the hypothesized change in the effects of age proves correct, then it is expected that age will have its maximum effect on the dependent variable at a much smaller level in the later years of the study than in the late 1960s and early 1970s.

The focus of attention for the remainder of this chapter is the second-stage analyses.[18]

Results for Perceptions of Inter-Party Conflict

The first set of results concern the models for people's perceptions about the scope of conflict between Democrats and Republicans. To begin, Table 3.1 reports the results of the analysis for the effects of *Inter-party*

[17] This follows simply by taking the derivative of Perceived Distance with respect to Age and solving for the maximum.
[18] The results from the first-stage models for the various dependent models by election year are available upon request.

conflict and *Off-year election* on *Perceived Distance* and *Important Differences*. For both models, *Inter-Party Conflict* has the expected positive, significant effect on people's belief that there are meaningful differences between Democrats and Republicans. In concrete terms, as *Inter-Party Conflict* moved from its minimum level in the 95th Congress meeting in 1977–8 to its maximum level in the 108th Congress of 2003–4, *Perceived Distance* between Democrats and Republicans moved around 2.25 points along the 7-point liberal conservative ideology scale. Similarly, as *Inter-party Conflict* shifted from its minimum level in the data set for *Important Differences* in 1967–8 to its maximum level in 2003–4, the probability that a "typical" person would report seeing inter-party differences would rise dramatically from 0.46 to 0.77.[19] Interestingly, the occurrence of an *Off-Year election* had no discernible effect on either *Perceived Distance* or *Important Differences* for the period considered here.

Over the past quarter-century, the social group seeming to bear the greatest incidence of conflicts between Democrats and Republicans has shifted from African-Americans over issues such as civil rights and anti-poverty programs during the 1960s to women over issues such as abortion and equal rights in the workplace during more recent years. It is therefore worthwhile to consider whether various social groups reacted differently to changes in the level of *Inter-Party Conflict*. To this end, the coefficients from the first-stage model are used to estimate the effect of contextual variables on different social groups in the manner described earlier, and these results are reported in Table 3.2. With respect to perceptions of the level of ideological conflict between Democrats and Republicans, the differences across groups is relatively small. Among women, African-Americans, and Southerners, only black opinion is notably different from the behavior of the population overall. Notably, even for the latter outlying group, *Inter-party Conflict* continues to have a significant positive effect. On the other hand, there are large differences across social groups in the effects of *Inter-Party Conflict* on people's responses to the *Importance Differences* question. As anticipated earlier, over the past forty years as women's issues have come to figure more prominently in national politics, *Inter-Party Conflict* appears to cause women to see greater differences between Democrats and Republicans than people on average. Meanwhile, African-Americans do not see the rise in *Inter-Party Conflict* to be *Important* even though the analysis on *Perceived Distance* analysis

---

[19] A "typical" person is defined to be a white male, age 40, unretired, non-Southern, in the middle income quintile, with low political sophistication in 2004.

Table 3.2. *Second-Stage Models for Inter-party Differences by Social Group*

| Dep. Var. | Perceived Distance (Intercept + Female coef.) | Perceived Distance (Intercept + Black coef.) | Perceived Distance (Intercept + South coef.) | Important Differences (Intercept + Female coef.) | Important Differences (Intercept + Black coef.) | Important Differences (Intercept + South coef.) |
Indep. Var.						
Inter-Party Conflict	6.87**	3.79**	6.53**	4.45**	1.27	3.95**
	(1.11)	(1.26)	(0.86)	(1.46)	(1.22)	(1.40)
Off-Year Election	0.03	0.02	0.06	−0.17	−0.41	−0.23
	(0.21)	(0.29)	(0.19)	(0.27)	(0.34)	(0.35)
Constant	−4.36**	−2.52**	−3.97**	−4.01**	−1.28	−3.41**
	(0.77)	(0.97)	(0.65)	(1.11)	(0.83)	(1.00)
R^2	0.76	0.38	0.79	0.49	0.19	0.43
n	16	16	16	15	15	15

Cell values are OLS regression coefficients (robust standard error estimates).
** Indicates statistically significant at $p < .05$ (two-tailed).

Table 3.3. *Second-Stage Models for Perceptions of Inter-party Differences for Individuals with High Political Knowledge*

Dep. Var. Indep. Var.	Perceived Distance (Intercept + Political Knowledge Coef.)	Important Differences (Intercept + Political Knowledge Coef.)
Inter-Party Conflict	7.83**	3.95**
	(0.99)	(1.63)
Off-Year Election	0.17	−0.15
	(0.18)	(0.32)
Constant	−3.95**	−2.59**
	(0.69)	(1.20)
R^2	0.86	0.39
n	16	15

Cell values are OLS regression coefficients (robust standard error estimates).
** Indicates Statistically significant at $p < .05$ (two-tailed).

shows that this social group is aware of the growing polarization of the party system along the dominant political-economic dimension identified by my measure of *Inter-Party Conflict*. The latter point is consistent with my finding in collaborative work (Grynaviski and Harris-Lacewell 2005) that Republicans had moved (prior to Obama's nomination) to catch up to Democrats on traditionally black issues such as education and foreign aid to Africa.

The second hypothesis drawn from the learning model with respect to inter-party conflict concerns the impact of political informedness on perceptions of party conflict. According to the learning model, people who are more informed about current affairs should be more sensitive to changes in party elite behavior than other Americans. The second-stage regressions for *Perceived Distance* and *Important Differences* designed to test for this effect are reported in Table 3.3. Consistent with theoretical expectations, the coefficient for *Inter-Party Conflict* is positive and significant in the second-stage analysis for both of the dependent variables that are considered, and the magnitude of this coefficient is larger than that observed for the baseline model reported in Table 3.1. However, the difference between the high-knowledge group and the entire sample on average is not enormous.[20] That said, if it is true that people judged

[20] It is not possible to assess the significance of this effect because the dependent variables in the various second-stage analyses are different, so coefficient standard errors are not directly comparable.

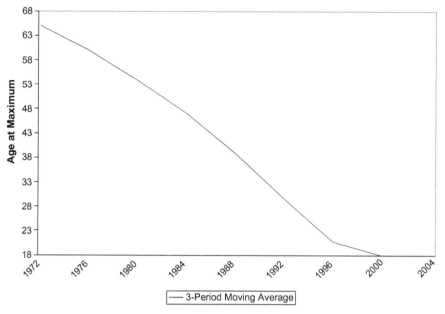

Figure 3.6. Age of respondents perceiving the greatest ideological differences between Democrats and Republicans, 1972–2004. *Source:* Author's calculations.

to be of high knowledge today have accumulated more political experience than other people their age over the course of their lifetime, then the attenuated nature of the political knowledge effects is entirely consistent with the learning model, which suggests that reactions to short-run information flows are moderated by the total amount of information that people have about the two parties, not just the amount of information received most recently.

The final hypothesis gleaned from the learning model is that there should be a marked change in the *Age* of individuals perceiving the greatest differences between the two parties. For the early years of the study, it is hypothesized that older individuals will see the largest differences between Democrats and Republicans, but that over time this relationship should reverse, with the youngest respondents in the latter of part of the sample coming to see the greatest inter-party differences. Evidence of this change is reported in Figures 3.6 for *Perceived Distance* and 3.7 for *Important Differences* which plot the three-period moving average (for only Presidential election years) of the estimated ages of individuals with, respectively, the greatest *Perceived Distance* and the highest probability of reporting an *Important Difference* between Democrats and Republicans.

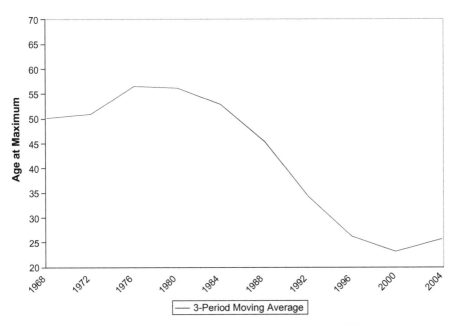

Figure 3.7. Age of respondents most likely to report seeing important differences between Democrats and Republicans, 1968–2004. *Source:* Author's calculations.

The figures provide dramatic evidence of the hypothesized shift. For *Perceived Distance*, individuals in their 60s perceived the maximum distance between Democrats and Republicans in the early part of the sample, and from the mid-1990s until today, it is the very youngest people who see the greatest differences between Democrats and Republicans. For *Important Differences*, during the late 1960s and early 1970s, it was individuals in their 50s who were more likely to see partisan choices as most consequential. By the mid-1990s, it was individuals in their 20s who had had the highest probability of reporting that they see *Important Differences* between the two parties. Although the impact of *Inter-Party Conflict* and *Political Knowledge* has been anticipated by other theorists, the clear reversal in the classic life-cycle model of political learning is an important original implication of my model.

Results for Partisan Certainty

The arguments of this book ultimately rest on the question of whether voters find partisan cues to be more relevant guides to their evaluations

Table 3.4. *Second-Stage Models for Democratic and Republican Certainty*

Dep. Var. Indep. Var.	Democratic Certainty[#] (Intercept-Only)	Republican Certainty (Intercept-Only)
Intra-Party Conflict	−12.14**	−14.87**
	(4.64)	(3.65)
Off-Year Election	−0.26	0.18
	(0.25)	(0.13)
Constant	3.90**	3.80**
	(0.98)	(0.64)
R^2	0.41	0.36
n	14	15

Cell values are OLS regression coefficients (robust standard error estimates).
[#] Models exclude outlying 1986 data.
** Indicates statistically significant at $p < .05$ (two-tailed).

of Democrats and Republicans when party unity is high. Evidence in support of this claim is provided in Table 3.4, which reports the results of the second-stage analyses of the consequences of internal party conflicts for *Democratic* and *Republican Certainty*. In the statistical analyses, higher levels of *Intra-Party Conflict* in both parties' caucuses had the hypothesized significant negative effect. With *Intra-Party Conflict* among Democrats varying from 0.23 in the 90th Congress of 1967–8 to 0.16 in the 108th Congress of 2003–4, changes in party elite behavior increased *Democratic Certainty* by around 0.9 units. With *Intra-Party Conflict* among Republicans varying from its peak in the series during the 92nd Congress of 1971–2 at 0.19 to its minimum level of 0.14 in the 103rd Congress of 1993–4, party elite behavior increased *Republican Certainty* by an estimated 0.7 units. Both of these changes are substantial given that survey respondents only provide about two or three answers to these kinds of open-ended questions on average (see Figure 3.5). Importantly, the large difference in the predicted effects of *Intra-Party Conflict* between Democrats and Republicans is due to the much larger increase in Democratic party unity (an effect anticipated by the theory), not a large difference across parties in the coefficients for *Intra-Party Conflict*. It is also notable that *Off-Year Elections* again have no discernible effects on public opinion.[21]

---

[21] In contrast to the models of *Inter-Party Conflict*, I do not have a good theoretical intuition about how changes in party unity over time would impact different social groups' *certainty* about the two parties. For readers who might be interested, for all

Table 3.5. *Second-Stage Models for Democratic and Republican Certainty
for High-Knowledge Individuals*

Dep. Var. Indep. Var.	Democratic Certainty[#] (Intercept + Political Knowledge coef)	Republican Certainty (Intercept + Political Knowledge coef)
Intra-Party Conflict	−15.27**	−19.82**
	(4.24)	(5.02)
Off-Year Election	−0.07	0.22
	(0.27)	(0.19)
Constant	5.28**	5.48**
	(0.85)	(0.84)
R^2	0.52	0.39
n	14	15

Cell values are OLS regression coefficients (robust standard error estimates).
[#] Model excludes outlying 1986 data.
** Indicates statistically significant at $p < .05$ (two-tailed).

The second hypothesis generated by the learning model concerning *Partisan Certainty* is that voters who are most informed will also be most sensitive to short-run changes in *Intra-Party Unity*. Evidence of the effects of *Intra-Party Conflict* on the *Partisan Certainty* of high-knowledge individuals is presented in Table 3.5. As anticipated, the effect of *Intra-Party Conflict* is significant and negative for both parties. More importantly for the theory, the coefficients reported in these models are once again noticeably larger in absolute magnitude than those reported in Table 3.4 for the population as a whole. For high-knowledge people, the change over time in the level of *Intra-Party Conflict* among Democrats moved *Democratic Certainty* by 1.1 units and changes in the level of *Intra-Party Conflict* among Republicans moved *Republican Certainty* by 1 unit. Compared to the baseline results in Table 3.4, the more highly sophisticated are roughly 20 percent more sensitive to changes in party elite behavior than the population as a whole. This effect is in addition to the greater *Certainty* that high-knowledge people naturally have because of the greater amounts of information they have about the political world which is identified in the first-stage model.

groups *intra-party conflict* had the hypothesized significant negative on *certainty*. Women, African-Americans, and Southerners are more sensitive than the average voter to changes in *Intra-Party Conflict* among Democrats. However, women and *African-Americans* are less sensitive than the average voter to changes in *Intra-Party Conflict* among Republicans, while Southerners are more sensitive.

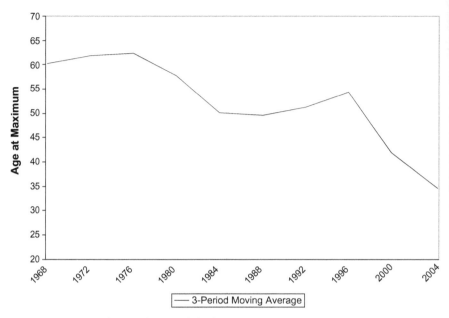

Figure 3.8. Age of respondents with highest Democratic certainty scores, 1968–2004. *Source:* Author's calculations.

The final question to be addressed in this section concerns the effects of *Age* on *Partisan Certainty* at different moments in history. To provide evidence of this relationship, Figures 3.8 and 3.9 provide plots of the estimated age group of people with the greatest *Partisan Certainty* at different points in time. As anticipated in the previous discussion, it was the oldest of the non-*Retired* members of the sample with the highest levels of *Partisan Certainty* during the late 1960s and early 1970s. For Democrats, there was an initial decline in the age of people reporting the highest *Partisan Certainty* scores; then as party unity stabilized at a fixed point during the 1980s, these age effects stabilized for a time, and as Democrats made further gains in party unity during the 1990s and 2000s, an even younger group of people had the greatest levels of *Democratic* and *Republican Certainty*. For Republicans, the rate of change in the age of people reporting the greatest *Partisan Certainty* was greater than that among Democrats. In contrast to a decade before, it was individuals in their early 30s who, during the 1980s, had the greatest *Republican Certainty* scores. Since that time, the age of people with the highest *Republican Certainty* has begun to creep back up, with individuals in their early 40s now having the least uncertainty about the two parties.

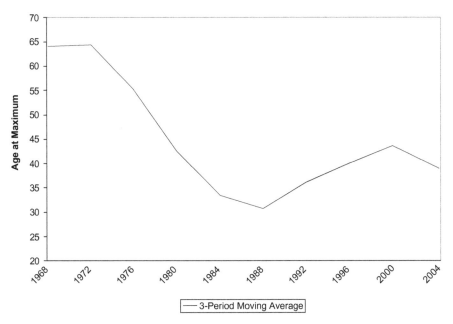

Figure 3.9. Age of respondents with highest Republican certainty scores, 1968–2004. *Source:* Author's calculations.

CONCLUSIONS

The familiar refrain among students of electoral politics is that if voters are offered "*Choices, Not Echoes*" by political elites, then the American voter will appear to possess more knowledge about the issues of the day and will be able to cast more informed ballots. In this chapter, this wisdom was refined with respect to party politics in two important ways. First, it has been shown that the amount of information carried by party labels is a function of the level of intra-party agreement. When intra-party unity is high, the evidence demonstrates that the public has more salient and accessible party images. Conversely, when intra-party unity is low, the public possesses relatively little accessible information about parties. The level of party unity in government is therefore important, in part, because it fosters the development of crystallized party images that allow voters to draw upon partisan cues in ways that reduce their uncertainty at the ballot box.

Second, it has been shown that except for the youngest, most politically aware citizens, people's beliefs about the national parties react slowly in response to changes in the positions of Democratic and Republican elites. As will become apparent in the next chapter, this claim proves important to my theory about voters' partisan preferences. For now, it is important to emphasize that this backward-looking behavior only makes sense from the rational-choice perspective if voters are gauging the credibility of campaign promises and the extent of pandering by the ruling party in relation to their prior experiences with a party in office. Thus, the inelasticity of voters' beliefs about parties over the short run is surprisingly consistent with the actions of a rational public who believes that their elected officials would promise them almost anything if they believed it would pay electoral dividends.

4

Party Unity and the Strength of Party Preferences

The thesis of this book is that an important function that political parties perform is that of a surety who offers guarantees to the public about how they will evaluate the performance of politicians in office who carry the organization's label. For a party's nomination to represent a credible signal, it must be the case that the organization places in jeopardy an asset that it values in the event that too many of its members act in a manner inconsistent with voter expectations. The argument developed in Chapter 2 suggests that when too many party members break ranks and act contrary to party principles, the organization risks losing the support of its strongest backers who deliver votes and other more material types of support to its candidates, and it is a party's preference to avoid this penalty that makes party endorsements credible. The purpose of this chapter is to develop and test the micro-logic for why voters may reward parties for high levels of party unity in government.

THEORIES OF VOTER PARTISANSHIP

The building block of my theory of voter behavior is a rational-choice model of party evaluation and choice based on how people view the activities of party members in government. A great deal has been previously written on the basis for people's partisan preferences, so before getting to my model, it is instructive to first consider the state of the literature on this subject.

The Michigan Model

The benchmark study for most work on voter partisanship is *The American Voter* (Campbell et al. 1960), which introduced the famous Michigan

Model. A central claim of that book is that the vast majority of Americans' political attitudes, at least as measured by many social scientific surveys, fluctuate considerably when considered from one study to the next. The one notable exception to this general pattern is people's description of themselves as a Democrat or Republican, which changes very little over time, even if they voted for candidates of the other party. Furthermore, it appeared to Campbell et al. that party preferences were transmitted from one generation to the next. The observation that a person's party preference is inherited from her parents and is largely unchanging over time gave rise to the idea that people have partisan *identities* in the same way that they may have religious or ethnic identities. Partisanship, by this account, is not a choice grounded in the platforms of the national parties, but is something you are born with and that is unlikely to change with political experience.

Over the past half-century, an accumulation of findings about how people's partisan preferences change over time has led scholars to reappraise the theoretical claim that party identification is a lifelong commitment.[1] In particular, there have been a number of occasions when a large number of individuals belonging to a particular social group changed their partisan allegiance in a manner inconsistent with the Michigan Model. The most famous example of social group realignment has been the conversion of Southern whites from Democrats into Republicans; however, substantial, sustained partisan realignments have also occurred among Catholics and African-American in the post-war period (Grynaviski and Harris-Lacewell 2005).

Contrary to one of the fundamental tenets of the Michigan Model, that voters are guided by leaders of their own party to hold a certain set of issue opinions, all three of these changes in voter partisanship were precipitated by a change in the policy positions of the national parties. The defection of Southern whites was initiated by Democratic President Harry Truman's 1946 endorsement (later incorporated into the national Democratic

[1] A great deal of scholarship also contradicts *The American Voter*'s claims regarding the instability of voters' issue opinions. Achen (1975) shows that unstable issue preferences in survey instruments are due to poorer measurement instruments for these variables than for party identification. Krosnick and Berent (1993) find that when party identification and ideology are elicited in similar ways, the level of test-retest stability is similar across the two concepts. Ansolabehere, Rodden, and Snyder (2008) report that when multiple survey measures are used in an index, response stability increases dramatically and that the predictive power of issue opinions for vote choices is on par with party identification.

Party platform) of the Committee on Civil Rights' recommendation that the federal government pass legislation to curtail lynching, the poll tax, and violations of voting rights for African-Americans. Over the next two decades, the Republican leadership adapted its small-government message to appeal to these dissatisfied Southern voters by framing opposition to civil rights legislation as a defense of states' rights (Black and Black 1987, 1992; Carmines and Stimson 1989). Perhaps not coincidentally, the shift in Republican strategy occurred at a time when growing numbers of Southern whites were already ripe for partisan conversion because of economic development in the region which created a growing pool of middle- and upper-income people of the sort who tended to favor the Republican Party in other parts of the country (McCarty, Poole, and Rosenthal 2005; Shafer and Johnston 2006).

The conversion of Catholic voters that occurred from the late 1960s through the early 1980s was sparked by a change in the platform of the national Republican Party under the leadership of Richard Nixon. During his second quest for the Presidency, Nixon came out in favor of public funding for parochial schools, which was quite popular among Catholic voters. Shortly thereafter, the Supreme Court decision *Roe v. Wade* was passed down, which further invigorated Catholics' entry into the Republican Party when the organization ramped up its efforts to appeal to religious conservatives. Furthermore, paralleling the case of Southern whites, this change in platform occurred in unison with the elevation of large numbers of Catholic voters into the middle and upper class, whose new economic circumstances had already made them more sympathetic to Republican policies (Prendergast 1999).[2]

---

[2] Many political scientists believe that the partisan realignment of Catholics can be explained by their preference for the Republican Party's position on issues related to race (e.g., school busing); however, this does not square with the facts because it fails to differentiate Catholic Republicans (the people who changed their partisanship) from so-called Reagan Democrats (the people who voted Republican while retaining their partisan loyalties). As Edsall and Edsall report in their astute analysis of the period: "Reagan Democrats clearly held more conservative stands on racial issues. . . . For a substantial percentage of defecting Democrats – all of them white – the redistributive policies of the Democratic party were no longer seen as benefiting their own families, friends, and neighborhoods, but were seen rather as benefiting minorities at the expense of the working and middle class" (1991, p. 164). Further supporting my interpretation of the importance of religious issues in this realignment is their observation that Catholics who regularly attended church services were almost 20 percent more likely to identify themselves as Republicans than those who did not (Edsall and Edsall 1991, pg. 179).

Finally, the realignment of African-American voters followed changes in the policy positions of both parties. To a considerable extent, the shift in black partisanship was a reward to the Democrats for passing the Civil Rights Act of 1964 under the leadership of President Lyndon Johnson. Meanwhile, following the lead of its Presidential candidates Barry Goldwater in 1964 and Richard Nixon in 1968, the Republican Party lurched to the right on the issue of civil rights in an effort to woo Southern whites.

Whatever the motivation may have been for the changes in the policies advanced by the national parties, the key point for the purposes of this book is that partisan realignments within each of these social groups can be interpreted as a rational response to changes in the positions of the national parties or changes in personal circumstances. Partisan conversion on either of these grounds is inconsistent with the Michigan Model.

Contemporary Theories

Contemporary approaches to voter partisanship come in two different flavors. One approach treats partisanship as a "standing decision," made upon reflection about which party is apt to provide the highest quality of governance from the individual's perspective, that is subject to change as new events transpire and voters update their beliefs (Key 1966). The classic description of this learning process, as described in the literature reviewed in Chapter 3, is that voters maintain a "running tally" based on political outcomes when a particular party is in power and that they identify with the organization that gives the better outcomes (Fiorina 1981). Other scholars in this tradition have argued that voters modify their partisanship in an effort to reconcile their current vote choices with their partisan identities (e.g., Franklin and Jackson 1983; Jackson 1975). According to both accounts, a party that performs well in office may reap future electoral rewards through the conversion of their opponent's supporters.

Another approach retains the Michigan Model's view that partisanship is fundamentally about social group relationships, but interprets it as grounded in people's belief that a party represents people like themselves (Green, Palmquist, and Schickler 2002). For example, a black voter is more likely to think of herself as a Democrat if she sees other African-Americans supporting the Democratic Party. The most important difference between this account and the classic Michigan Model is that party preferences are not themselves social group identities, thereby leaving open the possibility of partisan conversions if there is a large change in the social composition of the party's base. Green et al. describe the process of partisan change this way:

> Once a critical mass of people begin to shift parties, change in the parties' social imagery gains momentum. As conservative, devout Southerners became reticent about calling themselves Democrats, they less and less defined the social imagery of the party. As older party stereotypes faded, self-designated conservatives in the South gravitated steadily toward Republican affiliation. (Green et al. 2002, pp. 159–60)

Advocates of the two alternatives to the Michigan Model disagree sharply about which approach to party identification is correct, but compelling evidence in support of one approach or the other has proven fleeting. On the one hand, proponents of the interpretation of a party preference as a "standing decision" have struggled mightily to provide convincing micro-level evidence demonstrating the effects of short-run economic and political forces on people's partisan attachments (e.g., Green and Palmquist 1990; Green and Yoon 2002; Green and Schickler 1993; Schickler and Green, 1995).[3]

On the other hand, the best micro-level evidence that proponents of the social group-focused model of party preferences are able to provide in support of their argument is that (1) demographic variables predict partisan attachments (see all studies for all time) and (2) party preferences are stable over the short term, but not over the long term (Beck and Jennings 1991; Green et al. 2002; Jennings and Markus 1984; Jennings and Niemi 1978, 1981). However, both of these points are entirely consistent with a model of the voter who is making rational calculations about which party offers the best outcome for people "like her" when voter beliefs about parties are stable over time in the manner described in the last chapter. Supportive of this view, a number of studies report that group identities influence political behavior only when a group is worried that its concerns are not being addressed by the political process (Miller et al. 1981; Conover 1988). Koch (1994) argues that this explains why, for example, class identities exert themselves as politically salient during economic downturns, but when times are good, people focus on other concerns.

---

[3] Further, it is difficult for voters to assign credit or blame to a party in office for outcomes under its watch because of split partisan control of government, a phenomenon that has occurred in all but three sessions of Congress from 1981 through 2008.

Furthermore, Green et al.'s social group–focused model has difficulty explaining macro-level changes in party preferences, such as the partisan realignment of the South. In particular, their model confronts a time-consistency problem in that Southerners had to start identifying themselves as Republicans before people came to associate the Southern group identity with Republicans. This begs the question as to why people switched to the Republican Party to begin with. If the first movers out of the Democratic Party were motivated by issues or ideology, then why not believe that the same set of concerns caused later partisan conversions as well? Further, if white Southern group identity was key, why have only conservative whites changed their attachments?[4] If ideology is the key (as argued by Abramowitz and Saunders 2006), then Green's account begins to look very much like the rational-choice models they pooh-pooh. Crucially, by not accepting the interpretation that at least some individuals are making a calculated choice to leave one party in favor of another to advance private or group interests, sociological models of partisanship cannot explain partisan electoral realignments. (Perhaps the best way to reconcile the rational-choice and sociological traditions is to allow that ordinary voters look to trusted leaders of their social group to guide their voting behavior, and the leaders are responding to the parties' issue positions in a rational way, much in the manner described by Downs 1957).

A MODEL OF PARTY CHOICE

My model of party choice builds on the idea introduced in Chapter 3 that voters understand that an American political party is a team of politicians who may come into conflict with one another on important issues of the day. This observation gives rise to the idea that when someone evaluates a political party, what she is really doing is evaluating the entire set of professional politicians who call themselves Democrats and Republicans and deciding how she feels about that set of actors on average. Thus, if a person has strong positive opinions about the politicians in a party, this should lead her to have strong positive feelings toward the party as a whole. However, if a person only feels positively toward a small number of party members because they are united around a set of issues with

---

[4] Empirically, people almost never report that they like Republicans or dislike Democrats based on regional identities. In an analysis of open-ended questions from the ANES from 1972 through 2000, there was not a single Presidential election year when more than 3 percent of the respondents mentioned *any* region of the country or regional identity as a reason for why they liked or disliked either party.

which she disagrees, or because of conflict within the party on salient issues, then this should lead her to have less favorable evaluations of the party as an umbrella brand. My model clearly differs from sociological accounts like that offered by Campbell et al. and Green et al., in that I understand a person's party preferences to be a *choice* made upon reflection about which party's members best reflect a person's own preferences about the direction that government should take. My model of party choice also differs from previous rational-choice accounts in that it is not premised on voters simply assigning blame or credit to one party or the other for their performance in office in a political system where power is shared between parties and opinions are fragmented within parties.

The Formal Model

My model of people's evaluations of political parties builds upon the formal representation of voter beliefs about parties developed in Chapter 3 and familiar concepts from rational-choice theory (e.g., Hinich and Munger 1997). The model rests on the following assumptions. First, assume that people have a well-defined set of policy preferences that promotes either their own well-being or that of a salient social group to which they belong and that these preferences can be defined as a point along a left-right policy dimension. For ease of exposition, assume that there is only one issue dimension, but in practice there can be many, and define v_i to represent a voter's (indexed by i) most-preferred policy.

Second, assume that voters' utility for a candidate (indexed by j) is a decreasing function of their ideal point v_i along and the politician's actions in office y on that left-right issue dimension. To represent this relationship formally, the standard assumption of the spatial model that $U_i(y) = -(v_i - y)^2$ is used, which implies that the utility of voter i is a decreasing function of the distance between her ideal point and the candidate's issue position.

Third, to capture the idea that people's partisan preferences are based on their views of the organization's membership, assume that party evaluations are based on their expectations about the actions of a party member chosen at random. Drawing upon the formal model of voter learning developed in Chapter 3, assume that voters treat y as a draw from the distribution describing their beliefs about the policy positions of all party members. Simplifying the notation a bit from the last chapter, denote the expected value of a party member's issue position as μ and the uncertainty about that estimate as σ^2.

Fourth, assume that people are risk-averse expected utility maximizers in their party evaluations.[5] Voters are assumed to be risk-averse about their party evaluations because the theory is predicated on the idea that people value a party's label because it provides them with information about the behavior of party members in the same way that consumers value a brand name because it provide them with information about product quality. If a party exhibited a high "failure rate" in the form of intra-party issue conflict, then people would feel cooler toward the organization because its endorsement of candidates does not convey useful information. Because of the American two-party system, a person might retain a partisan leaning despite the fact that their preferred organization has fractured, but the greater uncertainty about which candidates were safe bets would weaken her brand loyalties.[6]

These four assumptions lead to two straightforward theoretical propositions.

> **Proposition One:** The expected utility that a person receives from a party member is a decreasing function of two factors: (1) the distance between the individual's ideal point and her beliefs about the policy position or ideological location of the average party member and (2) her perceptions of the variance in the positions of party members. Formally, $EU_i(y) = -(v_i - \mu)^2 - \sigma^2$.[7]

---

[5] This assumption is actually implicit in the assumption that people have quadratic expected utility functions.

[6] The standard critique of the assumption of risk aversion that derives from prospect theory (Kahneman and Tversky 1979) is that people are risk-taking in losses and risk-seeking in gains. I believe for decisions about whether to reelect an incumbent politician or an incumbent party, it might sense to apply prospect theory – a person might be risk-taking during a recession where they are choosing between a poor status quo thought to be known for certain and an alternative that might make things better or might make things worse, whereas a person might be risk-averse during an economic boom when choosing between a good status quo thought to be known for certain and an alternative that might make things better and might make things worse. However, I do not see party ID as a statement of which candidate a person intends to vote for. Instead, party preferences are grounded in people's evaluations of an organization's candidates when people do not have information specific to a candidate or current circumstances, which means that there is no zero-point that defines whether voters are in the domain of gains or losses. As a result, prospect theory does not apply to party identification, even though this approach could explain why large partisan tides are observed when the public is very satisfied or very dissatisfied with a ruling party.

[7] The proposition that people's expected utility towards a candidate is a decreasing function of ideological distance and uncertainty is standard in spatial models of politics (e.g., Alvarez 1998; Enelow and Hinich 1981). My innovation is applying

Proposition One states that people's evaluations about a party can be decomposed into two parts. The first part describes how favorably the individual views the characteristics of a typical party member. Specifically, the greater the distance between the individual's ideal point v_i and the ideology or policy position of the average party member μ, the less favorably she evaluates candidates in the party because she does not see them as being good advocates of her policy preferences. The second part of the expected utility function is related to the uncertainty about the party: because she is risk averse, the smaller the variance in the party's positions σ^2, the more confident she is in her assessment of the party's issue positions and the more positively she views the organization. Thus, people favorably evaluate a partisan brand if they see its average member as being close to them on the issue of the day and they think there is little chance that its candidates would deviate much from the party's norm.

Proposition Two: A person prefers the Democratic party if $-(v_i - \mu_D)^2 - \sigma_D^2 > - (v_i - \mu_R)^2 - \mu_R^2$, and she prefers the Republican party if $- (v_i - \mu_D)^2 - \sigma_D^2 < - (v_i - \mu_R)^2 - \sigma_D^2$, where μ_D and σ_D^2 are the mean and variance in Democratic Party positions and μ_D and σ_D^2 are the mean and variance in Republican Party positions.

Proposition Two simply states that people prefer the party that gives them greater expected utility for choices between unknown candidates in much the same way that people most prefer the brand that gives them the highest anticipated level of satisfaction among a set of unfamiliar products. This statement about the behavioral basis of partisan choice is trivial from the perspective of rational-choice theory but diverges from previous rational-choice models of party identification in three important ways. First, the proposition does not provide a role for a person's past partisanship when she decides which party she supports. Past partisanship may be highly correlated with current partisanship, but only because the factors giving rise to past partisanship (e.g., political preferences, beliefs about parties) are highly correlated with the factors giving rise to current partisanship, and this would especially be true for older individuals whose political beliefs are more stable for the reasons outlined in Chapter 3. In other words, lagged partisanship is predictive rather than explanatory. Second, although seemingly outside the scope of Proposition Two, it is

this logic to the study of party choice and identifying levels of intra-party conflict as an important contributor of voter uncertainty. Readers interested in a more rigorous proof of Proposition One result should consult Grynaviski (2006).

entirely plausible that demographic variables may explain variation in party preferences. In contrast to a number of previous rational-choice studies that used only variables such as race or religion as instrumental variables that explain variation within some set of independent variables (e.g., a person's issue positions: cf. Franklin and Jackson 1983; Franklin 1984), I see demographic variables as standing in for the issue preferences of a certain social or economic group in the population. For example, the coefficient *Black* may measure the average effect of differences between black and non-black respondents' opinions about an issue such as affirmative action or civil rights. Third, Proposition Two suggests that a person's party preferences may be affected by their uncertainty about the characteristics of Democrats and Republicans. Intriguingly, this means that a centrist voter who sees the two parties as being roughly equidistant from their ideal point may still have a partisan preference because they see one party as being the more certain option.

Empirical Support for Proposition One

To test Proposition One, a series of regression models of partisan evaluation are estimated using data from the American National Election Studies for general election years dating from 1978 through 2004. The dependent variables in these models, *Democratic Evaluations* and *Republican Evaluations*, are respondents' placements of the two parties on 101-point feeling thermometer scales. Larger values along these scales correspond to more positive evaluations of a political party.

There are two key sets of independent variables in the model representing the two terms in people's expected utility functions for a political party. The first set are measures of people's political preferences and how well they perceive the national parties as representing those interests. One set of variables that are used to get at this relationship are *Democratic Distance* and *Republican Distance*, which are measured by the perceived distances between respondents' self-placement on a 7-point liberal-conservative ideology scale and their placement of the two parties on these scales.[8] These ideological measures are used as an estimate of the set of issue positions that people hold because (1) they are the

[8] The Euclidean distance metric is used because this specification is closest to the functional form derived from theory. Respondents who are unable to place themselves or the party on these scales received *Partisan Distance* scores of zero. The conclusions reached about *Partisan Distance* and *Partisan Certainty* are not affected by these choices.

most commonly asked question in the ANES that gets at voters' beliefs about the political distance between themselves and the two major parties, (2) people's responses to issue questions cluster in such a way that their political beliefs can often be represented as points along a one-dimensional ideological continuum, and (3) this one variable in practice appears to explain almost as much variance in people's feelings toward a political party as a richer set of issue questions (Jackson 1983).[9] The research hypothesis is that the coefficients for *Partisan Distance* will be negatively signed so that greater perceived distances between the respondent and the party decrease people's *Partisan Evaluations*. In addition to *Partisan Distance*, a set of demographic variables are included that reflect variation in people's preferences based on their personal circumstances that are not captured by ideological proximity. These are *Age* and *Age²*, *Income*, and dummy variables for *South*, *Black*, *Catholic*, and *Female*.

The second key set of variables are the *Democratic* and *Republican Certainty* measures based on open-ended party likes/dislikes questions used in tests of the voter learning model in Chapter 3, the research hypothesis being that the coefficients would be positively signed so that greater certainty increases people's *Partisan Evaluations*. As noted in the previous chapter, *Partisan Certainty* provides only an indirect measure of people's beliefs about the level of conflict within a political party, but the evidence showing that when party unity is high people's party images crystallize and become more accessible in memory strongly supports the claim that the general public's uncertainty about parties is sensitive to the

---

[9] Following the methodological advice of Grynaviski and Corrigan (2006), the respondents' placements of parties on the 7-point liberal-conservative ideology scales is used rather than an estimate of the true party placement (e.g., the average placement among all respondents). The latter 'correction' for projection effects is not used because (1) Grynaviski and Corrigan (2006) show that this is a case where the cure is worse than the disease and (2) the evidence of substantial projection effects is unpersuasive. Briefly addressing the latter point, when considering the relationship between a person's party placement on the liberal-conservative ideology scale and their *Republican Evaluations*, the correlation coefficient for most years tends to only be around 0.03. Further, the strongest relationship between *Republican Evaluations* and party placement in terms of absolute magnitude occurs in 1992, and that relationship is negative, so that people with low Republican feeling thermometer scores (i.e., liberals) were more likely to describe the party as liberal, which is contrary to what one would expect based on projection theory! The relationship between *Democratic Evaluations* and Democratic liberal-conservative placements is stronger than that observed for Republicans, but absent a theory that explains why the phenomenon applies to one party and not another, it seems prudent to stick with the raw data (although I have estimated this both ways and the choice does not seem to matter).

level of intra-party conflicts. A more serious concern with this measure is that *Partisan Certainty* is an index that may include positive and negative components. This is potentially problematic because, if it is true that a positive image has a positive effect on *Partisan Evaluations*, a negative image has a negative effect on *Partisan Evaluations*, and people on average hold a greater number of positive party images than negative party images, then this could give rise to a positive *Partisan Certainty* coefficient for reasons unrelated to the theory. Therefore, as a robustness check, a second model is estimated including both the number of *Democratic* and *Republican Likes* and the number of *Democratic* and *Republican Dislikes* as separate independent variables. The theoretical expectation is obviously that the coefficients for *Party Likes* will be positive and the coefficients for *Party Dislikes* will be negative. The test of the uncertainty implications of the model will hinge on whether the coefficients for *Likes* will be greater in absolute magnitude than the coefficients for *Dislikes*. The *Likes* coefficients should be larger than those for *Dislikes* because each *Like* response indicates both an additional favorable consideration and more knowledge about the party, both of which should increase *Evaluations* of the party. On the other hand, each *Dislike* response indicates both an unfavorable consideration and more knowledge about the party, the first of which should reduce *Evaluations* of the party while the second is a positive for the party, so the two influences offset one another. Thus, each *Like* should move *Evaluations* in a strong positive direction while each *Dislike* should move *Evaluations* in a weak negative direction, so the absolute magnitude of the *Like* coefficient should be greater.

Data are available for all of these variables for every biennial ANES since 1978, except 1998 and 2002. These data are pooled into regression models estimated with dummy variables for each year to control for the fixed effects associated with particular elections.[10]

The results of the statistical analysis are reported in columns 1 and 2 of Table 4.1 for *Democratic Evaluations* and columns 3 and 4 for *Republican Evaluations*. The first row of the table reports the coefficients for

---

[10] The analyses broken down by year strongly suggest that constraining the coefficients to be constant across time to increase the models' efficiency was a prudent choice. For the core variables of interest, there is consistent support for the claim that people's expected utility for a party is decreasing in *Distance* and that party likes have a consistently larger effect in absolute magnitude than party dislikes. The only exception to the latter claim occurred in Democratic evaluations in 1988 and 1992, but in those cases the differences in the absolute magnitudes of the two coefficients were not significant.

Table 4.1. *OLS Models for Democratic and Republican Evaluations*

Dep. Var. Indep. Var.	Democratic Evaluations	Republican Evaluations	Democratic Evaluations	Republican Evaluations
Partisan Distance	−1.46*	−1.28*	−0.93*	−0.74*
	(0.03)	(0.03)	(0.03)	(0.03)
Partisan Certainty	1.35*	0.88*		
	(0.09)	(0.10)		
Party Likes			5.76*	7.35*
			(0.12)	(0.14)
Party Dislikes			−4.78*	−5.29*
			(0.14)	(0.13)
Age	0.30*	−0.21*	0.27*	−0.11*
	(0.06)	(0.06)	(0.05)	(0.05)
Age^2	−0.0016*	0.002*	−0.0014*	0.0014*
	(0.0005)	(0.001)	(0.0005)	(0.0005)
Catholic	3.31*	−1.39*	2.60*	−1.05*
	(0.40)	(0.43)	(0.36)	(0.39)
Income	−2.10*	1.49*	−1.53*	0.68*
	(0.16)	(0.17)	(0.15)	(0.15)
South	−2.10*	−2.16*	−2.53*	−1.06*
	(0.37)	(0.41)	(0.34)	(0.36)
Black	14.29*	−9.55*	10.58*	−6.16*
	(0.51)	(0.56)	(0.47)	(0.50)
Female	2.02*	−0.33	0.88*	0.38
	(0.33)	(0.36)	(0.30)	(0.32)
Constant	43.51*	74.30*	48.04*	65.76*
	(1.72)	(1.86)	(1.56)	(1.66)
R^2 n	0.31	0.16	0.43	0.34
	(13493)	(14216)	(13493)	(14216)

Cell values are OLS coefficients (standard errors). Year fixed effects are estimated but not reported.
* Statistically significant $p < 0.05$.

Partisan Distance. As hypothesized, the coefficients across the different models for *Partisan Distance* had a statistically significant and negative effect on both *Democratic* and *Republican Evaluations* in both specifications of the model. Being conservative and looking at the smallest of the coefficients for *Partisan Distance* across the four models, the difference in *Partisan Evaluations* between a person who perfectly agrees with a party and a person who places themselves and a party at opposite ends of the 7-point liberal-conservative scale is a movement of roughly 25 units along the party's feeling thermometer scale.

Turning to the effects of the various demographic variables, the results presented in the bottom half of Table 4.1 show that Catholics and African-Americans have significantly more positive *Democratic Evaluations* and significantly more negative *Republican Evaluations* than people of other faiths and other races. Conversely, Southerners and higher income people have significantly more positive *Republican Evaluations* and significantly more negative *Democratic Evaluations* than people from the rest of the country or individuals who are less affluent. Women, interestingly, have more positive feelings toward both parties than men, but this relationship is only significant for *Democratic Evaluations*. Finally, back-of-the-envelope calculations based on the coefficients for *Age* and *Age*^{2} reveal that older respondents have the least positive Republican evaluations and the most positive Democratic evaluations.

Proposition One's prediction regarding the effects of uncertainty on *Partisan Evaluations* is more novel and important for my theory. Considering first the models reported in columns 1 and 3 using *Partisan Certainty* as a measure of the theoretical concept of interest, I find the hypothesized significant positive effects.[11] However, as noted previously, a significant positive coefficient could be a statistical artifact of the measure. Columns 2 and 4 of Table 4.1 report the results of the data analysis breaking down *Partisan Certainty* into like and dislike categories, which makes it possible to disentangle the effects of the two classes of party images. A comparison of the *Party Like* coefficients in the third row of the table with the *Party Dislike* coefficients in the fourth row of the table reveals that there is the expected asymmetric effect of party likes and dislikes. For Democrats, each additional favorable party image moves a person almost 6 points higher along the Democratic feeling thermometer scale, while each additional dislike decreases Partisan Evaluations by only about 5 units. For

---

[11] Because *Democratic* and *Republican Certainty* are treated as dependent variables in Chapter 3, and because it is theoretically possible that *Partisan Certainty* is endogenous to *Partisan Evaluations* with people providing answers to party image questions to justify their partisan attitudes, I also estimate a pair of two-stage least-squares regressions to address the concern that *Partisan Certainty* is a random regressor. In one model in this system, I consider exactly the same model reported here. In the other model, I estimate the first-stage model reported in Chapter 3 for *Partisan Certainty* plus *Democratic* and *Republican Evaluations*. For one of the models, this analysis does reveal meaningful differences in the coefficients from what I report here; however, the substantive conclusions (i.e., the sign of the key variables is the same and the magnitude of the effect remains substantial) that I draw for evaluations of both parties remain intact. Consequently, I report only the simpler analyses here.

Republicans, the difference is even stronger, with likes increasing *Partisan Evaluations* by 7 points and dislikes decreasing that value by 5 points. An F-test of the null hypothesis that *Party Likes = −Party Dislikes* reveals that in both cases the differences in these effects is statistically significant at p < .05. This is evidence that people reward a more certain option and that when they evaluate a party that this greater certainty helps to offset the effect of negative party images (and adds to the effect of positive party images). The only other interpretation that I can think of for this result is that people place greater weight on party likes than on party dislikes; however, that explanation runs contrary to several generations of research demonstrating that "bads" loom far larger in human psychology than "goods," with one team of researchers characterizing the phenomenon as approaching "a general principal or law of psychological phenomena" (Baumeister et al. 2001, p. 323). To the extent that this body of scholarship is correct, the results just reported probably understate the impact of greater *Partisan Certainty* on partisan evaluations.

Empirical Support for Proposition Two

Proposition Two states that a person prefers the party that gives them the highest expected utility. Applied to the contemporary U.S. case, this means that a person will prefer the Democrats if her *Democratic Evaluations* are stronger than her *Republican Evaluations*; she will prefer the Republicans if her *Democratic Evaluations* are weaker than her *Republican Evaluations*; and she will be a political independent if she feels similarly toward the two parties. The hypothesis that a person prefers the party because they have more positive *Partisan Evaluations* toward it seems obvious, but stands in contrast to the claim by Green and his colleagues that voter partisanship is founded upon social-group attachments rather than being a rational choice. When confronted with competing theoretical accounts like this, I believe that the best approach is to compare the ability of the various models to predict the outcome of interest (see my discussion of this topic in de Marchi, Gelpi, and Grynaviski 2002). To that end, predictions of individuals' partisanship based on the two different theoretical perspectives are provided and compared to individuals' self-reported *Party Preferences*. People's *Party Preferences* are measured using their responses to the standard ANES party identification questions, which first ask them whether they think of themselves as Democrats, Republicans, or independents and then asks individuals who self-identify as independents whether they tend to favor the Democratic or Republican

Parties. People are defined to prefer a party if they self-identify with that organization of if they describe themselves as an independent who leans toward a party, and they are defined to be an independent otherwise.

Predicted party preferences are generated as follows. To generate predictions based on my theory, people's responses to the *Democratic* and *Republican Evaluations* questions are used: People with more positive *Democratic Evaluations* are predicted to prefer the Democrats, people with more positive *Republican Evaluations* are predicted to be Republicans, and people who reports having the same feelings toward both parties are predicted to be independents. To be sure that these predictions are driven by the variables included in my expected utility model of party evaluation rather than some omitted variable that determines a person's *Partisan Evaluations*, a second analogous set of predictions are generated based on the fitted values for *Democratic* (see Table 4.1, column 2) and *Republican Evaluations* (see Table 4.1, column 3). In the latter case, these predictions will only be as good as my model of *Party Evaluation*. Finally, to be sure that these fitted values are not simply picking up the predictive power of the social-group variables, the results of a third model are also reported where the social-group variables are excluded from the models of *Partisan Evaluations*. To generate predictions for a model based on a person's social-group memberships, an ordered probit model is fitted whose dependent variable is a person's *Party Preferences* to the same ANES data used in the *Democratic* and *Republican Evaluations* models, using the various demographic variables listed earlier to measure people's social-group memberships (plus year fixed effects). Based on the parameter estimates of this model, fitted values are calculated corresponding to the estimated probability that a person is a Democrat, Republican, or independent and predict that she identifies with the party that has the highest estimated probability. To allow for variation in the effects of social-group membership over time, a second model is estimated that interacts the set of year dummies with each of the different social-group variables. Notably, in comparing across the various predictions, the deck is stacked in favor of the social-group model because its predictions are generated from a model that has been fit to the *Party Preference* data, whereas the choice model predictions are pure forecasts fit only to the *Party Evaluations* questions.

Table 4.2 reports how well the five sets of predictions performed in order of their relative performance. The most important point to be gleaned from the table is that the three models using self-reports of *Partisan Evaluations* or fitted values from the foregoing models of *Partisan*

Table 4.2. *Forecast Results for Party Preference Models*

Actual Predicted	Democrat	Independent	Republican
Net evaluations forecasts – fitted evaluations basis			
Democrat	5448	214	250
Independent	1140	836	918
Republican	301	195	4139
Total Correct = 10,423, Total Incorrect = 3018			
Net evaluations forecasts – fitted evaluations basis			
Democrat	6107	822	1383
Independent	0	0	0
Republican	782	423	3924
Total Correct = 10,031, Total Incorrect = 3410			
Net evaluations forecasts – fitted evaluations basis with no social-group variables in first-stage model			
Democrat	6374	1011	1831
Independent	0	0	0
Republican	515	234	3476
Total Correct = 9850, Total Incorrect = 3591			
Social-group model – with year interactions			
Democrat	4736	746	2250
Independent	0	0	0
Republican	2153	499	3057
Total Correct = 7793, Total Incorrect = 5648			
Social-group model – without year interactions			
Democrat	4774	765	2367
Independent	0	0	0
Republican	2115	480	2940
Total Correct = 7714, Total Incorrect = 5727			

Source: Author's calculations

Evaluations to forecast *Party Preferences* performed much better than the pair of models using individuals' social-group memberships as predictors. Furthermore, the difference in fit across the two classes of models is striking. The worst performing model using *Evaluations* to predict *Party Preferences* successfully classified 73 percent of individuals. In contrast, the best performing model using social-group memberships to predict *Party Preference* only classified 57 percent of people accurately. For readers not convinced that the 16 percent difference in forecasting accuracy is impressive, I would note that if someone were to predict that everyone in the sample was a Democrat, they would be right 51 percent of the time, which means that my gain over this naïve forecast is three times that achieved by the alternative model. Overall, the evidence provided by the relative accuracy of these forecasts points strongly toward the theory of partisan choice grounded in rational evaluations of parties rather than a theory of party identification grounded in group memberships.

The Basis for Stable Partisan Preferences

The strongest rejoinder to the claim that party preferences are based on conscious reflection about parties' attributes rather than being grounded in social-group identities is the impressive over-time stability in people's expressions about which party they tend to support, a pattern that tends to persist even when people are voting contrary to their self-reported partisan identities (cf. Green et al. 2002). Fortunately, given my model of voter beliefs about parties, it is straightforward to show that, except for young adults, it is expected that people's partisan choices should remain quite stable over time.

There are two important parts of the explanation. First, unlike choices in the market for consumer goods where decision makers are frequently confronted with a large number of products competing for market share, there are typically only two parties fielding candidates for any given office. Consequently, the kinds of small changes in a brand's image or in uncertainty about its attributes that could move a product up or down in people's preference rankings within a market segment are unlikely to have a big impact on whether someone tends to prefer Democrats or Republicans. Thus, shifts in partisan preferences require much larger changes in beliefs about parties than would be required before someone changed brand preferences.

Second, as argued in Chapter 3, people's party images appear to be based on a lifetime of experiences – not just recent events. The logical implication of this is that as people receive ever greater amounts of information about the two parties over the course of their lifetimes, the receptivity of their beliefs to new information from political elites diminishes. Assuming that individuals' preferences for government action remain reasonably stable, the growing inelasticity of people's beliefs means that their partisan attachments will also become less labile as they age (see also Achen 1992).[12] The effect of the slow pace of belief change for

---

[12] This growing stability in partisan attachments would be magnified if, as seems likely, people's preferences for government action also become more stable over time as their own attitudes toward the appropriate rates of taxation, levels of income redistribution, and so forth also crystallize.

individuals past young adulthood is compounded by the United States' oligopolistic party system, which requires large scale changes in beliefs and/or preferences before a person's partisan choices would shift.

Thus, both Green et al.'s model of mass partisanship as reflecting social-group attachments and my rational-choice model generate very similar theoretical predictions about the stability of party affiliations for mature adults. As noted in the last chapter, the critical difference between these two accounts centers on the question of whether people's responses to current events are affected by their past political experiences. If Green and his colleagues are correct that people discount the past when evaluating party performance, then there should be relatively little difference in the stability of partisan attachments of younger or older individuals because everyone's beliefs are a function of the same set of information. Furthermore, there should be little difference in the partisan affiliations of people with similar social-group identities as a function of age because all group members should see the social composition of parties in the same way. On the other hand, if I am correct, then partisan attachments should be most labile among the young, and there may be meaningful differences across generations in the partisan affiliations of individuals with similar preferences because of the different sets of political events that people have observed. Because of these different implications of the two theories, it is possible to test which approach offers the better account of voter partisanship.

The first set of predictions to be addressed concerns the stability of young adults' partisan attachments compared to their elders. The extant literature provides very strong support for my claim that the partisanship of young adults is more labile than that of more mature individuals. Jennings and Markus (1984) examine data from a panel study of parents and children that spanned the period from the mid-1960s through the early 1980s. They report that "the results offer a strong endorsement of a learning model based on experiential history . . . the younger cohort scored a large gain in partisan stability during the 1973–1982 span. At the same time, the older cohort registered a very modest gain" (p. 1004). Although panel studies provide compelling evidence of growing stability within individuals, one might argue this was isolated to one generation and not part of a more general phenomenon. Compelling counterevidence to this point is provided by Miller and Shanks (1996), who use ANES data to track the behavior of cohorts from those first eligible to vote for President in 1896 through those first eligible to vote in 1992. They conclude: "Changes in social conditions and political context are more likely to produce changes in party identification among the young – or the newly identified – than among the old" (Miller and Shanks 1996, p. 184). Further support is provided by Bartels, who analyzes the ANES cohort data by adopting a flexible functional form able to estimate both age and period effects. While expressing considerable skepticism that simple Bayesian learning describes the mechanism for change, he still concludes:

> My estimates of the age-specific weights characterizing various points in the life-span are generally consistent (at least between the ages of 15 and 60) with a simple Bayesian model in which an individual's opinion at any give time is a simple average or "running tally" of past political experiences. I find no support for the hypothesis that more recent events receive disproportional weight, and only slight (and statistically uncertain) support for the notion that events experienced during a crucial period encompassing late adolescence and early adulthood have more powerful effects than those experienced later in life. (Bartels 2001, p. o)

The evidence in Chapter 3 about how age moderates the impact of new information together with the findings reviewed here about the growing stability of partisan attachments over the life cycle provides good support for my claim that the basis for partisan attachments is the experiences that people have accumulated over the course of their lifetimes.

The second set of predictions concerns the question of whether changes in the issue positions of party elites affect young people's partisanship differently than they do that of individuals who are more mature. If I am correct, then members of social groups most affected by a change in party strategy should exhibit substantial variation in their party affiliations across birth cohorts – with the youngest individuals exhibiting the greatest sensitivity, with older members of the group updating their party affiliations in a more gradual manner. To test this prediction, variation in the party preferences of different birth cohorts of Southern whites and Catholics who experienced a realignment in their party preferences as a function of changes in the issue positions of party elites is used.[13] For Southern whites, the research hypothesis is that prior to the mid-1960s, there should be little variation in party preferences across birth cohorts because party platforms with respect to this social group had remained

[13] A similar analysis for African-Americans is not conducted because generational differences for this group are complicated by a number of shifts in party positions on issues important to black voters over time. Prior to the New Deal, African-Americans favored Republicans as the party of Lincoln; then they joined Roosevelt's New Deal coalition; after the New Deal they briefly flirted with the Republican Party as Southern Democrats led the opposition to civil rights legislation, and then shifted strongly toward the Democrats under LBJ.

Table 4.3. *Percentage Republican among Southern Whites by Decade and Cohort, 1952–2004*

Birth Cohort	Percent Republican in Cohort (Weighted Cohort Sample Size)					
	1950s	1960s	1970s	1980s	1990s	2000s
1975–Present					60.59	37.63
Entry ~ 1995					*(n = 33)**	(n = 98)
1959–1974				48.00	48.95	57.27
Entry ~ 1979				*(n = 175)*	(n = 267)	(n = 173)
1943–1958		33.33*	35.03	45.24	44.77	55.34
Entry ~ 1963		*(n = 27)*	(n = 291)	(n = 389)	(n = 242)	(n = 185)
1927–1942	*18.99*	25.97	27.54	36.75	43.74	*56.13*
Entry ~ 1947	(n = 79)	(n = 190)	(n = 225)	(n = 234)	(n = 128)	*(n = 60)*
1911–1926	18.39	19.48	24.44	*28.10*		
Entry ~ 1931	(n = 261)	(n = 283)	(n = 200)	*(n = 121)*		
1895–1910#	17.65	23.64	*25.00*			
Entry ~ 1915	(n = 170)	(n = 181)	*(n = 36)**			
Before 1895	*11.90**					
	(n = 42)					

* Indicates that these estimates are based on fewer than 50 respondents in cohort.
# These respondents may have been Hoover supporters in 1928.
Source: ANES Cumulative Data File, 1952–2004. Cell values represent the percentage of respondents less than 65 years old during Presidential election years who self-identify as a Republican or an Independent Leaning Republican.

reasonably static until this time. Beginning during the mid-1960s and 1970s, it is hypothesized that Republican Party strength will become greater among the youngest birth cohorts and that these generational differences will persist through the 1990s as Republicans' positions on the salient issues of the day such as school busing, abortion, and gun control appeal to large numbers of Southern whites. By the 1990s, it is hypothesized that the differences across birth cohorts will begin to vanish, with older people having had time to update their beliefs about which party is committed to the policy outcomes that Southern whites prefer. For Catholic voters, a similar pattern is hypothesized to occur a decade later, as the Republican Party came to support Catholic issues such as public support for private schools and pro-life measures with respect to abortion.

Table 4.3 reports the percentage of Southern white ANES respondents during Presidential election years who report a Republican Party preference by decade and birth cohort. Table 4.4 reports the similar set of results for Catholic voters. The italicized cells correspond to the first or

Table 4.4. *Percentage Republican among Catholics by Decade and Cohort,*
1952–2004

Birth Cohort	Percent Republican in Cohort (Weighted Cohort Sample Size)					
	1950s	1960s	1970s	1980s	1990s	2000s
1975–Present					29.83	40.27
Entry ~ 1995					(n = 27)*	(n = 117)
1959–1974				38.43	40.07	43.39
Entry ~ 1979				(n = 242)	(n = 306)	(n = 284)
1943–1958		22.92	30.30	37.52	32.98	39.88
Entry ~ 1963		(n = 42)*	(n = 411)	(n = 541)	(n = 297)	(n = 198)
1927–1942	27.27	20.98	27.48	33.69	33.53	40.21
Entry ~ 1947	(n = 110)	(n = 301)	(n = 312)	(n = 282)	(n = 174)	(n = 49)
1911–1926	26.63	20.05	28.05	24.48		
Entry ~ 1931	(n = 338)	(n = 319)	(n = 293)	(n = 143)		
1895–1910	25.65	22.62	17.86			
Entry ~ 1915	(n = 191)	(n = 145)	(n = 25)*			
Before 1895	28.26*					
	(n = 46)					

* indicates that these estimates are based on fewer than 50 respondents in cohort.

Source: ANES Cumulative Data File, 1952–2004. Cell values represent the percentage of respondents less than 65 years old during Presidential election years within a decade who self-identify as a Republican or an Independent Leaning Republican.

last year a birth cohort was in the sample so a substantial share of the cohort's members may not have been in the sample because they were too young or too old (deceased or over age 65), which restricts my ability to compare that cell to values for that cohort in other years, but not to other cohorts.[14] With respect to the data for Southern whites, as expected, during the 1950s the differences across generations of Southern whites were very small. However, during the 1960s, it was the youngest members of the sample who were most receptive to Republican Party appeals, with 33 percent of the Baby Boom generation, 26 percent of the New Deal generation, and just 19 percent of the pre–New Deal generation Southern whites indicating a preference for Republicans. This pattern of generational differences persisted through the 1990s, and it was only during 2000 and 2004 that differences in the partisan attachments of Southern whites across birth cohorts became attenuated, with the exception of the

[14] I exclude individuals over age 65 because people's responses to survey questions become quite unstable as they age (see Chapter 3).

youngest birth cohort who were substantially *less* likely to self-identify as Republican than older people.

With respect to Catholic voters, the data reported in Table 4.4 reveal small differences across birth cohorts through the 1970s. Beginning during the 1980s, sizeable generational differences began to emerge, with 38 percent of the youngest cohort born between 1959 and 1974 describing themselves as preferring the Republican Party, compared to just 24 percent of individuals in the oldest birth cohort who reached adulthood during the New Deal. By the 2000s, these generational differences had largely dissipated, with the oldest members of the sample finally coming to prefer the Republican Party at rates comparable to that reached by the younger birth cohorts the decade before. The most important point to be gleaned from this analysis is that for both of these cases of partisan realignment, it was the youngest people who broke most strongly from the traditional Democratic allegiances of their social group, with the older birth cohorts slowly coming to prefer the Republicans at comparable levels.

THE STRENGTH OF PARTY PREFERENCES

Thus far this chapter has established that people's feelings toward a political party are positively related to how close they think the party's candidates are to them on the issues of the day and their level of certainty about the party. Furthermore, it has shown that people's partisan preferences are grounded in their evaluations of the Democrats and Republicans. Left unanswered is the question of why someone would come to develop such strong partisan commitments that they are willing to incur personal costs contributing to an organization's electoral success.

The strength of a person's party attachments is hypothesized to be influenced by three main factors. First, the strength of a person's party preferences is hypothesized to be an increasing function of the difference in the expected utility she receives from the election of candidates from her more-preferred party compared to that received from the election of members of the less-preferred party. Thus, a person who thinks very highly of her more-preferred party and very poorly of her less-preferred party will have stronger attachments to the former organization and may be more likely to incur private costs in order to contribute to its electoral fortunes. On the other hand, a person who is largely indifferent between the two parties will have weaker party preferences. My rationale is that a person who sees big differences in the importance to herself of electing a

Democrat or Republican will be more eager to contribute to her preferred party's electoral fortunes. Unless there are big differences in people's uncertainty that would tip people's party evaluations strongly toward one organization or the other, this claim is quite similar to that offered by researchers such as Wattenberg (1981, 1994) who argue that the strength of people's party attachments is a function of whether they have positive opinions about one party and negative opinions about its opponent.

Second, *ceteris paribus*, an older person is hypothesized to have stronger partisan commitments than a younger person (at least through their working years). This occurs because as a person ages, she becomes more confident that her personal situation will not change in such a way that it will change her mind about which party she prefers. That is, an older person will generally have a clearer sense about her occupation, income level, whether she will have children in school, etc., five years from now than a young adult. As a result, the older person will be much less likely to regret contributions to a party's electoral fortunes and will therefore tend to think of herself as a strong partisan. In contrast, a person first entering adulthood really has no idea whether five or ten years from now they will be financially well off and personally benefit more from low federal income taxes or if they would be better served by a higher tax rate and greater government largesse. Consequently, a young person is unlikely to be a committed partisan. This argument has a similar flavor to that advanced by Campbell et al. (1960) in *The American Voter*, who argued that as people become older they move from political independence to strong partisan. The important difference between my work and theirs is that I believe that it is possible that as people become older, their party preferences could become weaker if, for example, party unity breaks down as it did during the middle twentieth century, thereby increasing voter uncertainty about the organization and lowering evaluations of the group.

Third, the strength of a person's partisan attachment is hypothesized to be an increasing function of her evaluation of her more-preferred party, regardless of what she thinks about its opponent. As a result, a person who favorably evaluates both parties, perhaps because they value both Democrats and Republicans for being effective in their own area of issue ownership, might still possess a strong partisan attachment to just one organization. This is likely to occur because a person who holds a party in high regard may be extremely loyal to the organization in the same way that a consumer might be loyal to, say, Ford pick-up trucks and be insensitive to price fluctuations for those vehicles, even though they know Chevy makes fine trucks, too. Conversely, a person who feels only lukewarm toward her preferred party is unlikely to have very strong attachments to the organization or to contribute beyond voting to its electoral successes, even if they strongly dislike its opponent. In this latter instance, a person's partisan preferences reflect her beliefs about which organization is the lesser of two evils, and she is therefore likely to be open to independent candidates or third-party challengers and unlikely to incur private costs to boost the electoral prospects of her preferred party. In effect, the stronger support for a highly evaluated party is the price premium that people pay their preferred party to provide the organization with incentives to act in accord with their self-interest.

The Asymmetric Effect of Party Evaluations on the Strength of Party Preferences

Drawing upon these three claims, it is possible to derive a series of testable hypotheses concerning the effects of party evaluations on the strength of people's party preferences. First, if the strength of people's party preferences are a function of the difference in Democratic and Republican Party evaluations, then it must be true that (1) the more positively someone evaluates her more-preferred party, the stronger her party preferences and (2) the more positively someone evaluates her less-preferred party, the weaker her party preferences. Second, if there are the anticipated life-cycle effects, then age will have a positive effect on the strength of a person's party preference. Third, if evaluations of a preferred party affect the strength of a person's party preferences in a process that is distinct from the process of comparing across parties, then it must be true that her evaluations of her more-preferred party will have a larger absolute effect on the strength of her party preferences than her evaluations of their less-preferred party.[15]

To test these hypotheses, a multinomial logit model is estimated with the dependent variable being whether an individual self-identifies as a strong partisan, as a weak partisan, as an independent leaner, or as an

[15] This logic has a similar flavor to that advanced by Weisberg (1980) who suggests that people's evaluations of the two parties may not be perfectly correlated in the sense that a person who likes the Republicans may not necessarily dislike the Democrats. The value added of my account is the claim that voters place greater weight on their evaluations of their more-preferred party compared to their less-preferred party.

independent without partisan leaning.[16] Two independent variables of interest are *Favored Party Evaluations* and *Unfavored Party Evaluations*, where the former variable is the *Partisan Evaluations* score of the party with the higher feeling thermometer score and the latter variable is the *Partisan Evaluations* score of the party with the lower feeling thermometer score. Using the category *Weak Partisan* as the baseline category, it is hypothesized that *Favored Party Evaluations* should be positively related to *Strong Identifier*, *Unfavored Party Evaluations* should be negatively related to *Strong Identifier*, and the absolute magnitude of the coefficient for *Favored Party Evaluations* should be greater than that for *Unfavored Party Evaluations*. Conversely, it is hypothesized that *Favored Party Evaluations* will decrease the probability that a person is an independent leaner or pure independent rather than a weak partisan, that *Unfavored Party Evaluations* will be positively related to being an independent leaner or pure independent, and that the coefficients for *Favored Party Evaluations* regarding the two sets of predictions will be larger than that for *Unfavored Party Evaluations*. To test the hypothesis that age has a positive effect on the strength of a person's party attachments, the natural log of a person's *Age* is included as an independent variable in the model. For purposes of statistical control, *Income*, *South*, *Black*, *Catholic*, and *Female* are included as control variables as well as year fixed effects.

Table 4.5 provides multinomial logistic regression results which provide good support for my research hypotheses. Not surprisingly, people were more likely to be a *Strong Identifier* than a *Weak Identifier* the more highly they evaluated their own party and less likely to be a *Strong*

---

[16] Treating independent leaners and weak partisans as equivalent categories has been the norm since Keith et al. (1992) demonstrated that the voting behavior of these two groups is almost identical. However, because of concern over treating independent leaners and weak partisans as identical, a multinomial logit model was also estimated with the dependent variable Strength of Identification on a three-category scale: independent leaner, weak partisan identifier, and strong partisan identifier. Confirming the results presented in the text, *Evaluations* toward the more-preferred party make individuals more likely to be a strong partisan compared to a weak partisan, *Evaluations* toward the less-preferred party make individuals more likely to be a strong partisan compared to a weak partisan, and the coefficients for *Evaluations* toward the more-preferred party are greater than that for the less-preferred party. Interestingly, only *Evaluations* toward the preferred party had a significant effect on identification as an independent leaner rather than as a weak partisan. The data therefore appear to show that people cross the threshold from a preference for a party to self-classification as a Republican or Democrat only if they place greater value on evaluations of their more-preferred party relative to that of the opposition.

Table 4.5. *Multinomial Logit Models for Strength of Party Preference*

Effects Relative to Baseline Category	Coefficients (standard errors)
Pure Indep. Identification	
Favored Party's Evaluations	−0.087* (0.002)
Unfavored Party's Evaluations	0.056* (0.003)
Ln(Age)	−0.409* (0.074)
Catholic	−0.014 (0.069)
Income	−0.143* (0.026)
South	0.008 (0.066)
Black	0.004 (0.099)
Female	−0.288* (0.058)
Constant	3.797* (0.342)
Indep. Leaner	
Favored Party's Evaluations	−0.021* (0.001)
Unfavored Party's Evaluations	0.004* (0.001)
Ln(Age)	−0.268* (0.051)
Catholic	−0.061 (0.048)
Income	0.001 (0.018)
South	0.026 (0.045)
Black	−0.044 (0.067)
Female	−0.262* (0.040)
Constant	2.042* (0.245)
Strong Partisan	
Favored Party's Evaluations	0.054* (0.002)
Unfavored Party's Evaluations	−0.026* (0.001)
Ln(Age)	0.766* (0.054)
Catholic	−0.002 (0.050)
Income	0.055* (0.019)
South	0.013 (0.046)
Black	0.377* (0.061)
Female	−0.160* (0.041)
Constant	−6.193* (0.274)
χ^2_{40}	6525.66*
n	18,295

Cell values are multinomial logit coefficients (standard errors). Year fixed effects were estimated for this model, but are not reported here.
* Statistically significant $p < 0.05$.

Identifier the more highly they evaluated their less-preferred party. Similarly, people were less likely to be an *Independent Leaner* or a *Pure Independent* the more highly they evaluated their more-preferred party and more likely to be an *Independent Leaner* or a *Pure Independent* the more highly they evaluated their less-preferred party. The more interesting feature of the analysis concerns the question of whether partisans place

greater weight on evaluations of their own party than that of their opponent. Consistent with this hypothesis, the reported model estimates reveal
that the magnitude of the coefficient for *Favored Party Evaluations* is
substantially larger in absolute magnitude than that for *Unfavored Party
Evaluations* in predictions for all classes of the strength of a person's
partisanship. Finally, the positive significant coefficient for log(Age) in
predicting whether someone is a *Strong Partisan* and the negative significant coefficient for this variable in predicting whether someone is an
Independent Leaner or *Pure Independent* relative to the baseline category
of *Weak Partisan* is consistent with the hypothesis that older people have
stronger partisan attachments. However, this finding is also consistent
with the Michigan Model, which claims that individuals' partisanship
grows inexorably with age – a later section of this chapter provides evidence in support of the claim that older people within each period will
tend to have stronger partisan attachments than younger people, but that
it is not necessarily true that the strength of a person's partisan attachments grows inexorably stronger with age.

Party Elite Behavior and the Strength of Party Preferences – Period Effects[17]

The statistical analyses presented to this point in this chapter have been
quite far removed from the question of whether voters are responding
to changes in the behavior of party elites, which I believe is the factor
ultimately responsible for over-time variation in the strength of voters'
partisan attachments. This deficiency is potentially quite troubling given
that my measure of people's certainty about the positions of party elites
only indirectly reflects their beliefs about the level of internal party conflicts. Fortunately, given the model of the voter developed over the course
of the last two chapters, it is straightforward to generate a set of predictions about how aggregate partisanship would change over time as a
function of party elite behavior in government. To the extent that these
predictions comport well with empirical data, then it is possible to be

---

[17] Wattenberg (1982, 1991) argues that the decline in the strength of party identifica-
tions during the 1960s was caused by the rise of candidate-centered elections, which
he believes lessened the importance of party labels as guides to decision making.
The problem with Wattenberg's account is that it can only can explain the decline
of parties – the candidate-centered nature of campaigns has not changed appre-
ciably in the past decade, but it has become increasingly clear that the electorate's
partisan attachments have rebounded over the past two decades.

more confident in the validity of the analyses presented in this book that focus on specific stages in the logical development of my argument.

The first theoretical implication of my model is that aggregate partisanship will be stronger during periods with high levels of intra-party unity and weaker during periods with lower levels of party unity. The logic behind this argument depends on a rather lengthy chain of argumentation that proceeds as follows. First, according to the learning model, the level of public certainty about the Democrats and Republicans depends on the level of ideological conflict within the national parties: when parties are highly unified, voters are certain about the policy positions of candidates in the party; when parties are divided, voters are uncertain. Second, the choice model tells us that the expected utility that people receive from a political party is an increasing function of public certainty about that party. Thus, when parties are unified, voters will have more positive evaluations of political parties than when parties are internally divided. Third, and finally, the strength of partisan preferences is an increasing function of the strength of people's evaluation of their more-preferred party. Because earlier steps in the logical chain show that party unity improves partisan evaluations, it follows that party unity should also increase the strength of party preferences.

The decline and resurgence in levels of party unity discussed in Chapter 3 provides a nice test-bed for this prediction. If the model is correct, then the number of strong partisans should decline from the 1950s through the mid-1970s during the period when parties were becoming internally divided. Conversely, the number of strong partisans should begin to increase once levels of party unity began to increase in the late 1970s and continue to rise through the present. The evidence for this hypothesis is presented in Figure 4.1, which reports the percentage of ANES respondents over time who describe themselves as strong partisans and as pure independents. As anticipated by the theory, during the 1960s and 1970s, the proportion of respondents who considered themselves strong partisans declined. Meanwhile, the number of independents refusing to acknowledge any partisan attachments began to rise during the 1950s and reached its maximum level during the mid-1970s. Then, as the movement in the level of Congressional party unity changed direction, the trends in the strength of partisanship also reversed, with growing numbers of strong partisans and declining numbers of pure independents through the 2000s.

The argument that people are responding favorably to rising levels of party unity at the elite level seems counter-intuitive given that most people

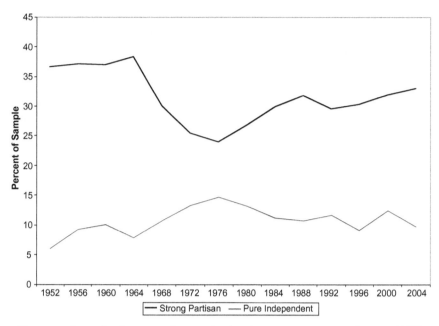

Figure 4.1. Strength of party preferences in the electorate, 1952–2004. Source: ANES Cumulative Data File, 1952–2004.

seem to view the rise of party polarization in Congress in an unfavorable light. One might think instead that a more logical explanation is that people's political preferences are such that they view the movement of the Democrats and Republicans toward ideological polls favorably. For this to be true, one of two things must have occurred – either people's political preferences must have changed such that they view a party more favorably, or the parties must have changed issue positions in a way that appeal to larger numbers of American voters.

The first of these alternative explanations is commonly advanced in the media and scholarly accounts in terms of the emergence of a culture war among rising numbers of people who have non-centrist attitudes on social issues. However, this explanation is not very compelling because the evidence is non-existent that the American public's attitudes on social issues have changed in this way. In a detailed study of long-term trends in public opinion on a variety of social issues, Dimaggio, Evans, and Bryson (1996) find:

Between-group differences in social attitudes have steadily declined. Although many remain great in absolute terms, social-attitude polarization by age, education, race, religious faith, region, and (except for abortion) political ideology, declined between the 1970s and the 1990s. Only the gap between Republicans and Democrats grew, suggesting that the party system, which has conventionally been expected to moderate social divisions, has been exacerbating them. (p. 739)

Along these same lines, Fiorina (2006) reports that: "there is little evidence that the country is polarized even on 'hot button' issues like abortion. On the whole the views of the American citizenry look moderate, centrist, nuanced, ambivalent – choose your term – rather than extreme, polarized, unconditional, dogmatic" (p. 65).

It is of course possible that the public's preferences have realigned on non-social issues. To demonstrate that the numbers of liberal and conservative extremists are not growing on other kinds of issues, ANES data from 1972 through 2000 on individuals' preferences on six different issues as well as their ideological orientation are used. The six issues are *Government Aid to Minorities, Defense Spending, Government Services and Spending, Government Sponsored Health Insurance, Government Guarantees of Jobs and a Good Standard of Living,* and *Women's Role in Society.* The issue scales and ideological orientations are measured on 7-point issue scales. To assess whether the number of extremists is growing, the proportion of respondents who hold a conservative viewpoint and the proportion of respondents who hold a liberal viewpoint is calculated for each year and each issue where data are available. Someone is considered to have a liberal (conservative) opinion if they placed themselves on the political left (right) side of each 7-point scale's midpoint. "Don't Know" responses on the issue scales are considered to be without a liberal or conservative position because someone who does not know their position on an issue is unlikely to have their political behavior determined by that issue.

Table 4.6 reports the proportion of liberal and conservative members of the electorate for the seven different issue and ideology scales. If the electorate were polarizing along ideological grounds, then one would expect to see in the table growing numbers of liberals and conservatives (i.e., the trends for the number of liberal and conservatives should both move upward). However, looking across seven different issue and ideological scales, there is not a single instance where the number of both liberals and conservatives has increased noticeably over time. Nor is there a situation where the number of liberals or conservatives increased meaningfully, while the number of members of the other group remained the same. The only exception, and it appears to be a small exception

Table 4.6. *Percentage of Population with Liberal or Conservative Issue Opinions*

		1972	1976	1980	1984	1988	1992	1996	2000
Gov't Job Guarantees	Lib %	31.5	30.0	30.5	33.5	28.4	30.1	27.3	24.8
	Con %	45.2	48.3	48.6	43.8	50.3	47.4	51.6	56.1
Health Insurance	Lib %	37.3	34.9		30.9	35.7	44.6	34.8	40.5
	Con %	32.9	34.3		34.0	32.5	24.1	35.1	32.0
Aid to Minorities	Lib %	34.0	34.9	21.8	31.8	26.4	22.6	18.5	18.9
	Con %	42.5	43.4	48.7	37.5	49.5	50.4	58.0	54.3
Women's Role	Lib %	48.9	55.4	62.1	59.6	68.7	74.8	77.4	79.1
	Con %	30.7	24.9	20.8	16.8	14.8	11.3	10.9	10.1
Gov't Svcs. & Spending	Lib %				33.5	32.1	31.3	36.8	22.8
	Con %				35.3	38.6	37.3	33.5	47.4
Defense	Lib %			11.2	32.2	33.4	47.0	31.0	16.2
	Con %			71.1	35.6	33.2	19.6	36.5	56.4
Liberal/Conservative	Lib %	25.8	24.1	25.3	25.6	23.4	27.6	24.3	27.0
	Con %	36.8	38.2	44.1	41.0	45.3	40.9	43.6	41.5

Source: ANES Cumulative Data File, 1948–2000. Cell values represent the percentage of the population who place themselves on the liberal or on the conservative side of the various issue and ideology scales.

indeed, is that the number of liberals and conservatives on the ideology scale has increased very modestly over the past thirty years, but certainly not enough to justify the substantial increase in party attachments in the general public. Even in this one exceptional case, the general pattern appears to be one in which the proportion of conservatives increases while the number of liberals falls and vice versa, so that the number of political moderates remains relatively stable over time.

An alternative explanation based on voters' issue preferences is that the parties have changed their issue positions to appeal more strongly to the public and people (whose policy preferences have largely remained static) adjust their partisan attachments accordingly (Fiorina 2006; Hetherington 2001). Thus, the Democratic Party's shift to the political left has increased its appeal among liberals while the Republican Party's shift to the political right has made it more satisfactory to conservatives, which one would expect to result in an increase in the total number of strong partisans in the electorate among people with non-centrist issue positions. Importantly, this prediction is fully in accord with the model presented earlier, with people rewarding parties for taking positions close to them on the issues of the day. However, if voters were obeying this kind of simple spatial logic of party evaluation, then centrist voters should be alienated by the polarization of party elites and therefore exhibit weaker partisanship. On the other hand, if my theory is correct, then the positive effects of party unity on voters' party evaluations should counteract the negative effects of party polarization among moderates. A useful test for my claim that strengthening party preferences are due, at least in part, to growing levels of party unity is therefore to examine whether political moderates are also becoming stronger partisans during the contemporary period of party elite polarization.

To demonstrate that partisan attachments are not weakening among political moderates, the proportion of voters placing themselves at or near the center of six different issue scales and the liberal-conservative ideology scale who self-identify as strong partisans is calculated. The results of these calculations are reported in Table 4.7, which provides clear evidence that party attachments have not weakened among those individuals who places themselves at the midpoint of a 7-point issue scale.[18] To the contrary, it appears that partisan attachments of moderate

---

[18] A similar conclusion would be reached considering individuals who place themselves at 3, 4, or 5 on these scales.

Table 4.7. *Percentage Strong Partisan among Respondents with Centrist Issue Positions by Issue and Year*

Year	Health Insurance	Guarantee Job & Standard of Living	Gov't Services & Spending	Defense Spending	Women's Role	Aid to Minorities	Lib-Con
1972	19.23	25.41		25.44	23.92		22.30
	(156)	(492)		(511)	(464)		(574)
1976	26.34	22.54		24.41	24.31		18.28
	(224)	(386)		(340)	(399)		(558)
1980		28.51		28.44	23.05	23.24	21.52
		(242)		(218)	(347)	(241)	(302)
1984	28.05	25.24	27.30	28.91	29.49	27.12	22.24
	(165)	(420)	(575)	(467)	(590)	(612)	(508)
1988	28.53	25.21	27.10	29.68	28.24	28.10	23.69
	(319)	(361)	(465)	(310)	(425)	(580)	(439)
1992	25.00	27.73	25.91	36.05	25.55	29.89	24.78
	(432)	(476)	(629)	(319)	(595)	(706)	(569)
1996	28.40	26.69	30.28	34.90	31.13	29.71	22.50
	(324)	(341)	(459)	(192)	(363)	(488)	(400)
2000	32.46	29.41	30.40	31.07	26.72	32.34	20.56
	(191)	(170)	(250)	(103)	(247)	(235)	(214)
2004	28.17	27.23	25.90	34.58	27.51	28.11	24.54
	(213)	(224)	(278)	(107)	(269)	(281)	(273)

Source: ANES Cumulative Data File, 1948–2004. Cell values represent the proportion of respondents who place themselves at 4 on the 7-point issue scale who self-identify as a strong partisan (number of centrists).

voters have actually strengthened over time.[19] This observation is much more strongly in accord with my theory in which voters are rewarding parties for greater levels of party unity in government than with other approaches emphasizing only party platforms.[20]

Party Elite Behavior and the Strength of Party Preferences – Cohort Effects

As a final look at the data on voter partisanship, it is important to demonstrate empirically the validity of two additional theoretical implications of my model. First, the model predicts that there will be a positive relationship between age and the strength of partisan identities at different moments in history (i.e., age and strength of party preferences will be correlated in each year – a prediction also consistent with the Michigan Model). Second, in contrast to the claims made by proponents of the Michigan Model, the model predicts that people's partisan attachments will not necessarily strengthen over time, depending on whether party unity is on the upswing or on the decline.

To provide empirical support for these predictions, a cohort analysis is conducted that allows me (1) to examine over-time changes in the behavior of a random sample of people across birth cohorts at different moments of history and (2) to compare differences in the behavior of individuals at similar stages of the life cycle at different moments in history. The data needed to conduct such an analysis are provided in Table 4.8, which reports the percentage of the population who describe themselves as a *Strong Partisan* in ANES surveys by birth cohort for each election year from 1952 through 2004. Reading across the rows to highlight differences across birth cohorts in a given election year, it is clearly true that older people generally have stronger party preferences

---

[19] The same pattern also occurs among ideological extremists, but that is to be expected, with ideologically extreme voters rewarding their more-preferred party with stronger attachments.

[20] Some might argue that even moderates might form stronger party attachments in response to growing differences between the average Democrat and the average Republican that crystallizes differences between the two parties (e.g., Hetherington 2001, Pomper 1972). However, this explanation is inconsistent with the empirical finding (Table 4.1) that *Partisan Evaluations* are negatively related to *Partisan Distance*, which implies that moderates dislike extreme parties. The incorrect inference in previous studies is surely a result of the correlation between *Intra-Party Unity* and *Inter-Party Conflict* in government.

Table 4.8. *Percentage Strong Partisan by Birth Cohort and Year, 1952–2004*

Birth Cohort Year	1975–Present	1959–1974	1943–1958	1927–42 Entry	1911–26 Entry	1895–1910	Before 1895
1952				32.37	28.14	39.39	*50*
1956				25.26	33.67	40.77	*45.45*
1960				34.34	32.02	39.92	
1964			*25*	31.69	36.06	48.54	
1968			*12.24*	26.49	28.16	*38.51*	
1972			*15.84*	21.12	31.05	*34.25*	
1976			15.1	21.47	30.8		
1980		*24.14*	18.85	26.8	33.94		
1984		*21.21*	23.83	31.63	39.09		
1988		25.42	28.36	37.32	37.76		
1992		18.36	28.75	34.08			
1996		24.81	31.6	34.65			
2000	*19.05*	27.03	34.94	40.83			
2004	28.06	28.92	36.05	*39.92*			

Source: ANES Cumulative Data File, 1948–2004. Cell values represent the percentage of respondents between age 21 and 65 by Presidential election year who self-identify as a strong Democrat or Republican. For cells in italics, the entire birth cohort is not included in the sample because some members are too young or too old.

than younger people – a prediction made by both myself and Campbell et al. in *The American Voter*.

A key implication of my theory that differs from the Michigan Model is that I expect that within all birth cohorts there should be a decline in the proportion of strong identifiers during the post-war period as party unity in government continued to unravel, whereas the Michigan Model predicts strengthening partisanship during this period. Evidence of this relationship is provided by reading across rows of the table that describe changes in the proportion of strong identifiers within each birth cohort. The table clearly shows a marked decrease in the number of strong partisans during this period of time across birth cohorts, with all groups reaching their minimum proportion of strong partisans in the period 1972–6, when party unity in government also reached its nadir (see also Abramson 1976, 1979). Since that time, as party unity in government rose, partisan attachments in the electorate across cohorts also steadily rebounded (see also Miller and Shanks 1996).

CONCLUSIONS

This chapter offered a major revision to current models of party-in-the-electorate and in doing so provides important insight into the incentives that politicians have for seeking unified national parties. It argued that a crucial feature of the development of partisan reputations is the consistency of messages that citizens receive about the party. During periods of conflict within the parties, citizens will find that party labels convey less useful information about the attributes of candidates within the party. As a result, people may evaluate the parties as a whole less favorably, in much the same way that consumers are less likely to choose pay a price premium for umbrella brands whose different products are of uneven quality. On the other hand, if parties are highly unified and stable, then citizens will find party labels useful tools for informing their votes and are likely to reward their most-preferred party by incurring private costs to advance its electoral interests. Examined in light of changes in the national political system over the past half-century, this approach seems to account for the stability in respondents' partisan preferences over the life cycle and also seems to explain the decline and resurgence in the number of strong party identifiers in the post-war period.

Placing these findings within the broader theoretical claims of this book, the argument that party unity encourages the emergence of strong partisans who are more likely to turn out to vote and participate in other ways on a party's behalf provides parties as teams of politicians with incentives to cooperate within the government. All party members benefit from the emergence of strong partisans in their district who help their own campaigns, and they benefit from strong partisans in other parts of the country who boost the party's prospects of winning legislative majorities. As argued in Chapter 2, it is the benefits that parties receive from the existence of brand loyalists that establish the credibility of partisan cues at the ballot box.

5

Reconciling Candidate and Party Brand Names

Over the last few chapters, it was argued that parties benefit from acting as unified teams in government because it reduces the uncertainty of voters about the characteristics of party members. Consequently, it is rational for citizens to cast votes based on candidates' party affiliations because they know that if the party fails to corral its members in the future, then it jeopardizes its valuable reputation in the same way that a franchiser stakes its brand name on the performance of its local franchisees. This provides a rationale for the empirical fact that voters tend to rely primarily on politicians' party affiliations in Congressional elections rather than other decision-making cues (including candidates' own policy positions) and explains why it is rational for the public to hold the national parties collectively responsible for their actions in government – a notion essential to the surety model of party government.

This account of the importance of partisan cues is not easily reconciled with the notion that American elections are candidate-centered (Agranoff 1976; Wattenberg 1982, 1994). Seminal studies of Congressional elections strongly suggest that politicians endeavor to develop and campaign on the basis of private brand names established via their legislative record that have particular appeal in their home districts and that differentiate them from other members of their party (Fenno 1978; Mayhew 1974a). In the language of the spatial model of political competition, politicians have strong incentives to establish a reputation that is appealing to the median voter in their districts regardless of what the other members of their party are doing.

The claim that politicians are able to campaign on the basis of private brand names established through their legislative record has the capacity to challenge the central arguments of this book in two fundamental ways. First, it raises questions about whether voters view congressional elections through the prsim of which party they prefer to control the government. If politicians develop well-defined private brand names that they value, then these reputations might differentiate office-motivated types of candidates from ideologues. With information about individual politicians revealed through their performance in office, over time, parties might become unnecessary to correct for the problems created by the adverse selection in legislative elections. Furthermore, legislators focused on appealing to local interests might harm the party's reputation for providing the public with a certain type of candidate, thereby weakening partisan attachments in the general public in the manner described in the last several chapters. With too many legislators acting in this way, the national parties would lose their ability to use party brand names as a credible signal because the electorate would no longer see the Democrats or Republicans as placing a valuable reputation in jeopardy when they run candidates for office.

Second, fears that other legislators might bow to electoral pressures from their constitutents might jeopardize intra-party cooperation in government. The argument developed in Chapter 2 suggests that parties are organizations whose members tend to have similar policy preferences and that these preferences tend to be are extreme compared to that of ordinary voters. Members of this organization might be willing to cast votes contrary to district interests to secure policy gains, especially on procedural votes, but they will be much less inclined to do so if they do not expect their co-partisans to reciprocate on later votes.

The purpose of this chapter is to demonstrate that the American system of candidate-centered elections is consistent with the surety model of party government. Its first part is dedicated to addressing the two theoretical challenges posed to my theory that were just described. The remainder of the chapter describes the strategic choice that politicians confront when choosing to campaign on the basis of their party's record or to differentiate themselves from their party in order to compete on the basis of private brand names.

CANDIDATE REPUTATIONS AS A SUBSTITUTE FOR PARTY LABELS?

The first challenge to the surety model of party government posed by the possibility of private candidate brand names is that their existence might undermine the rationale for parties developed in Chapter 2. In support of the argument for private brand names is the overwhelming impression given by politicians to both the public and to scholars that they believe that personal reputations are important. Even prior to the period of party decline during the 1950s that scholars believe gave rise to the modern era of candidate-centered politics, 85 percent of incumbent candidates standing for reelection to the House believed that their "personal standing and record" was "very important" or "quite important" to their electoral fortunes (Stokes and Miller 1962, p. 542). Although this belief may be genuine, just because politicians talk about the desirability of personal reputations that are appealing in their home district does not necessarily mean that they are able to successfully appeal to the vast number of ordinary Americans on the basis of a private brand name. For a politician's reputation to inspire confidence that she will not behave opportunistically in the event of her election, it must be the case that she has "equity" in her brand name that would be sacrificed if she behaved badly. At a minimum, this requires that voters know the candidate's name and some useful attributes that differentiate her from opponents. If these conditions are not satisfied, then the politician does not place a valuable personal reputation in jeopardy if she pursues extreme policies once in office. At the very least, if a tremendous number of ordinary voters do not know who the politician is, then they have no way of knowing whether she has a private brand name to value. Similarly, if name recognition is sufficiently low, then the handful of voters who do recognize the candidate but who understand that most other voters do not may also infer that the candidate's current reputation is not a particularly valuable asset.

A logical starting point for assessing whether individual politicians have reputations that the general public believes they value is to determine whether people are able to recall or even recognize their names. One useful measure of this is to ask people in an open-ended question to provide a candidate's name. Based on evidence from the ANES, the public's ability to *Recall* the name of incumbent members of the House of Representatives who are running for reelection is remarkably low. As reported in the first column of Table 5.1, the percentage of ANES respondents unable to recall the name averaged over 68 percent over the last three decades. The low name recognition of American politicians is incredibly damaging evidence for the claim that voters rely on candidates' private brand names when casting their votes – a person would have to be able to identify the candidate before trusting her brand name.

To put in perspective the weakness of Americans' ability to recall their incumbent Representative's name, Cain, et al. (1987) report that when citizens in the United Kingdom were asked to recall their incumbent MP's name, only 35 percent of respondents were unable to do so. The striking

Table 5.1. *Incumbent Name Recognition*

	Percent Who could not Recall Incumbent's Name	Percent Who could not Place Incumbent on Feeling Thermometer	Percent Who could not Place President on Feeling Thermometer
1970	66.55		
1974	62.74		
1978	67.42	21.58	2.18
1980	66.51	17.87	0.58
1982	65.20	20.39	1.33
1984	69.16	17.85	1.29
1986	74.62	22.72	0.68
1988	69.58	15.36	2.07
1990	75.84	19.28	0.88
1992	68.06	16.49	0.68
1994	69.64	17.12	0.44
1996	52.06	23.00	0.37
1998	77.38	26.28	0.33
2000	74.82	22.34	0.59
2002		15.96	0.28
2004		18.90	0.52
Overall	68.61	19.81	0.94

Source: ANES Cumulative Data File and Gary Jacobson. Cell values are the weighted percentages of respondents who either were able to recall the House incumbents' name or were able to place politicians on feeling thermometers.

thing about this fact is that the United Kingdom has a parliamentary system of government in which legislators' party-line votes on most measures prevent MPs from differentiating themselves in any meaningful way from their party. Thus, in a country where one would expect personal reputations to have minimal effects on voting behavior, the public actually knows individual candidates better than they do in the United States. While there are important institutional and cultural differences between the United States and the United Kingdom that could explain these differences, the cross-national comparison still makes the point compellingly that (1) there is nothing inherently hard about recalling the identity of an incumbent politician and (2) the United States' weak partisan institutions do not translate into higher levels of name recognition.

Market research suggests that it might nevertheless be rash to conclude from name recall questions that a brand name lacks value if people's decisions are made at the point of purchase (Keller 2001). Mann (1978) and Jacobson (2004) make a similar case with respect to politicians – arguing that the public might recognize the name of a candidate on the ballot even if they are unable to pull that information from memory. There is good reason to be skeptical about this claim because most people probably know that they are going to vote for the Democrat or the Republican when they arrive at the polls even if they do not know those candidates' names (which implies that candidate brand names are irrelevant to the decision), but it is at least plausible that elections to Congress are sufficiently far down the ballot that a person arriving at the polls has not already come to a decision about how to vote. If the latter scenario were true, then that would require that the public could recognize the incumbent's name on the ballot and assess their feelings toward the candidate. As a rough measure of candidate name recognition, I use ANES respondents' ability to place their incumbent House member on 100-point scales describing how warmly or coolly they feel toward this individual. These data are reported in the second column of Table 5.1 along with feeling thermometer scores for the President, which provides a useful benchmark. In contrast to the recall questions, where just two-thirds of respondents could not identify their incumbent, the data from feeling thermometer scores suggest that just 20 percent of the American public either fail to recognize the name of their sitting Congressman or their opinion of this person is so poorly formed that they are unable to place him or her on the feeling thermometer scale when given the Congressman's name.

If the actual level of incumbent name recognition hovers around 80 percent, then that would be much more supportive of the claim that politicians have equity in their private brand names than the 32 percent figure reported earlier. The question that follows is whether people who are able to place their incumbent on feeling thermometers really do have reasonably well-informed opinions about the candidate and her issue positions, or if this is simply evidence of what market researchers call "spurious awareness," which is said to occur when someone mistakenly reports being able to recall something (Keller 2001). To assess whether the public knows something about legislators' records in Washington, I look at ANES respondents' placements of their incumbent on 7-point issue scales on a number of important public policy questions as well as her political ideology. The issues included whether men and women should have an equal role or if women's place is in the home; whether government should help blacks (minorities) or if blacks (minorities) should help themselves; whether government should provide many fewer services and reduce spending a lot or if government should provide many more services and increase spending a lot; and whether government should see to

Table 5.2. *Percentage of Respondents Able to Place Both the Incumbent and Themselves on Scale*

	Liberal-Conservative	Women's Role	Aid to Blacks	Government Services and Spending	Gov't Guaranteed Jobs and Std of Living
1978	54.25	56.51	52.30		52.27
1980	54.12	55.68	48.26		54.42
1982	55.75	53.40	54.62	54.17	52.29
1984				44.70	47.78
1986	45.77			48.22	
1990	52.28			49.51	
1994	39.18			39.62	35.40
1996	49.52			48.81	
1998	44.59	43.87		40.66	42.18
2000	45.58			50.76	
2004	42.25			35.60	
Overall	48.80	53.16	51.77	46.14	47.58

Source: ANES Cumulative Data File, 1952–2004. Cell values are weighted percentages of respondents able to answer questions about both themselves and the incumbent.

people having a job and good standard of living or if government should let each person get ahead on their own. Table 5.2 reports the percentage of respondents for each election year since 1978 who were able to place both themselves and their incumbent Representative on these scales when asked to do so. Considering the various topics, roughly half of all respondents failed to place both themselves and an incumbent candidate who ran for reelection on these scales when given the candidate's name. This is an incredibly low standard by which to measure the information that people possess about candidates because it does not speak to the accuracy of their candidate perceptions, yet only about half of all people surveyed were able to offer an answer to these questions – even for seemingly easy questions such as whether the incumbent is liberal or conservative.

This general pattern of low levels of public awareness about their incumbents also adheres when people are asked about specific measures before Congress. For example, Ansolabehere and Jones (ND) find in their study of public knowledge about recent salient votes in the House that "57% [of respondents] placed their Representative [i.e., offered a guess about her vote] on the Prescription Drug Importation bill, 64% on the Partial-birth Abortion Ban, and 62% on the Gay Marriage Amendment (p. 12)." Of the roughly 60 percent of people offering guesses about their incumbent's votes, they find that the rate of correct predictions was also quite low, with only 64 percent, 74 percent, and 62 percent of people correctly identifying their Representatives' votes on the respective scales. Putting the data together, their study finds that only about one third of people were able to correctly guess their Representatives' votes on these high-profile bills. These findings echo the seminal studies by Miller and Stokes (1963; Stokes and Miller 1962), who report, "Our constituent interviews indicate that the popular image of the Congressman is almost barren of policy content.... By the most reasonable count, references to current legislative issues comprised not more than a thirtieth part of what the constituents had to say about their Congressmen" (Stokes and Miller 1962, pp. 542–3; see also Jacobson 2004)."

My purpose here is not to disparage the American public for their lack of information about the identities and actions of their elected officials. For reasons that will be laid out in greater detail later in this chapter, most Americans have little information about their MCs and relate to their Representative (if at all) in terms of her personal qualities and service to her district because the Representative has little incentive to provide information about her legislative record to her constituents: her party's brand name already conveys that information. Most people are able to make reasonably good decisions about how to vote based on their own preferences about the direction of government, the positions of the national parties on these issues, and candidates' party affiliations – people just infer that the politicians vote with the rest of their party (Miller and Stokes 1962; Ansolabehere and Jones 2007). Taking this argument a step farther, one factor contributing to voters' lack of knowledge about specific candidates may be that they do not trust the information that individual politicians provide and therefore do not undergo the cognitive effort needed to store this information. This perspective is supported by the evidence in Chapter 2 that ordinary Americans believe that politicians are "experience goods" and by experimental studies showing that subjects who are actually given candidate-specific issue information and then asked to recall shortly thereafter a candidate's issue positions are more likely to provide the party's position than the candidate's (Rahn 1993). That insight aside, the essential point for the purposes of this chapter is that if people are drawing upon partisan cues or other stereotypes and they have little specific information about the candidates running for office, that strongly supports my claim that politicians' private brand names are not a substitute for partisanship in American elections.

CANDIDATE INCENTIVES TO DIFFERENTIATE THEMSELVES FROM THEIR PARTY

The second challenge posed by politicians' desire to develop private brand names is that incumbents who believe that their personal reputations affect electoral outcomes may split with their party to cast votes that satisfy district interests. This argument is much more relevant for my work than the claim that candidate reputations provide a substitute for partisanship in American elections, because not all voters need to know an incumbent's record for politicians to believe that it is consequential. For example, it is possible that an incumbent believes that it is in her electoral interest to satisfy an influential group of voters who place considerable weight on an issue and pay heed to their Representative's actions, and that by giving into this pressure they divide the party, thereby damaging its reputation.

In considering politicians' electoral motivation to cast votes that disagree with that preferred by a majority of other members of their party in government, it is useful to consider three different strategic situations that candidates confront given their district's preferences (either the district writ large, or a group of high demanders) on an issue and the actions of other MCs. First, there are legislators who represent districts who approve of the votes cast by the majority of other members of the incumbents' party in government. For these politicians, electoral considerations provide scant motivation for defecting from the party line – voting with the party is equivalent to voting with the district. Second, there are legislators who represent districts who disapprove of the votes cast by majorities of both parties. For politicians representing this group of constituents, it is unlikely that they will feel compelled to bow to electoral pressures to vote against the party. Ultimately, there is not much to be gained by taking credit for being on the bottom of a 415–20 vote in the House, so MCs whose votes reflect district tastes have little reason to campaign on this issue, and a challenger would not make much political hay by claiming that they would have cast the twenty-first vote opposing Congressional action. In fact, pointing to this kind of legislative failure would presumably be damaging to a politician's reputation because it creates the impression that she is unable to move policy in the direction preferred by her district. Third, there are legislators who represent districts whose policy preferences place them at odds with their own party and in agreement with the opposition party. This group of legislators obviously have the strongest incentives to vote against their party for electoral purposes, especially given that challengers could point to their party's support of the district as evidence for how they might have voted regarding this issue.

Given this (I think uncontroversial) statement about the electoral concerns that incumbents face with respect to their vote choices, it is possible to inquire into the types of issues that create incentives for politicians to differentiate themselves from their party as well as the characteristics of the districts who encourage this type of behavior.[1] In pursuing this inquiry, it is helpful to begin from the assumption (following Mayhew 1974a; Krehbiel 1993) that the national parties have relatively weak levers to manipulate the voting behavior of party members so as to bias the findings against my theory. Proceeding from this assumption, it would seem to follow that if the Congressional parties are not able to offer much to compensate members for casting hard votes against constituent interests, then office-motivated MCs (1) would vote with their district and (2) would strive to differentiate themselves from their party's positions on the issues in the manner described earlier. However, viewed through the theoretical lens about legislator incentives presented previously, this argument is a bit of a red herring, because a party does not necessarily need to be able to coerce its members to prevent them from defecting from the party line. A key variable motivating a politician's decision to differentiate herself from her party is the appearance of issues on the legislative agenda that force her to choose between the party line and the interests of her district. From this observation, it obviously follows that the exercise of agenda control has the potential to significantly influence the incentives for politicians to defect from their party for electoral purposes.

The Implications of Agenda-setting Powers for Private Brand Names

Cox and McCubbins (2005) present a pair of models to illustrate how the exercise of gate-keeping power by the majority party affects the kinds of policies that Congress adopts. The first model, what they call the Floor Agenda model, considers legislator behavior when the Committee of the Whole controls the legislative agenda in Congress. This represents the type of agenda control portrayed by Mayhew (1974a), who sees appointees to agenda-setting offices (i.e., Speaker, majority-party leader, and members

---

[1] Egan (2007) offers strong support for this assumption. He shows that MCs are most sensitive to their districts in cases where their party has an issue position at odds with constituent interests and the opposition party's issue position is viewed more favorably in the district.

of the Rules Committee) as agents for the entire House of Representatives who looked after the well-being of the chamber as a whole. The second model, what Cox and McCubbins call the Party Cartel Model, considers legislator behavior when the majority party in Congress also exercises agenda control. In practice, this means that appointees to agenda-setting offices do not allow legislation to reach the floor for a vote if it is opposed by a majority of majority-party members (even though there may be a Congressional majority in favor of that legislation). In this section, these models are used to illustrate how the simple exercise of gate-keeping powers by majority-party leaders greatly limits the opportunities that MCs have to cast votes that differentiate themselves from their party for electoral purposes. (A subsequent section introduces a model consistent with a more expansive view of party government where the leader of the majority party uses her agenda-setting powers to secure the more extreme public policies favored by ideologues in her party).

Model Preliminaries. There are five key assumptions shared by the two models. First, legislators are assumed to confront a single public policy question, where the different policy choices can be represented as points along a left-right political continuum or issue dimension. There is a status quo point q that represents the reversion point that remains in force if the legislature fails to pass an alternative policy. Second, there are n members of the legislature. Each member of the legislature has an ideal point in the policy space representing their most preferred policy outcome, and their utility for a public policy falls as the distance increases between their ideal point and the policy's location along the left-right continuum.[2] To best flesh out how electoral pressures might weight on MCs' voting decisions, in an abuse of terminology (especially given the assumption that some legislators may be uncompromising ideologues), it is assumed that each legislator's ideal point corresponds in some vague sense to the position that she believes maximizes her reelection chances in the district, perhaps because it represents the policy position most preferred by the median voter in her district or because it is the policy most preferred by high demanders on that issue dimension back home. Third, there exists a coalition of legislators (to be defined later) with the ability to block bills from floor consideration, but once a bill reaches the floor, all members may introduce amendments. Fourth, the legislative process occurs in four stages: (1) an MC or MCs introduce a bill on the policy

[2] Specifically, legislators have city-block utility functions.

domain in question (presumably, the bill is referred from committee), (2) the agenda setters decide whether to allow the bill onto the floor for further consideration, (3) if the bill receives floor consideration, amendments are offered and decided by majority rule, and (4) the floor chooses between the reversion point q and the bill as amended. Fifth, all players in the game know each other's preferences, the status quo point q, and the rules of the game.

Nicely, these assumptions allow for the application of the median voter theorem for each issue considered by a session of the legislature. That is, for each issue that the agenda setter allows to reach the floor for vote consideration, some member (perhaps the median voter herself) will introduce the policy proposal most preferred by the median voter in the chamber as the bill or as an amendment. By the assumptions of the model, no proposal can defeat the policy most preferred by the median voter in a pairwise vote. Consequently, the spatial location of the bill (as introduced or as amended on the floor) considered for final passage is at the ideal point of the median voter in the chamber. Let F represent the location of the floor median in the policy space; the final passage vote is between q and F; and F wins a majority of the votes in the legislature.

Since it seems likely that the electorate cares much more about final passage votes than about procedural maneuvers leading up to that vote, I will focus my attention for now on the question of when legislators feel electoral pressure to cast votes that differentiate themselves from the rest of their party when choosing between q and F.[3] To begin, it is useful to identify who sincerely prefers (recall the abuse of terminology whereby MCs' "preferences" are equivalent to constituency opinion on an issue dimension, not their personal values) to vote for F and who prefers to vote for q as a function of their location in the policy space: the spatial locations of legislators supporting and opposing F are identified

---

[3] One could argue that votes on amendments could also be considered potential campaign issues. I do not dwell on this possibility, because procedural rules have shielded MCs from publicly casting tough votes on floor amendments. It was not until the early 1970s that roll-call votes taken in the Committee of the Whole were recorded teller votes, so, prior to that time, MCs had little reason to be concerned that these votes would come back to haunt them. Shortly after that reform, the House made more frequent use of restrictive amendment procedures, including the closed rule. Bach and Smith (1988) tell us that part of the rationale for operating under these restrictive rules is that they prevent MCs from being forced to cast votes on amendments that embarrassed party leaders, by revealing either the extreme positions favored by some party members or severe internal party divisions on key issues.

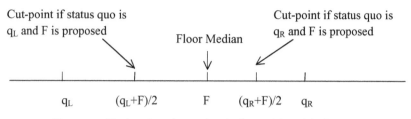

Figure 5.1. The location of cut-points in the spatial model of voting.

in Figure 5.1 for the case where the status quo policy q_L is on the left side of F and for the case where the status quo policy q_R is to the right of F. Considering first legislators' choices between q_L and F, the standard spatial logic of voting implies that the midway point between these two policy choices represents a cut-point such that any actor to the left of $(q_L + F)/2$ prefers q_L and anyone to the right of $(q_L + F)/2$ prefers F. Similarly, the midway point between q_R and F is the location such that any legislator to the left of the cut-point $(q_R + F)/2$ prefers F to q_R and any legislator to the right of $(q_R + F)/2$ prefers q_R.

Building upon these insights, it is also possible to identify the set of policies that are majority- and minority-party preferred. A policy x is defined to be preferred by a party over a policy y if a majority of party members prefer x to y. It follows from this definition and the assumption of single-peaked preferences that a party-preferred policy must also be preferred by the party member with the median ideal point on that issue dimension. Assuming that M is the ideal point of the median majority party member and m is the ideal point of the median minority party member, Figure 5.2 summarizes the set of majority- and minority-party preferred policies with respect to q. Addressing the case of the majority party (the minority-party case is symmetric to that of the majority party and not addressed here), if q is to the left of the point 2M − F, then the cut-point is to the left of M, which means that the median majority-party member and every party member to the right of M (which together constitute a majority of the majority party) prefer F to q. On the other hand, if q is between 2M − F and F, then the cut-point(q + F)/2 is between M and F so that the median majority-party member and every member of her party to the left of M (which together constitute a majority of the majority party) prefer q to F. Finally, for status quo locations to the right of the floor median, the cut-point is to the right of F so that M and every legislator to the left of M prefers F to q.

144

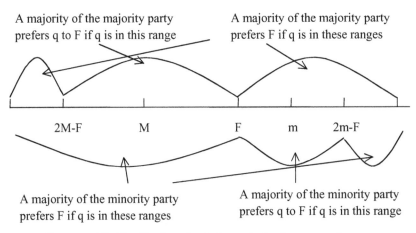

A majority of the majority party prefers q to F if q is in this range

A majority of the majority party prefers F if q is in these ranges

| 2M-F | M | | F | m | 2m-F | |

A majority of the minority party prefers F if q is in these ranges

A majority of the minority party prefers q to F if q is in this range

Figure 5.2. The identification of majority- and minority-party preferences.

Given this set of results regarding the voting behavior of each MC and the action favored by each party when choosing between q and F, it is possible to identify the set of conditions that must be satisfied for a legislator to cast final-passage votes that differentiate herself from the rest of her party in order to advance her electoral interests under different agenda-setting models.

Floor Agenda Model. Agenda-setting by the Committee of the Whole refers to the case where a majority of the entire chamber must vote to allow a bill (and its amendments) to come to the floor for consideration – if they exercise their gate-keeping powers, the status quo point q remains law. Following Shepsle (1979), the main value of gate-keeping by the Committee of the Whole is to restrict the introduction of non-germane amendments that may create social choice problems in the legislature. For expositional purposes, however, the exercise of gate-keeping powers by the Committee of the Whole can be largely ignored because it is always true that a majority of the Committee of the Whole (weakly) prefers to allow the bill to come to the floor for a vote. This follows from the fact that the median voter can always introduce her ideal point as an amendment, and there is always a legislative majority who prefers the median voter's position to the status quo, so that the coalition favoring F to q ensures that legislation on that issue area reaches the floor.

To identify the spatial locations of legislators whose constituents want them to vote in accord with their party's preferred position and those who do not, it is useful to first decompose the policy space into six distinct

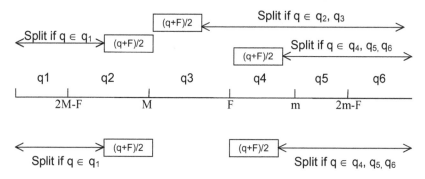

District ideal points of majority party members with divided loyalties under Floor Agenda Model as a function of q

District ideal points of majority party members with divided loyalties under Party Cartel Model as a function of q

Figure 5.3. Divided or unified party-district loyalties: the majority-party case.

parts that represent different possible ranges of values of the status quo point q. These six regions are presented in Figure 5.3 as $q_1, \ldots, q_6$, where q_1 represents the set of points to the left of $2M - F$, q_2 the set of points between $2M - F$ and M, and so forth. Having decomposed the space in this way, it is possible to identify which legislators have split district-party loyalties on final passage votes as a function of q's location.

Beginning with the left-most extreme region of the policy space, if $q \in q_1$, then by the results summarized in Figure 5.1 it follows that only those legislators representing districts to the left of $(q + F)/2$ prefer q to F, and by the results presented in Figure 5.2 it also follows that F is preferred to q by both the majority and minority parties. Thus, as depicted in the top half of Figure 5.3 for the majority party and 5.4 for the minority party, all legislators representing districts whose ideal point is to the left of $(q + F)/2$ have split party-district loyalties and all legislators representing districts whose ideal is to the right of $(q + F)/2$ have unified party-district loyalties. Figures 5.3 and 5.4 also depict the symmetric results for the case where $q \in q_6$ and legislators to the right of $(q + F)/2$ support q and have split party-district loyalties and legislators to the left of $(q + F)/2$ have unified party-district loyalties. Given the incentives discussed earlier, neither legislative supporters or opponents of F have incentives for credit claiming on the issue if q occupies an extreme location of the policy space because (1) they voted with their party and free-ride on the organization's stance, (2) they voted against their party on an issue where they lost a

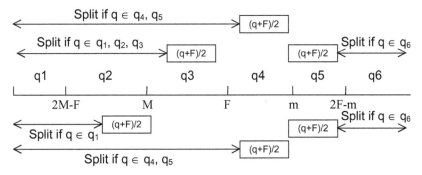

District Ideal points of minority party members with divided loyalties under Floor Agenda Model as a function of q

District Ideal points of minority party members with divided loyalties under Party Cartel Model as a function of q

Figure 5.4. Divided or unified party-district loyalties: the minority-party case.

lopsided vote, or (3) they voted against their constituency's preferences and prefer not to communicate that information.

Repeating this logical procedure for the case where q ∈ q2 or q3, only those legislators representing districts with ideal points to the left of the cut-point $(q + F)/2$ have constituencies that prefer q to F, the majority party prefers q, and the minority party prefers F. As portrayed in Figures 5.3 and 5.4, majority-party members representing districts with preferences to the right of $(q + F)/2$ and minority-party members representing districts with preferences to the left of that cut-point have split party-district loyalties, and the resulting incentives for publicly distancing themselves from their party's position on the issue or for explaining their decisions. (The figures also portray the symmetric results for the case where q ∈ q4 or q5 where majority-party members to the right of $(q + F)/2$ and minority-party members to the left of that cut-point have split loyalties.) On the other hand, majority-party members representing districts with preferences to the left of $(q + F)/2$ and minority-party members representing districts with preferences to the right of that cut-point have unified party-district loyalties and the weak incentives for credit claiming that this implies.

Taken together, the important implication of these results from the Floor Agenda model for my purposes is that except for issues where the status quo point is at either the far left or far right ends of the policy space, large numbers of politicians have incentives to vote against the preferences of their party in order to best represent their districts. Thus, with agenda setting by the Committee of the Whole, familiar arguments about legislators' incentives to vote against their party and to communicate those votes to constituents are sound.

Party Cartel Model. Agenda-setting by the majority party describes the case where Congressional leaders are granted gate-keeping powers to keep issue areas that divide the majority party from coming to the floor for consideration. Following Cox and McCubbins (2005), this is the case where Congressional leaders exercise gate-keeping powers when a majority of majority-party members prefer the status quo point q to the floor median F to prevent a bill or amendment from being introduced – as it inevitably would by the median voter logic – that shifts policy to F. As anticipated by Figure 5.2, this implies that legislative action is not allowed on issue dimensions where the status quo is located between $2M - F$ and F, or the area that Cox and McCubbins describe as the majority-party "blackout" zone. With the majority party exercising gate-keeping powers in this manner, legislator behavior on measures reaching the floor will not change. Thus, if $q \in q_1, q_4, q_5$, or q_6, then the results derived from the case where agenda control is exercised by the Committee of the Whole apply. If $q \in q_2$ or q_3, on the other hand, then the majority party prevents legislative action on the floor on that issue dimension, and no voting take place.

According to the formal structure of this model, the voting behavior of legislators who aspire to best represent their constituents' preferences for reelection purposes is unchanged by majority-party agenda control – it is just that the legislative gates remain closed in some issue areas. Consequently, it is not immediately apparent that investments in private brand names would be meaningfully affected by this kind of behavior. However, it is straightforward to show that the exercise of gate-keeping power by the majority party has an important effect on the extent to which district pressures encourage MCs to defect from their party on roll call votes.

Consider first the incentives for majority-party members to vote against their party as a function of q and their district's ideal point. For issues where $q \in q_1$, then no majority-party member has an electoral incentive to vote against her party. If her district agrees with the party, then the member votes the party line and the district is satisfied with the decision. If her district disagrees with the party, then the member should still feel free to vote with the party because there is little reward to her from being on the bottom of a lopsided vote. For issues in the majority party's blackout zone (i.e., $q \in q_2$ or q_3), then majority-party leaders exercise their gate-keeping powers to prevent divisive issues from reaching the floor. Finally, for issues where the status quo is to the right of the Floor median (i.e., $q \in q_4$, q_5, or q_6), those majority-party members to the right of $(q + F)/2$ may have incentives to communicate their disapproval of the majority party's actions. Assuming that politicians do not represent districts whose preferences are more extreme (at least on important issues that divide the majority party so much that its leaders exercise their gate-keeping powers) than those of the median member of the opposition party, that means that only a small group of majority-party members representing centrist districts whose ideal point is between $(q + F)/2$ and m when the status quo is to the right of the floor median feel strong electoral pressures to vote against their party. I summarize these results graphically in the bottom half of Figure 5.3.

Consider now the case of minority-party members. For issues where the status quo point is extreme such that $q \in q_1$ (or q_6), minority-party members representing districts whose ideal points are to the left (or right) of $(q + F)/2$ lack electoral incentives to communicate differences with their party, because their vote places them on the bottom of a lopsided outcome; other MCs vote with the position preferred by their party, and their district is pleased with that choice. For issues where the status quo is in the majority-party blackout zone, majority-party leaders exercise their agenda-setting powers to prevent a floor vote, so there is no voting record to campaign on. Finally, for issues where the status quo is to the right of the floor median but not extreme (i.e., $q \in q_4$ or q_5), minority-party members who represent districts to the left of $(q + F)/2$ do possess incentives to vote against their party. Echoing the majority-party case, assuming that minority-party members are very unlikely to represent an extreme district whose preferences are closer to those of the majority party (i.e., minority-party members do not represent districts whose ideal point is to the left of M), it is once again a narrow range of centrist legislators who have electoral incentives to communicate their voting records to their districts. These results are summarized in the bottom half of Figure 5.4.

Evidence for the Party Cartel Model. The comparison of the *Floor Agenda Model* and the *Party Cartel Model* clearly demonstrates that the locus of agenda-setting powers in Congress has important ramifications for incumbents' incentives to cast votes to appeal to district tastes.

If Mayhew's ideas about the responsiveness of agenda-setting agents to the Committee of the Whole are correct, then MCs might frequently be placed in a situation where they would feel strong electoral pressure to vote against their party to advance the interests of their district, thereby buttressing the argument that parties cannot maintain reputations for being unified because of incumbents' preference to vote with their district. On the other hand, if Cox and McCubbins are correct that majority-party leaders are agenda-setting agents who prevent measures opposed by a majority of its caucus from reaching the floor, then there will only be a relatively small group of centrist MCs in both parties who have electoral incentives to vote against the party line.

In support of the surety model, the evidence seems quite persuasive that agenda-setting agents do protect the majority party in the manner described by the *Party Cartel Model*. As noted in Chapter 2, party leaders in the House have had recourse to Reed's Rules, adopted in the 1890s, which grant the Speaker (and her partisan allies on the Rules Committee) the ability to restrict the flow of legislation onto the floor. Since that time, there have been very few instances where the Speaker, as head of the majority party, has allowed issues that are opposed by a substantial part of her party's members from reaching the floor, and of those issues where the majority party gets "rolled" by the minority, they find that it is rarely the case that the measure is of any consequence (Cox and McCubbins 2005). The key implication of the majority party's exercise of gate-keeping powers for the purposes of this chapter is that most issues reaching final-passage votes on the floor of Congress provide scant electoral motivation for most MCs to cast votes to protect private brand names that differentiate their activities from those of their party. Thus, parties can maintain high levels of party unity in government – a necessary condition for the creation of strong brand names – without asking politicians to sacrifice their electoral interests and without resorting to coercive disciplinary tactics.

Special Rules and the Theory of Conditional Party Government

So far, this part of the chapter has argued that the exercise of gate-keeping power by the majority party – a power that most scholars will readily admit the majority party possesses – is sufficient to maintain party brand names. I argued in Chapter Two for a more expansive view of party influence in the policy-making process than simple "negative" agenda control might suggest. Building on the intuitions of the theory of conditional party government (cf. Rohde 1991), I argued that members of Congress – although keenly aware of how their roll-call votes might impact their reelection chances – want to pass public policies that are as close as possible to their personal ideals. Furthermore, I argued that a person who chooses to make politics her career will often have policy preferences that are more like those of their party's leadership than those of the median voter in her district. If an MC finds herself in such a position, then she may find that cases arise where she would prefer a non-centrist policy outcome (the policy most preferred by her party leader, say) over both the status quo and the policy preferred by the median voter in Congress. If enough MCs find themselves in this situation, so that there is a high level of preference agreement within the majority party (and well-defined cleavages between majority- and minority-party members), then majority-party leaders will be empowered by their back-benchers to pull policy away from the center of the chamber, toward policy positions favored by the center of their party.

The most important of the powers granted to majority-party leaders appears to be the ability to introduce restrictive special rules that control amendment activity in the Committee of the Whole – a power that gives majority-party leaders the ability to prevent floor consideration of the median voter position (Rohde 1991). This implies that there are circumstances, in contrast to the *Floor Agenda* and *Party Cartel* models, where the alternative to the status quo considered at the final passage vote is non-median. This possibility raises the question as to whether MCs are confronted with greater incentives to defect from the party line when the conditions of conditional party government are satisfied – a matter of particular concern for the argument of this book, which suggests that party brand names should be strongest when party unity is high.

To flesh out how the exercise of positive agenda control affects legislators' incentives to cast votes that differentiate themselves from the rest of their party when party unity is high, a model of positive agenda control is developed that captures the main insights of conditional party government. To make this model comparable to that described previously, the shared assumptions of the *Floor Agenda* and *Party Cartel* models are adopted, with the exception that now MCs are not free to introduce whatever amendments they like. It is assumed instead that the legislature uses a closed rule where MCs are forced to choose between a proposal B and q; that B is chosen by the median member of the majority party

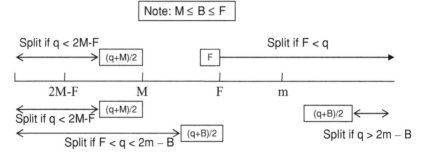

District ideal points of majority party members with divided loyalties with Positive Agenda Control as a function of q

District ideal points of minority party members with divided loyalties with Positive Agenda Control as a function of q

Figure 5.5. Divided or unified party-district loyalties with positive agenda control.

located at M; that the agenda setter can propose that B be anywhere in the policy space so long as it is sincerely preferred by a majority of majority party members; that the agenda-setting agent exercises her gate-keeping powers to prevent floor consideration of issues where there is no alternative to q that receives majority support of the majority party in a manner akin to the *Party Cartel* model; and that the agenda-setting agent seeks to maximize her own electoral well-being (i.e., she chooses B to be as close to M as possible).[4]

Given these assumptions, it is helpful to first identify the conditions where the majority party's agenda-setting agent exercises her gate-keeping powers to prevent floor consideration of an issue where there exists no viable alternative to the status quo preferred by a majority of majority-party voters. As depicted in Figure 5.5, if the status quo point is located anywhere to the left of M, then the agenda setter will allow floor consideration of the issue area because there is a proposal (M, for example) that receives majority support of the majority party and majority support of the entire chamber. If the status quo is located between M and F, then the agenda setter prevents floor consideration of that issue area because the only policies preferred by a majority of the majority party

---

[4] This is obviously not the most general model possible, but it suffices to illustrate the consequences of the exercise of "positive" agenda-setting by the majority party for legislators' incentives to cast votes that differentiate themselves from other members of their party.

over q are to the left of q, whereas the only policies preferred by a legislative majority over q are to the right of q. Finally, if q is to the right of F, then the agenda setter allows floor consideration of the bill because there exists a proposal (F, for example) that is preferred by a majority of the majority party and by the entire legislature. Thus, there are two regions outside the majority-party blackout zone that should be considered when determining the possible effects of positive agenda control on legislators' incentives to cast votes that differentiate themselves from their party.

For the case where q is to the left of M, the electoral incentives for legislators to cast votes that differentiate themselves from their party are incredibly small under positive agenda control. In this case, the agenda-setting agent proposes B to be her ideal point M, knowing that M defeats q and receives majority support from her party – she could personally do no better. The spatial location $(q + M)/2$ represents the cut-point such that all legislators to its left prefer q and all legislators to its right prefer B. Because $(q + M)/2$ is in an extreme region of the policy space, majorities of both parties prefer B to q. Following the logic developed for the *Party Cartel* and *Floor Agenda* models, it follows that neither party's members have strong electoral incentives to cast votes that differentiate themselves from their co-partisans in this circumstance: even if a legislator represented a district preferring q to B, she would have been on the bottom of a lopsided vote that provides little opportunity for credit claiming. It is also noteworthy that if $q < M$, the range of spatial locations where legislators might have split party-district loyalties is *smaller* because of the exercise of positive agenda control when compared to the *Party Cartel* and *Floor Agenda* models for both the majority and minority party.

For the case where q is to the right of F, positive agenda control has the potential to increase the number of majority-party legislators and to decrease the number of minority-party legislators with electoral incentives to differentiate themselves from their party. To illustrate this, it is necessary to first identify the proposal B introduced by the majority party's agenda-setting agent. Since $q > F$, the agenda setter can propose any policy (weakly) to the right of both $2F - q$ and M and secure majority support for her proposal from the entire legislature and the majority party. She therefore proposes B to be the leftmost winning proposal, $2F - q$, if $M < 2F - q$, and she proposes B to be M otherwise because her ideal point defeats q in a pairwise vote and there is no other winning proposal that makes her better off.[5] In the former circumstance, all legislators to the left of the floor median F vote for B so that B is the majority-party preferred proposal, and all legislators to the right of the floor median vote for q so that q is the minority-party preferred proposal. In the latter circumstance, all legislators to the left of $2F - q$ vote for B so B is the majority-party preferred proposal, and all legislators to the right of $2F - q$ vote for q so q is the minority-party preferred proposal (except in the extreme cases where $q > 2m - B$.

With these preliminary results for $q > F$, it is possible to assess whether a legislator has split party-district loyalties as a function of her ideal point. For the majority party, the analysis is straightforward: all majority-party members to the right of F (or $(q + M)/2$ for extreme q or very centrist M) have electoral incentives to vote against the policy preferred by a majority of their own party, whereas all majority-party members to the left of F lack these pressures. Notably, majority-party members located between F and $(q + F)/2$ did not have split party-district loyalties under the party cartel model, but they do have electoral incentives to vote against the rest of their party because of the exercise of positive agenda control. Thus, on balance, the effect of positive agenda control on majority-party members' electoral calculations is to increase the number of centrist legislators who have incentives to cast votes that differentiate themselves from the rest of their party and to communicate those differences to the public; however, it is still true that, as in the party cartel model, it is only centrist members of the majority party with these kinds of incentives.

Turning to the minority party, it is necessary to consider both the case where a majority of its members vote for B and the case where a majority of its members vote for q (recalling that the focus is on the situation where $q > F$). With regard to the former case, a majority of minority party members prefers B to q only if $q > 2m - B$. If q is in this area (a very extreme part of the policy space even compared to region q_6, which I considered in the models without positive agenda control), minority-party members lack electoral incentives to buck their party and vote for q either because they can vote with their party for B or because they will be on the bottom of a badly lopsided vote. If q is in the part of the policy space to the right of F where a majority of

---

[5] Note that if the majority party chooses its median member to be the agenda-setting agent in the manner described here, it ensures that a majority of its members are made better off by the application of the closed rule compared to the party cartel and floor agenda models.

minority-party members vote for q over B, then minority-party members to the left of $(B + q)/2$ do have electoral incentives to cast votes to differentiate themselves from the rest of their party. In contrast to the majority-party case where it increased member incentives to vote against their party, for minority-party members between $(B + q)/2$ and $(F + q)/2$, the exercise of positive agenda control removed the electoral incentives to cast votes to differentiate members from the rest of their party.

In sum, the exercise of positive agenda control by the majority party does have the potential to create situations where majority-party members have electoral incentives to vote against the position favored by the rest of their party in a manner detrimental to their shared brand name; however, this does not undermine the argument that agenda control by the majority party prevents it from maintaining high levels of party unity in Congress. To understand why, it is important to reiterate that the only circumstance when positive agenda control encourages defection from the party line occurs when the reversion point q and the median member of the majority party are on opposite sides of F, in which case majority-party members with centrist ideal points between q and $(q + F)/2$ (or $(q + M)/2$ for extreme q or centrist M) may have split party-district loyalties on final-passage votes under positive agenda control that they did not have under the basic *Party Cartel* model. In all other cases, the incentives of MCs from both parties to cast votes contrary to the party line are either unchanged or weakened by positive agenda control. Furthermore, in the one exceptional case, it is also important to remember that, according to the theory, positive agenda control is most likely to be granted with sharp inter-party cleavages and high levels of intra-party unity in Congress. This means that there will be relatively few majority-party members on the "wrong" side of the floor median – in fact, the number of majority-party members with split party district loyalties on those kinds of issues would not much exceed the surplus legislators the majority party needs to pass the measure, and many of these legislators would have had split party-district loyalties without positive agenda control. Thus, even if Congress were to be confronted with a large number of issues where the status quo point was far away from the policies preferred by large numbers of majority-party members (a situation most likely to occur after a change in the identity of the ruling party), the use of positive agenda-setting power would be unlikely to encourage substantially greater defection rates than observed under simple negative agenda control because that power is only granted when a party is highly unified on the issues of the day.

WHO DEVELOPS PRIVATE BRAND NAMES?

To this point, this chapter has focused on responding to various arguments that could be made in support of the claim that party brand names cannot be used as signaling devices because electoral politics in the United States is candidate-centered. Accordingly, it has been demonstrated that relatively few voters have sufficient knowledge about individual politicians to cast votes based on private brand names. It has also been shown that agenda control by the majority party greatly increases the credibility of partisan cues because the exercise of gate-keeping powers by party leaders protects the party's collective reputation by reducing the need for most MCs to cast votes contrary to the party line because of electoral considerations. Thus, in the absence of contrary information, it may be rational for voters to trust a candidate's party affiliation as a predictor of her future behavior in that it provides information about the distribution of possible positions that she might take in office despite the fact that not all party members act in the same way.

The argument of the remainder of this chapter is that the reason that voters have such poor knowledge about their Representatives in Congress is that incumbents have very weak incentives to invest in private brand names because they can campaign on their party's record. This argument proceeds from the following pair of observations. First, there may be tradeoffs between actions that raise a candidate's political profile, strengthening her brand name, and other types of activities that improve her reelection prospects. For example, someone who spends all of her time raising money for large ad buys come reelection time is not securing federal money for her district and is not developing a reputation as a hard worker deserving of advancement within the party ranks. Thus, a politician who does not often disagree with her party on key issues may find the opportunity costs of securing a private brand name are greater than the benefits of publicly differentiating herself from her co-partisans. Second, incumbent politicians' voting records may not be perfect reflections of constituency opinion in their districts, especially for ideologically motivated citizen-candidates. Consequently, many legislators may prefer to not make their legislative records a campaign issue.

Given these two observations, it is possible to generate some straightforward predictions about how a legislators' voting record relative to the rest of her party affects her incentives to invest in private brand names. Considering the entirety of House members' voting records, centrist legislators are by definition actors who sometimes vote in accord with the preferences of their party and sometimes vote against their party and with the preferences of the opposition party. These individuals have a voting record that differentiates themselves from their party, and, if they vote with their district, their record is preferred by their constituents to the position of the opposition party, which means that they have incentives to inform the public that they do not share the party's position on the issue. If they develop a centrist record by voting against constituent interests, then they have a lot of explaining to do about their actions, especially when facing a viable challenger who is pointing to that record as a reason to reject the incumbent's reelection bid. A partisan legislator, on the other hand, is someone who typically votes with her party, regardless of what the opposition does. Legislators who closely toe the party line have weaker incentives to invest in private brand names than centrists because their voting records do not provide information that usefully differentiates their actions from those of their co-partisans, so their time might be better spent on other types of activities. Finally, an extremist legislator is someone who votes with her party most of the time, but when she defects it is on issues where her action diverges from that of both their party and the opposition. These individuals have the weakest incentives to invest in private brand names. On most issues, they vote with their party; however, when they vote contrary to its preferences, they will typically be on the bottom of lopsided votes. Consequently, on those issues where there are differences between their voting record and that of their party, they do not want to communicate that information to the public. At best, their voting record (relative to the rest of Congress) creates the impression that they are ineffective coalition builders, and at worst, they are extremists out of step with the preferences of their district and their party.

Campaign Contacts and Candidate Extremism

If the theoretical intuitions just developed are correct, then legislators such as Chris Shays (R-Connecticut) and Heath Shuler (D-North Carolina) with centrist voting records will have the strongest incentives to engage in costly efforts to boost their name recognition and to communicate differences with their party, and extremists will have the weakest such incentives. As a first cut at testing this claim, it is investigated whether individuals who are represented by legislators with centrist voting records are more likely to report some sort of contact with their incumbent while people who are represented by legislators with extremist voting records are less likely to do so. To test this hypothesis, a series of probit models are estimated where the dependent variable is whether a respondent to the ANES reports having some sort of *Contact* with an incumbent candidate using data from 1978 to 1994, except for 1982 and 1992, which were years when redistricting makes it more difficult to match incumbents with their district. Contact includes everything from having met the incumbent personally, to attending a meeting with her, to talking to her staff, to receiving mail from her, to reading about her, to hearing radio about her, or to seeing her on television. Initially, only year fixed effects to capture the consequences of over-time variation in the political context and the main independent variable of interest – the *Ideological Extremism* of the respondent's incumbent House member, which is measured using the absolute value of the politician's DW-Nominate score for the current Congress – are included as predictors for *Contact*. The research hypothesis is that *Ideological Extremism* is negatively related to an incumbent making *Contact* with her constituents because extremists have the weakest incentives to invest in a private brand name.

In subsequent analyses, the model is elaborated to ensure that the original model estimates are not especially sensitive to the presence of other variables that may affect *Contact*. The variables considered are the presence of a *Quality Challenger* in the election and whether the respondent and the incumbent are of the *Same Party*. Following common practice in the literature, a candidate is defined to be a *Quality Challenger* if she had previously held elective office, which provides some evidence of her ability to organize a political campaign and muster public support for her candidacy. A *Quality Challenger* is hypothesized to be positively related to *Contact* between the incumbent and the respondent because the presence of a serious electoral threat may force incumbents to campaign harder, thereby making contact with more people (see also Jacobson 2004). *Same Party* is hypothesized to be positively related to *Contact* because incumbents may be likely to target campaign appeals to partisan audiences who are more favorably disposed toward their candidacy in order to turn out the vote and because voters are more likely to seek out help from candidates who belong to the same party (see also Box-Steffensmeier et al. 2003).[6] Other respondent-level variables are not included in the analysis because factors such as a survey respondent's political interest or socioeconomic status are likely to be uncorrelated with the behavior of

---

[6] A person is defined to be a Democrat (Republican) if she self-identifies as a Democrat (Republican) or as someone who leans Democratic (or Republican).

Table 5.3. *Probit Models for Contact with an Incumbent*

Coefficient (standard error)	Contact by Incumbent	Contact by Incumbent	Contact by Incumbent	Contact by Incumbent
Ideological	−0.46*	−0.46*	−0.49*	−0.51*
Extremism	(0.08)	(0.08)	(0.08)	(0.09)
Quality		0.09*	−0.03	−0.02
Challenger		(0.04)	(0.09)	(0.09)
Qual Chal *			0.41	0.40
Extremism			(0.28)	(0.28)
Same Party				0.18*
				(0.03)
Constant	0.95*	0.94*	0.95*	0.87
	(0.05)	(0.05)	(0.05)	(0.05)
χ^2	37.61*	42.54*	44.69*	86.71*
n	10,595	10,584	10,584	10,584

Cell values are probit coefficients (standard errors). Year fixed effects are estimated, but are not reported here.
*Statistically significant at $p < .05$ (two-tailed).

politicians trying to appeal to a wide audience and are only a distraction from my arguments.[7]

The first four columns of Table 5.3 report the results from the various statistical analyses testing whether *Contact* is a function of the incumbent's *Ideological Extremism* and other variables. Reading across the first row of the table reveals that *Ideological Extremism* is a statistically significant, negative predictor of candidate contact in every specification of the model, just as hypothesized. Confirming the results of previous studies, the presence of a *Quality Challenger* and a respondent's membership in the *Same Party* as the incumbent both have a significant positive effect on *Contact*. To give some substantive meaning to the effect of *Ideological Extremism* on *Contact*, predicted values from the fullest specification of the model (column 4) are used. For the case where there is no *Quality Challenger* and the incumbent and the respondent are of different parties, the predicted probability of *Contact* by the incumbent varies from 0.85 when *Ideological Extremism* is at its minimum value to 0.70 when *Ideological Extremism* is at its maximum value.[8] For the case where there

[7] Box-Steffensmeier et al. (2003) find that respondent-level variables do not interact with legislator characteristics in models of contact.
[8] The baseline year for the predicted values is 1980, and *Same Party* takes the value 1.

is a *Quality Challenger*, the probability of *Contact* remains at 0.85 for centrist legislators, but increases for extremist legislators to 0.82.[9] Thus, the extremism of an incumbent's legislative record has about five times the effect on their probability of making *Contact* with a resident in their district than the presence of a viable opposition candidate who, one might expect, would induce greater campaign efforts by the incumbent because of the presence of a stronger electoral threat.

Candidate Message and Incumbent Extremism

A second perspective on candidates' investments in private brand names that differentiate themselves from their party in government is provided by the content of the messages they send to their district. If the theoretical claims provided previously are correct, then incumbents will typically communicate positive messages about Congressional actions when they are in the majority and negative messages when they are in the minority. However, centrist MCs will endeavor to communicate to constituents their support for Congressional actions opposed by their party if they belong to the minority and their opposition to Congressional actions supported by their party if they belong to the majority. More loyal partisans, on the other hand, will simply try to persuade voters that their party supported desirable public policies.

Nice support for this set of arguments is provided in Lipinski (2004)'s careful study of Congressional communications as reflected in franked mail for the period from 1991 through 1995. Contrary to the popular view that MCs run against Congress, Lipinski shows that this phenomenon broke along purely partisan lines – fewer than 5 percent of majority-party members sent negative messages about Congress in any given year, and that includes 1994 when, in anticipation of a Republican Congressional takeover, Democratic Party members would have had particularly strong incentives to campaign against the chamber. Meanwhile, he finds that more than 60 percent of majority-party members said positive things. In contrast, he finds that, on average, fewer than 20 percent of minority-party members said positive things about Congress while

---

[9] I consider the possibility that *Ideological Extremism* is a better measure for safe seats than the presence of a quality challenger – the logic being that a legislator could take more extreme positions if she did not fear a general election threat. When incumbent lagged vote share is added, its coefficient is significant, but the large significant effects from *Ideological Extremism* persist.

more than 40 percent of majority-party members did so. Thus, the messages sent by the overwhelming number of MCs were partisan in content (Lipinski 2004, p. 42). Consistent with my theoretical expectations, Lipinski (2004, p. 51) notes that the exception to this general pattern is party members who most often vote against the rest of their party on key issues: he finds that majority-party members in this situation are less likely to communicate positive messages to their district and that minority-party members are more likely to do so.[10]

Name Recognition and Candidate Extremism

Taking a different approach to the question of whether an incumbent's ideological extremity affects the strength of her private brand name, I address whether ideologues have lower name recognition than centrist politicians. The conventional wisdom would presumably be that ideologues stick out like sore thumbs in government and would be well known by the residents in their district as a result; according to my account, however, name recognition should be a decreasing function of ideological extremism because of the incentives that they provide candidates to invest in the development of private "brand names."

To adjudicate between these rival hypotheses, a series of probit models is estimated where the dependent variable is whether a respondent to the ANES is able to *Recall* the name of their incumbent House member (who was running for reelection) using data from 1978 through 2004. As before, *Recall* is measured using a respondent's ability to elicit from memory the name of their House incumbent. Initially, the only variables included are the main independent variable of interest – the *Ideological Extremism* of the respondent's incumbent House member, which is again measured using the absolute value of the politician's DW-Nominate score for the current Congress – and year fixed effects. The research hypothesis is that *Ideological Extremism* will be negatively related to respondents' ability to *Recall* their incumbent's name.[11] A second model tests the

---

[10] Lipinski does find that incumbents who represent a district that is more hostile toward their party are more likely to send negative (positive) messages about Congress if they are in the majority (minority); however, he also demonstrates that this effect is limited to district-wide mailings, and that when incumbents find themselves in this situation, they increase their use of targeted mailings that bolster their party's image to the most loyal partisans in their district (2004, p. 54).

[11] The results of models with respondent-level covariates are not reported because the characteristics of individual voters are very poorly correlated with the attributes of

hypothesis that non-centrist incumbents' name recognition will be greater if they confront *Quality Challengers*, based on the logic that the challenger has incentives to campaign against the incumbent's record in office (for much the same reason that ideologically extreme legislators do not want to do so), which requires them to inform the public about the incumbent's name so that people do not vote based simply on party labels. To test for the effects of competent challengers on incumbent candidates' name recognition, a third probit model is estimated with *Recall* as the dependent variables that includes as independent variables the incumbent's *Ideological Extremism*, whether the incumbent faces a *Quality Challenger*, and a variable measuring the multiplicative interaction of *Ideological Extremism* and *Quality Challenger*. The research hypothesis is that the interaction between *Ideological Extremism* and *Quality Challenger* will be positive. Finally, as a robustness check, additional probit models are estimated, which includes a host of variables that previous research (e.g., Jacobson 2004; Box-Steffensmeier, et al. 2003) suggests might affect an incumbent's name recognition, including the *Total Spending* on the election campaign in millions of dollars, whether the incumbent is a freshman or more *Senior*, and whether the respondent reported having *Contact* with the incumbent. It also includes year-spending interaction terms to control for changes in purchasing power and technology that might impact the relationship between spending and name recognition.

Table 5.4 reports the results of the statistical analyses for candidate name recognition as a function of her political extremism and other variables. Across all specifications of the model, *Ideological Extremism* has the expected effect on a respondent's ability to *Recall* the name of her incumbent. In concrete terms (based on coefficients from the most fully specified model and a "typical" 1980 election), for respondents living in a district without a *Quality Challenger* represented by a centrist incumbent with an *Ideological Extremism* score of zero, the probability that they successfully *Recall* the name of their incumbent is 0.45.[12] If they are represented by a representative with an *Ideological Extremism* score of zero who does not have a *Quality Challenger*, the probability that they *Recall* their incumbent's name falls by about one-third, to 0.32. In the

House members, so their exclusion will not bias my results, whereas their inclusion would be distracting. The results are not changed in any meaningful way if I add individual-level data.

[12] A "typical" respondent in this case was represented by a Senior incumbent with the median amount of spending on the election and reports having had some contact with the incumbent.

Table 5.4. *Probit Models for Incumbent Name Recognition*

Coefficient (standard error)	Recall Incumbent	Recall Incumbent	Recall Incumbent	Recall Incumbent	Recall Incumbent[#]
Ideological Extremism	−0.33* (0.06)	−0.33* (0.06)	−0.39* (0.06)	−0.37* (0.09)	−0.34* (0.10)
Quality Challenger		0.17* (0.03)	−0.02 (0.06)	−0.07 (0.09)	−0.16 (0.09)
Qual Chal* Extremism			0.48* (0.11)	0.60* (0.27)	0.54* (0.27)
Senior				0.02 (0.04)	0.05 (0.04)
Contact				1.26* (0.04)	1.26* (0.05)
Total Spend (Millions)					0.69* (0.22)
Constant	−0.40* (0.04)	−0.38 (0.04)	−0.35* (0.04)	−1.42* (0.07)	−1.60* (0.10)
χ^2	441.31*	534.45*	542.32*	1166.68*	1006.44*
N	19,467	17,935	17,935	10,402	8,557

Cell values are probit coefficients (standard errors). Year fixed effects are estimated, but are not reported here.
[#] Year-Spending interaction terms were estimated but are not reported here.
* Statistically significant at $p < .05$ (two-tailed)

presence of a *Quality Challenger* who can score political points by labeling the incumbent an extremist, these effects reverse themselves. In this case, for the "typical" survey respondent the probability that they *Recall* an incumbent's name increases from 0.39 when she is a centrist to 0.46 when she is ideologically extreme. The conclusion that I draw from these analyses is that incumbents with the most extreme voting records prefer to run simply as partisans, and that they are exposed as ideologues by quality challengers hoping to capture their seats.

The Incumbency Advantage and Incumbent Extremism

Perhaps the most striking thing about more ideologically extreme incumbents making less of an effort to contact constituents, campaigning as partisans, and having lower name recognition is that they are sacrificing many of the benefits commonly associated with the incumbency advantage. This naturally raises the question whether candidates' behavior is really a strategic response given their voting record – perhaps they are just in safe districts so they do not need to exploit their office to its fullest potential when running for reelection.

There is pretty strong evidence in the extant literature that supports the argument that ideologically extreme incumbents perform less well than centrist politicians when running for reelection (e.g., Canes-Wrone et al. 2002; Erikson and Wright 2000),[13] which is inconsistent with the notion that seat security alone drives this behavior.[14] The standard explanation provided in these studies for why extremist incumbents perform less well at the polls is that voters are holding them accountable for their legislative record. I agree that this kind of direct relationship may exist; however, the effect that legislative records have on the strategic choices of incumbents (and challengers) with respect to their relationships with constituents may also have an indirect effect on their electoral prospects. Previous work has established that candidate name recognition has an effect on vote choices that is on par with a voter's party identification and greater than incumbency status (e.g., Jacobson 2004, p. 135). Given the findings presented earlier regarding how ideological extremism affects the probability that incumbents make contact with residents in their district, their overall name recognition, and the content of their campaign messages, it is entirely possible that extremist incumbents fare so poorly in elections because their legislative records prevent them from reaping the full rewards of incumbency status. The value-added of my account of indirect effects is that it explains why voters who know very little about their incumbent's actions in office are less likely to vote for MCs with extremist records.

The Decline of Party?

The main point of this chapter has been to show that incumbent politicians typically have weak incentives to invest scarce campaign resources trying to communicate to the public that their legislative record provides credible information that they are somehow distinct from the rest of their party. At a glance, the well-documented breakdown in party-line voting in Congressional elections that took place during the 1960s and 1970s (e.g., Bartels 2000) and the attendant rise in the incumbency advantage

---

[13] Similarly, Brady et al. (1996) and Jacobson (1996) find that Democrats with higher party unity scores were more prone to electoral retaliation in the 1994 election.
[14] Some analysts suggest that this may be a pattern restricted to the period since the 1960s (Ansolabehere et al. 2001).

(Mayhew 1974b; Gelman and King 1990; Cox and Katz 2002) would seem to challenge this argument.

The arguments developed in this book can be reconciled with the breakdown in party-line voting in two very different ways. One possibility is that candidate partisanship ceased to be seen as a credible signal of their legislative intentions during the 1960s and 1970s. As noted in Chapter 3, during this period the level of internal party disagreements within both the Democratic and Republican Parties' Congressional caucuses grew markedly, and there was an attendant decline in the number of strong partisans in the electorate. Consequently, voters may have come to believe either that the national parties lacked the institutional capacity to maintain discipline in government or that the party organizations no longer valued their reputations sufficiently to incur the costs of policing their memberships.

An alternative explanation for the decline in party-line voting that also accords with the arguments in this book is that during the middle-twentieth century a large number of incumbents found themselves belonging to parties that were not a good match ideologically with their electoral districts. This was especially true of Southern Democrats, who increasingly found themselves representing conservative constituencies with policy preferences at odds with their national party. Following the formal logic presented earlier, these ideologically mismatched MCs had very strong electoral incentives to cast votes that differentiated themselves from the rest of their party and to invest heavily in private brand names that communicated that disagreement to constituents. As a result of investments in private brand names, it was possible for these incumbents to successfully win the votes of people who might normally have supported the other party's candidates, especially in light of the fact that their challengers would have been at a disadvantage (compared to challengers at other points in history) because the high levels of internal party conflict would have increased risk-averse voters' uncertainty about the attributes of candidates within that party. Party brand names therefore may have still existed during the period of party decline, but they were viewed by professional politicians as being less valuable than in the generations before and after.

Overall, I tend to favor the latter explanation for the decline in party-line voting because the evidence that voters ceased to find candidates' party affiliations to provide a credible signal of their political positions is not very strong. This is because one would not expect to observe partisan electoral tides if voters ceased using party labels at the ballot box.

As argued in earlier chapters, if voters do not depend on party labels, then they should simply cast votes in retaliation against incumbents who voted for an unpopular (or against a popular) policy regardless of their party ties. Because partisan electoral tides persisted during the period of party decline (e.g., Claggett et al. 1984; Cox and McCubbins 1993), in many cases occurring when candidates from both parties supported unpopular programs (e.g., the tide against Reagan during the 1982 recession, whose economic policies received strong Republican and Southern Democratic support), it seems reasonable to believe that voters continued to depend upon partisan cues to establish that the out-party might be the better option. Furthermore, if partisanship ceased to convey credible information about candidates, it seems likely that there would have been a dramatic increase in the number of successful independent and third-party candidates who could compete with little disadvantage against their partisan opponents. However, there is little evidence to support the claim that third-party candidates had become more viable in Congressional elections during this period. To the contrary, by some measures the 1960s and 1970s marked the nadir in public support for candidates not belonging to one of the major political parties (Aldrich 1995).

CONCLUSION

The goal of this chapter was to explain why it is that, even though all politicians would like to have a reputation perfectly suited to their district, many of them do not compete on the basis of private brand names. It argued that the establishment of private brand names involves opportunity costs to legislators or, given how out of step their legislative record is with their constituents, may even prove damaging. With the Congressional leadership exercising control over the legislative agenda to prevent MCs from having to choose between partisan and constituent interests, this chapter showed that most incumbents campaign on the basis of their party record rather than incurring the costs of creating a private brand name. The exception to this general rule is those (typically centrist) politicians whose legislative record gives them an advantage over less experienced challengers who cannot offer credible signals of their commitment to a set of principles other that provided by their party affiliation.

6

Brand Names and Party Strategy

One of the central themes in previous chapters of this book was that the Democrats and Republicans in Congress are able to maintain their brand names through a combination of agenda control by the majority party and a system of reward payments to party members who toe the party line. It was asserted that one reason that party elites favor these kinds of institutions is that they value the appearance of party unity because it is a necessary condition to maintain their brand name. However, previous researchers have argued that party elites agree to the establishment of institutions that secure some level of party discipline in government because they value belonging to a legislative team that secures partisan logrolls which are mutually beneficial to all organization members, and partisan institutions prevent individual legislators from free-riding on this collective good when it is in their short-run self-interest to do so (cf. Schwartz 1977). The motivations identified in previous research for forming institutions to enforce these logrolls are that party members value the policy achievements as desirable ends in and of themselves (e.g., Aldrich 1995; Rohde 1991) or as a means to further their electoral interests through credit-claiming back home (e.g., Kiewiet and McCubbins 1991; Cox and McCubbins 1993, 2005). The purpose of this chapter is to demonstrate that, in addition to enforcing partisan logrolls, an important factor shaping the choice of a party's control apparatus is the desire to convey to the public how votes for its candidates might translate into policy outcomes.

To demonstrate that party elites value the ability to convey this information, a series of case studies is presented reflecting a variety of strategic situations that parties might confront. In each case study, it is shown that incumbent politicians value party labels as way of communicating information about unfamiliar politicians because they see party brand names as a vehicle for capturing majority control of government. Further, it is shown that political elites choose leaders and institutions because they believe that maintaining party discipline in government is a necessary condition for maintaining these shared brand names. The value of this approach is that it provides detail about the unique strategic contexts that political elites confronted at different moments in history, and shows how the desire to exploit party brand names shaped their behavior in predictable ways given that strategic environment. By establishing through these case studies that politicians understand the role of party brand names as a signaling device and see party unity as necessary to preserve that function, a strong case can be made that party elites recognize and value formal party organizations for performing the role of a surety in American elections.

INCENTIVES FOR FORMAL PARTY ORGANIZATION

One implication of the arguments of this book is the idea that American politicians benefit from the presence of a party brand name because it helps organization members secure the public support necessary to win elective office. To the extent that this is true, then office-motivated politicians without a party brand name should form organizations whose purpose, at least in part, is to achieve levels of party discipline sufficient to obtain a brand name that provides credible signals of the attributes of group members. Given that the two major American political parties are almost 200 years old, to examine the impetus for forming party organizations able to create and maintain a brand name requires going back to events surrounding the advent of the mass political parties in the first decades of the American republic.

In this part of the chapter, it is shown that from the very advent of the first mass party organizations in the United States, American politicians were aware of the importance of maintaining some level of party discipline in order to use party labels as a signal about candidates' political traits. The value of this demonstration is twofold. First, showing that party organizations worked to develop, maintain, and exploit the rewards of brand names at the start of the American republic, in combination with evidence from the modern period provided elsewhere in this book that party brand names have had staying power in the United States, strongly suggests that politicians recognize the desirability of party brand names. Second, it is a difficult case for the theory. Because the first mass parties emerged concurrently with mass suffrage, it is surprising that leaders with limited experience in competing before the general public were aware of the electoral benefits of clearly articulated partisan ideologies and possessed the knowledge and ability to develop a set of institutions necessary to protect the value of their common reputation.

The historical case that is used to illustrate the role of partisan brand names is that of the Bucktail Party in New York. The value of studying party organization within a state, rather than at the federal level, is that the Bucktails emerged decades prior to the advent of strong national parties in the U.S. Congress with the capacity to discipline group members (Silbey 1967), and as will become apparent shortly, conceived of their role in a manner similar to that theorized in this book for modern political parties. The New York case provides an especially useful example because it is generally accepted to represent archetypal organizational behavior both during the early antebellum period when personalistic factions were the norm, and in later years when groups that we would today recognize as parties with reasonably stable memberships, standardized nomination procedures, and so forth, prevailed in state legislatures (McCormick 1966; Wallace 1969).

The Politicians' Strategic Problem

Prior to the American Revolution, New York had two political parties – the Tories and the Whigs (or the popular party) – competing for seats in the colony's General Assembly. As their names suggest, the Tories supported the actions of the provincial governor, whereas the Whigs did not (Levermore 1896).

These organizations bore little resemblance to modern political parties with their stable membership structures and institutions to regulate internal party conflict (e.g., rules regulating the nomination of candidates). The colonial organizations tended instead to be transient factions that emerged in response to the actions of the governor on a specific set of concerns. The building blocks of these factions were coalitions, formed along familial lines and cemented through inter-marriage, of large landowning families in the state (who themselves controlled the votes of residents in their community). A family's support of the Tories or Whigs was a function of whether its members benefited from or were harmed by the actions of the crown. Thus, as the issues before the government shifted over time, families shifted allegiances in response to their self-interest (Becker 1907).

During the two decades of the first American party system born after independence, the political organizations in New York changed in three fundamental ways. First, and perhaps obviously, the state's political organizations ceased to be structured by patterns of support and opposition to the crown's policies and instead formed around policy debates between the newly emergent national Federalist and Democratic-Republican parties. Second, with the emergence of popular control of government, members of the state's middle class began to enter the ranks of the newly created national parties with the hopes of making their careers in politics (cf. Goodman 1967). Third, as politicians came to see political parties as vehicles to promote their professional ambitions, the membership of the two parties became somewhat more stable. Institutions to maintain harmony within the two parties, such as the use of party caucuses to nominate candidates and the distribution of federal patronage to reward loyalty to the organization, were created (Friedrich 1937).

As the Federalist Party began its precipitous decline during the first decade of the nineteenth century, political conflict within New York occurred increasingly among Democratic-Republicans. Without the stabilizing force of two-party competition, parochial allegiances to large land-holding families began to reassert themselves.[1] For members of the traditional elite (who had the good fortune to ally with the Democratic-Republicans during the first party system), this was in many respects a welcome change. Most importantly, they no longer required the unified support of the Democratic-Republican Party to defeat a Federalist candidate. As a result, they were less beholden to the party caucus's decisions regarding candidate nominations, which gave them the opportunity to choose which office they wished to contest. Because their family ties provided them with a sort of brand name, members of the state's elite did not depend on a party label to convey information to the electorate about their political beliefs (Wallace 1969).

For members of the newly emergent group of middle-class politicians, on the other hand, the demise of the two-party system in New York created a number of problems. With electoral competition increasingly occurring between factions of the Democratic-Republican Party, they were no longer able to contest elections on the basis of their party's brand

---

[1] The Clintons and Livingstons set aside their historical rivalry and together formed the Jeffersonian Republican Party in 1800, when Aaron Burr (the famous American pariah) negotiated a balanced ticket of Clintons and Livingstons in statewide elections. Once the threat of defeat from the Federalists receded, this organization fractured along familial lines (Niven 1983, pp. 13, 16).

name and, as members of the middle class, lacked the family connections of the state's traditional elite that conveyed information about their ideological convictions. Their initial strategy was to align with one of the strong families in the state and lean on the endorsements of these factions' leaders. The problem with this approach was that the middle-class politicians' livelihoods were subject to the whims of the large families – as alliances among these factions changed, these politicians confronted the possibility that their support from the family could be lost because of some trade brokered by their patron to advance his own interests (Hofstadter 1969; Wallace 1969).

These concerns came to a head in events surrounding the 1812 presidential election. That year, James Madison – the incumbent President belonging to the Democratic-Republican Party – was running for reelection. He was seen by many in the United States as too weak to lead the country in the War of 1812. However, with the Federalist Party in its death throes, it was unable to field a viable challenger. In a manner emblematic of the opportunistic behavior of New York's landed elite, DeWitt Clinton, who inherited his uncle's (the Governor of New York during the Revolution and Jefferson's second Vice President) mantle as head of his family's political organization, ignored his party's Congressional caucus and took advantage of this opportunity to run against Madison for President. To compete nationally, Clinton solicited the help of the remnants of the Federalist Party. In New York, that support was cemented by agreeing to back Federalist Party member Rufus King's successful reelection bid to the U.S. Senate. Clinton ultimately lost his bid for the Presidency, and the result for many of his backers was severe because Madison retaliated by reallocating his administration's patronage resources from the Clinton family to its opponents (Hofstadter 1969; Niven 1983; Remini 1951).

Party Brand Names as a Solution

In reaction to Clinton's rupture with the national party, many of his middle-class allies, including a newly elected state senator named Martin van Buren, defected from his organization. Rather than realigning themselves with another large family, these individuals decided to form their own faction within the Democratic-Republican ranks; however, they faced a critical strategic problem. In contrast to the earlier period when the dominant figures in New York state politics belonged to the economic and social elite, the leaders of the anti-Clinton faction were members of the state's middle class. Van Buren, for example, was the son of a tavern keeper, while many other members of his faction were the children of yeomen farmers, immigrants, and so forth. Van Buren's faction needed some mechanism to identify group members and to signal their commitment to the faction's principles that could be used in place of the name of a powerful individual or family.

To compete with the Clintons and other prominent families, van Buren's faction pursued a two-pronged approach. First, it worked to establish a reputation that differentiated its members from those of its opponents – in particular, the faction tried to portray itself as being the party of the common man, while branding Clinton with a reputation as being a supporter of the economic and social elite. To accomplish this task, van Buren's organization embraced the factional identity "Bucktail," originally a pejorative term linking the group to the New York City political machine run out of Tammany Hall, as a kind of party label that they used to identify organization members (cf. Wallace 1969; Hofstadter 1969). With that identity, they were able to connect faction members to the policies they supported, such as the development of a common set of standards to limit bias in the approval of corporate charters, and they opposed government intrusion into the private sphere through activities such as the regulation of whiskey. The reputation as being the "party" of the common man was crystallized in 1821, when van Buren's faction pushed for a convention to amend New York's constitution in order to enact a series of democratic reforms, including the expansion of the franchise. Clinton opposed the new state constitution because his family identity forever linked him to New York's traditional aristocracy, and he recognized that he could not appeal to the farmers and city workers entering the electorate better than could the middle-class Bucktails. Clinton's history of backing the Federalist Party (seen as favoring commercial interests), together with his opposition to the new constitution, cemented his reputation as being a supporter of the economic elite, while the Bucktails purported to be the party of ordinary New Yorkers (Remini 1959).

For party endorsements to act as a substitute for endorsements by prominent figures in elections required a high level of unity within the organization: if the Bucktails had divided over the new state constitution, for example, their claim to be the party of the common man would not ring true. Thus, the second key to the ascendance of the Bucktails was their strict adherence to party discipline. One manifestation of the group's organizational strength was strict adherence to the caucus doctrine, a doctrine that was based on the idea that the faction should be able to control which members were nominated as its candidates for elective office. Rather than splintering into rival personalistic factions each election, the party debated behind closed doors its choice of candidate, and once the decision was made, the minority was expected to publicly embrace the choice of the majority (Remini 1959).

Another feature of Bucktail organization was a rigid structure of career advancement. Individuals with political ambitions were expected to provide loyal service to the party during an apprenticeship period, before being provided with opportunities to run for higher offices (Wallace 1969). The historian Robert Remini describes the group's political organization this way: "A theory underlying the establishment of this machine was that all men who would attain political prominence must do so within the framework of the organization, recognizing the authority of those in control" (1951, p. 8). Although unusually distinctive, the political career of Silas Wright nicely illustrates the pattern by which candidates advanced through the Bucktail ranks. Initially elected as surrogate of St. Lawrence County in 1821, Wright soon became his party's nominee for state senate, winning a seat in 1824. After three years in that office, Wright was elected to the U.S. House of Representatives. He then served as New York state comptroller and later as U.S. Senator. He finished his political career as Governor of New York, after declining the Democratic nomination for Vice President of the United States in 1844 out of loyalty to Martin van Buren, whose reelection bid for the Presidency was thwarted at the national convention. Over time, loyalty to the party was rewarded with opportunities for future advancement.

A third feature of Bucktail organization was their use of patronage. In general, the Bucktails were conscientious in their management of government offices, trying to avoid the impression that competent officials were replaced for personal or political gains. However, occasionally they went a bit overboard, such as the time when the party seized control of the legislature from Clinton's faction, together with New York's Council of Appointments. Niven describes the aftermath:

At its first meeting on January 12, 1821, the council removed eleven county sheriffs, the comptroller, the treasurer, the attorney general, secretary of state, all the chief officers of the militia, until then considered to be nonpartisan posts, the mayors and recorders of New York City and of Albany, and the superintendent of common schools.... Over the next six weeks, the council systematically combed through the six thousand minor posts, removing the few Federalists yet remaining, all the Clintonians and even some Bucktails considered ineffective or doubtful politically. (pp. 90–1)

It should be noted that this was perhaps their most extreme abuse of the patronage system, provoking a public outcry that was partially responsible for a constitutional convention that dispersed this power among local governments, the governor, and legislature. These reforms, however, only strengthened Bucktail control over patronage, by making its distribution more sensitive to the wishes of the legislative caucus (McCormick 1966).

Finally, many of the Bucktails were close friends, fiercely loyal to one another. One contemporary noted in his diary that "their families interchange civilities, their females kiss each other when they meet – their men shake each other heartily by the hand – they dine, or drink, or pray, or take snuff... with and in each other's company" (James Gordon Bennett, quoted in Remini 1959). It is easy to understand the origin of this loyalty. Many politicians during this period were lawyers who rode the state's judicial circuit. They therefore traveled from town to town together, separated from their families. It is inevitable that as they lived and dined together, friendships would form that could approach familial proportions. These relationships were then reinforced among like-minded politicians when they returned to Albany for the state's legislative sessions. The confluence of shared political interests and good company created strong bonds within the Bucktail ranks.

Discussion

For the purposes of this book, the example of the antebellum Bucktail faction of the Democratic-Republican Party makes two main points. First, one of the key motivations for the organization of this faction was the desire of middle-class politicians to have a brand name that equipped them to challenge at the polls the state's wealthy land-owning elite and their allies. Second, to develop this brand name, these middle-class politicians devised a set of institutions that restricted what types of politicians might be considered Bucktails, and they created an incentive system to ensure that those politicians receiving the organization's endorsement toed the party line once in office.

In closing this section, it is worthwhile to note that there are striking similarities between the political situation in New York during the late 1810s and early 1820s and that nationally a decade later, and between politicians' response to these circumstances. Echoing the strategic problem in New York, the organization of the national Democratic Party was viewed as a solution to the political uncertainty associated with transient factional alliances in national politics. Following the breakup of the Democratic-Republican Party in 1824 over the choice of Presidential candidate, which ultimately resulted in the election of John Quincy Adams, a candidate denied pluralities of the popular or the Electoral College votes by Andrew Jackson, national politics came to be focused on personalistic coalitions, much like that observed in New York prior to the emergence of the Bucktails (Baker 1998; McCormick 1966). After the election, the four-way cleavage between Democratic-Republican supporters of the presidential candidates Adams, Jackson, Henry Clay, and William H. Crawford simplified into a two-way division between supporters of Adams and Jackson.

The problem with the organization of parties around the identities of candidates was that the President was effectively term-limited by the tradition of not holding that office longer than George Washington. Thus, when choosing the successor to the leadership of the Adams and Jackson factions, politicians confronted the very real possibility of having to build a national coalition anew at least once a decade. Martin van Buren, later Jackson's Vice President and anointed successor, recognized the problem and the solution. Drawing from his experiences in New York, van Buren identified party brand names as a means of transferring reputations from one individual to another.[2] Thus, the Democratic Party under van Buren's leadership developed a set of institutions that in many respects mirrored those used by the Bucktails in New York. Baker writes: "After Jackson, however, the practice of identifying parties with leaders' names disappeared, a casualty of structured nominating conventions, official platforms, and statewide organizations less dependent on a central figure" (1998, p. 112).

PARTISAN BRAND NAMES AND THE
RESPONSIBLE-PARTY MODEL

The "responsible-party model" is a normative standard advocated by the American Political Science Association (1950) during the mid-twentieth

---

[2] Support for this argument is given in van Buren's famous letter to Virginia newspaper editor and party organizer Thomas Ritchie, which laid out his plans for the party, known today as the Democrats. Remini describes the letter as follows: "This letter of Van Buren's admits of no doubt that he was intent on 'forming' the Democratic party. He said he wanted to produce a coalition between the great sections of the country, substitute principles [of party discipline] for personalities, and 'draw anew the old Party lines' based on natural divisions between the followers of Hamilton and those of Jefferson" (Remini 1959, p. 131).

century whereby the party system in the United States is to be judged according to whether each party (1) presents a coherent national platform and (2) works as a unified team in government so that voters might hold the ruling party accountable for its performance in office. For the most part, scholarly observers over the past half-century have accepted the fact that the American party system falls far short of this normative ideal: even when the Democratic and Republican parties have exhibited high levels of party unity in government, neither organization consistently presents the public a coherent national agenda supported by its elected members in Washington. In fact, according to standard models of electoral politics in the United States emphasizing the candidate-centered nature of campaigns and elections, it would be disadvantageous for an American politician to be bound by a national party platform because their rival could easily find a platform that better appeals locally. National parties hoping to secure legislative majorities would, therefore, not want to act in the manner of a responsible party because it would not be in their long-term electoral interests.

Perhaps the most provocative claim of this book is that by establishing the credibility of opposition candidates, party brand names make it rational for the American public to hold incumbent politicians from a single party accountable for their performance in government in a manner consistent with the classic responsible-party model. The mechanism that I propose is that in the run-up to an election, out-party leaders have the opportunity to establish what their party's candidates would do in the event of their election. Voters judge the credibility of these promises based on the consistency of current promises with the party's past policy positions and their beliefs about party leaders' ability to discipline their members based on their past observations of party unity in government. If voters find party leaders' pledges to be credible, and they prefer those promises to those offered by the incumbent, then they may vote for the challenger in a manner consistent with the responsible-party ideal. (Meanwhile, challengers from the in-party cannot credibly differentiate themselves from their co-partisans.) To the extent that this argument is correct, then it is incentive compatible for party leaders who believe that they could secure additional seats in Congress by running as a responsible party to adhere to the normative ideal.

Over the past half-century, there have only been two instances when majority control of Congress has changed hands. The first of these switches occurred in 1994 when the Republicans secured a legislative majority in the House for the first time since 1949. The second occurred in 2006 when the Democrats recaptured control of the House. In this part of the chapter, it is shown that in both instances, the out-party's leaders went to great lengths in the run-up to the election to (1) provide demonstrable evidence of the party's ability to maintain high levels of discipline within its Congressional caucus and (2) offer a national campaign platform that they promised to pursue in the event of their election, thereby acting in the manner of a responsible party. The observation that the national parties acted in the manner of responsible parties in these two pivotal elections is telling evidence that the conventional wisdom about party strategy is incorrect and that it is incentive compatible, at least in the circumstances described here, to act in a manner that is consistent with the responsible-party ideal. Importantly, the factor that makes it rational for party leaders to act in this manner is their ability to credibly convey to the public how votes for unfamiliar members of their party would affect policy outcomes in the next government.

The Strategic Environment in 1994 and 2006

There were a number of features of the 1994 and 2006 elections that made them ripe for a partisan tide able to catapult the out-party into majority control of the legislature. First, in both years the ruling party held unified control of the House, Senate, and Presidency, making it easy for the public to attribute responsibility for the performance of government to the Democrats in 1994 and to the Republicans in 2006. Second, they were both midterm elections, which meant that it would not be possible for a change in the identity of the President to lead to a shift in the direction of government independent of which party controlled the House. Third, in both years the majority party in Congress was perceived as being very vulnerable. The question that confronted the Republicans in 1994 and the Democrats in 2006 was how to exploit this vulnerability when they could not ride the coattails of their own party's presidential candidate.

To provide a little more context, consider first the problem of the Republicans in 1994. That year, the Congressional Democrats' majority status was in jeopardy for one of the first times in forty years. With a Democratic President in power for the first time in more than a decade, Congressional Democrats pushed through a liberal policy agenda that turned off a great number of centrist voters. Measures that fueled the notion that the Democrats had tilted too far to the left included tax hikes, a crime bill that included provisions for programs such as "midnight basketball" in inner-city neighborhoods, the Brady Bill, and a failed attempt to institute universal health care (Rae 1998). The question that Republican Party leaders confronted (and it was a question they had obviously been asking themselves for some time) was, how does a party removed from power for forty-eight years secure the national support it needs to wrest majority control of government?

In 2006, the Democrats faced a similar challenge. In the months prior to the Congressional elections in that year, Democratic Party leaders foresaw an opportunity to capture a legislative majority in the House. The Republicans in Congress had become extremely unpopular because of their support for an increasingly unpopular war in Iraq and a worsening economy under their stewardship. However, just four years before, Democratic Party leaders had believed that they were ripe to recapture the House, because the national economy was in the doldrums, and many Americans seemed to blame the Republican leadership, with its close ties to big business, for a series of corporate scandals (e.g., Enron, MCI). They were far from deluding themselves: public opinion polls throughout 2002 gave Democrats a slight edge in respondents' statements about which party they intended to vote for,[3] and media outlets including the *New York Times,* the *Washington Post*, and CNN all forecasted Democratic gains. In discussions with other members of his party's senior leadership, House Minority Leader Richard Gephardt claimed that Democrats might pick up as many as forty seats (Brady and Pope 2002). After Democrats lost four seats in 2002 despite this optimism, it was widely said that they came up short because "they didn't have a message, and they didn't have a messenger," or, as former President Bill Clinton argued in a 2004 speech to the Democratic National Committee: "We need to brand ourselves better. There were too many people who didn't know why we were Democrats except that we were against Bush's policies."[4] The question that Democrats found themselves asking in 2006 was what they needed to do to finally recapture control of the House.

The Role of Congressional Party Discipline

The parties' strategy to recapture control of the House can usefully be decomposed into short- and long-term components. The long-term

---

[3] (http://www.zogby.com/features/featuredtables.dbm?ID=51. Link active February 16, 2008).
[4] Quoted by Scott Shepard, February 10, 2005, "Dems Moving On after Disappointing 2004 Election," Cox News Service.

strategy was to instill higher levels of party discipline in government, and to frown on efforts to reach across the aisle and strike bipartisan compromises in order to set the table so that they might someday take advantage of a vulnerable ruling party at some unknown point in the future. In the language used elsewhere in the book, the Democrats and Republicans were establishing that they could make credible promises to wrangle their rank-and-file members to adhere to the principles supported by the national party.

For Republicans, the groundwork for taking this approach was laid in 1989, when the party's Congressional caucus elected Newt Gingrich as party whip (cf. Harris 2006) following an election year in which their party won the Presidency for the third consecutive time, but *lost* seats in the House. Gingrich's platform in that contest was that the Republicans would better realize their policy goals over the long term if they recaptured control of the House, and that this could not be accomplished if they continued working across the aisle with Democrats to negotiate the best deal possible on any given piece of legislation. He advocated instead a more confrontational style of partisan politics that was inconsistent with the old way of doing business, and his election to the post of Whip over Michael Madigan (who favored the party's previous approach) empowered Gingrich to implement this strategy. Richard Armey, later majority-party leader, explained the Republicans' choice this way: "I've long since thought that we need a little more emphasis on the word 'opposition' and a little less emphasis on the word 'loyal.' "[5]

The expected benefit of pursuing this more confrontational style was that it would clarify for the public the differences between the two parties. As RNCC Chair Guy Vander Jagt put it in a 1996 interview for *Frontline*:

You'll see them more energized, more involved in drawing the line to show the difference between Republican and Democratic behavior, and therefore you'll see more sharply defined confrontational votes that we can play to. One of my frustrations has been you do not change public perception by issuing press releases from the Republican National Committee. You change it by headlines that result from action under that Capitol dome and votes that are taken there.[6]

He continued to explain that this was deemed critical for a Republican victory because a majority of the public was unaware of the fact

---

[5] Quoted by Robin Toner, March 23, 1989, "House Republicans Elect Gingrich of Georgia as Whip." *New York Times*.

[6] http://www.pbs.org/wgbh/pages/frontline/newt/boyernewt4.html. Link active February 27, 2008.

that Democrats controlled the House – by voting as a team against the Democrats on key issues, the Republicans believed that ordinary citizens would be better able to assign credit or blame to the ruling party. Since Republicans thought that the general public had become dissatisfied with liberal policies (as evidenced by their string of victories in Presidential contests), they believed they could win in many districts with Democratic incumbents if they were more successful in signaling to the public the unified Democratic support for and unified Republican opposition to these programs.

For Democrats, the move to instill higher levels of party discipline came about in 2002, largely in response to their disappointing performance in the Congressional elections that year. In a manner reminiscent of the Republicans in the late 1980s, the effort to instill party discipline began with the replacement of a leader who did not believe that sharp inter-party conflicts were to the out-party's benefit with someone who did. For the Democrats, this meant the election of Nancy Pelosi (who had only months before been elected minority whip)[7] to the position of minority-party leader. Echoing Gingrich, Pelosi's platform in the leadership contest was: "To win back the House in 2004, we need a unified party that will draw clear distinctions between our vision of the future and that espoused by the Republicans."[8] That position stood in stark contrast to that of Harold Ford and Martin Frost, her rivals for the position, who both argued that the party would be better off selecting someone who would not use the resources of her office to pull the party to the left, further alienating moderate voters who had seemingly abandoned the party in the most recent elections.

Two sets of interests motivated these efforts. First, the Democrats saw party discipline as a way of communicating to the public the party's unified support on key issues. In describing why she was exhorts House Democrats to remain united on floor votes, Nancy Pelosi states that: "Unity is a message in itself. . . . The public will begin to see us as united

[7] Smith (2007) notes that the election of Pelosi as Speaker was an almost foregone conclusion given that she had already defeated her most serious rival for leadership of the Democrats in the House, Steny Hoyer, the previous spring in the contest for Whip. Notably, Hoyer's pitch to House Democrats as a "legislative pragmatist" during the Whip contest was very reminiscent of the pitches made by Ford and Frost in 2006.

[8] http://www.pbs.org/newshour/updates/pelosi_11–702.html. Link active February 27, 2008.

behind some core principles."[9] Second, given the Republicans' modest majority in the chamber, minority-party discipline forced vulnerable majority-party members to choose between casting votes contrary to the interests of their district or against the policy preferred by other party members. If Democrats were steadfast in their opposition to a Republican policy, this meant that many Republicans were forced to choose between casting a vote that would be unpopular in their district and seeing their party's program in Washington fail.

The common elements of both parties' long-term electoral strategies in the House was to choose party leaders who were willing to drive their organization to act as a unified team in opposition to the policy programs of the ruling party. The change in both party organizations' behavior after the election of Gingrich and Pelosi is consistent with this story. For Republicans, the average percentage of members voting with their party on roll calls that divided the two parties was 76 percent in the first Congress with Gingrich as Whip (he held the position for just part of this Congress), 82 percent in the second, and 87 percent in the third. For Democrats, party unity scores rose from 88 percent in Gephardt's last term to almost 91 percent party unity scores during Pelosi's two Congresses as minority leader (the smaller Democratic gains were likely a consequence of the fact that they began Pelosi's Speakership already more unified than the Republicans in 1989).[10] This change in party tactics was important because it conveyed to the public that party leaders in Congress could credibly promise to deliver votes on key issues.

The Role of National Party Platforms

Whereas the parties' long-term electoral strategy was to identify leaders willing to discipline the organization's rank and file, their short-term electoral calculations concerned how to best profit from the ability to commit organization members to a particular set of principles in the event of their election. For both the Republicans in 1994 and the Democrats in 2006, the key questions that the parties had to answer given the "candidate-centered" nature of American campaigns and elections were (1) how to

---

[9] Quoted by Juliet Elperin in the *Washington Post*, November 3, 2003, "House Minority Leaders Commended for Focus on Party Unity."

[10] Republican Party unity scores had also risen notably during Pelosi's time as Minority Leader, with its members voting together on 93 percent of party unity votes.

link individual incumbents in the ruling party to the unpopular policies of their national organization (especially the President) and (2) how to convey what the out-party intended to do in the event it won procedural control of the House. Although the two parties had different responses to the first of these questions, a common element in both parties' efforts to capture majority control of the House in the months immediately prior to the national election was to introduce a national platform.

The Republicans in 1994 and the Contract with America

Considering the election-year tactics of the Republican Party in 1994, the two key elements of their electoral strategy were to link vulnerable local Democratic incumbents to their party's policies by pointing to their legislative records and to introduce the *Contract with America*, the Republicans' national "platform." The first critical component of the Republican strategy was to link Democratic MCs to their party by conveying to their constituents that the incumbent backed its policy program. In speech after speech and advertisement after advertisement, Republicans pointed to votes by Democratic House incumbents in support of their party's programs – such as the Crime Bill and national health insurance – as proof that they too were big-government liberals. In perhaps the most notorious of these types of advertisements, pictures of House Democrats were digitally "morphed" into an image of the Democratic President (Balz and Brownstein 1996). As a result, the Republican challengers provided credible information (the incumbents' own roll-call records) about the incumbent Democrats' support of unpopular policies in such a memorable way that it was hard for incumbents to "run away" from the positions of the national party.

The second element of the Republican leadership's strategy to capitalize on the Democrats' weakness was to nationalize the election, making it a choice between the Democrats' unpopular policies and a well-defined Republican alternative. As a result, voters who did not like Clinton's policies would have confidence that a vote for a Republican Congressional candidate might influence the direction of government. The Republicans' approach to nationalizing the election was inspired by "Governing Team Day," and understanding what this earlier event entailed, and why it failed to accomplish its intended ends, provides a great deal of insight into the Republican Party's strategy in 1994 (Gimpel 1996). "Governing Team Day" was a campaign event staged in October 1980 by Representative Jack Kemp (assisted by Gingrich, his lieutenant at the time), who believed that Congressional Republicans had an opportunity to make big gains in the House by riding Ronald Reagan's coattails in his Presidential election contest against unpopular incumbent Jimmy Carter. To maximize these potential gains, Kemp staged an event on the steps of the Capitol building where Ronald Reagan appeared, in a public display of party unity, with the Republican Party's Congressional candidates. As originally conceived, the idea of the event was to have Reagan announce his economic and national security programs and to have the Republican Congressional candidates pledge that they would implement those policies if given an opportunity to "govern." However, the goal of a joint platform never reached fruition because the Congressional Republicans – divided between tax-cutters and budget balancers – could not reach agreement on the policies to put forward, especially with regard to the supply-side tax cuts that Kemp wanted to feature (Sinclair 2006).

To nationalize the election in 1994, a midterm election when the Republicans did not have a Presidential candidate to serve as the party's standard bearer, Gingrich believed that it was necessary to commit the party to a common platform so that voters would know precisely what the alternative was to Clinton. He paid considerable attention when formulating this national platform to identifying a set of issues that would not divide the party and that would not prove harmful to large numbers of Republican candidates in close races. To avoid a repeat of 1980, where "Governing Team Day" fell short of aspirations in part because of intra-party divisions between tax cutters who supported the Kemp-Roth tax cuts and deficit hawks who opposed them, Gingrich delegated to House ally Dick Armey the responsibility of identifying which issues Republican candidates as a whole could get behind. Taking for granted party support for a balanced-budget amendment and line-item veto, the leadership circulated a questionnaire to Republican candidates identifying which issues were seen as important in the campaign and whether there was sufficient agreement within the party to include it in their national program. Tellingly, more controversial issues such as abortion, the flat tax, and school prayer were excluded from the document (Gimpel 1996; Balz and Brownstein 1996). Once those issues were identified, Gingrich and Armey assembled working groups, composed mostly of younger members of the party with a strong interest in a legislative area, to draft the legislation (Armey 1995).

Having identified the set of issues that his party could agree upon, Gingrich's team formulated the Congressional Republicans' national platform. The key element of Gingrich's strategy was his plan to commit the

Republican Party to a particular policy direction with the *Contract with America*. The *Contract* was a campaign document that listed ten bills and three resolutions that all but seven House candidates endorsed, in an unprecedented show of party unity during a campaign, on the Capitol steps a month before the election.[11] The measures included things to appeal to the party's traditional base, such as tax cuts, crime prevention, and welfare reform. It also included term limits, a balanced-budget amendment, and a line-item veto to attract the support of the large number of anti-government voters who had supported the third-party candidate Ross Perot in 1992; these were issues generally consistent with traditional Republican values. The signers of the document pledged to put each of its different components to an up-or-down vote in the first 100 days of the 104th Congress if the Republicans won a legislative majority. The logic behind the *Contract* and the impressive display of party unity was that it provided voters with a clear signal about the direction of government if they threw the Democrats out that November – exactly what one would expect from a "responsible" opposition party.

The Democrats in 2006 and The New Direction

Fortunately for the Democrats in 2006, the Republicans had made it easy to connect its incumbents to the unpopular policies of their President. In the three Congresses preceding the 2006 election, Republicans voted together on party-unity roll calls (i.e., votes where Republicans and Democrats took different positions) 93 percent of the time – the highest levels in a century. If public opinion on key issues changed in a district previously disposed to vote for a conservative candidate, the high levels of Republican discipline in government therefore made it difficult for vulnerable incumbents to credibly differentiate themselves from the newly unpopular policies of the national party. The Democratic Congressional Campaign Committee drove that message home in districts with vulnerable Republicans, labeling them, variously, Bush's "crony of the week" or "rubber stamp of the week" in an effort that the *Chicago Tribune* reported as being surprisingly effective in generating local media coverage.[12]

---

[11] Gimpel notes that of the seven defectors, only four objected to particular pieces of legislation; the other three just did not attend the official ceremony (p. 27).

[12] The Chicago Tribune. http://www.chicagotribune.com/news/politics/chi-0611120215nov12,1,2323509.story?page=2&cset=true&ctrack=1&coll=chi-news-hed. Link active April 1, 2008.

Recognizing that it had faced a similarly unified party four years before with disastrous results, the Democratic leadership in 2006 drew upon the lessons learned from 1994 and 2002 when formulating its electoral strategy. To take advantage of Republican vulnerability, they came to the conclusion that it was in their interest to be a "responsible" opposition party and to provide voters with a statement of what they intended to do if elected. Taking a page from Gingrich's 1994 playbook, the Democrats therefore tried to capitalize on the Republican Party's vulnerability by introducing a national platform that could be supported by virtually all of the organization's members both in the general election and once in office.

After months of internal debates over whether this kind of thing was necessary or even beneficial, in late July, the Democrats introduced their *New Direction for America*, a national platform of sorts that provided a clear statement of the direction that party leaders intended to take the country in the event that they secured a legislative majority in the House. The *New Direction* identified the six issues (or campaign themes), what they termed the "Six for '06," which the Democrats would push if elected. They included traditional Democratic issues such as raising the minimum wage, protecting Social Security, and raising taxes on big business (oil companies and companies who outsourced jobs in particular), along with a promise to force the President to redeploy troops from Iraq. Notably absent from the "Six for '06" were controversial issues such as abortion and gun control that divided the party and that were especially unpopular in more rural parts of the country where Democrats were hoping to pick up seats held by ultra-conservative Republicans.

Party leaders wanted the public to believe that on these six issues, they were committing their party's nominees to advancing the "Six for '06." In fact, they were forceful in advancing this view. Rahm Emanuel, who as chairman of the Democratic Congressional Campaign Committee was the architect of the party's electoral strategy, stated that: "This 100 days is about drilling in the different direction we as Democrats will take this country." Similarly, in an interview about the *New Direction*, Nancy Pelosi stated: "This is a unified Democratic message.... This is a national message about core values that the Democratic Party will fight for and take us in a new direction. Democrats are wedded to that. It defines us, rather than have the Republicans define us."[13] Thus, much like the

---

[13] Quoted by Kathy Kiely, June 16, 2006. "'New Direction' is new theme for Democratic plan." *USA Today*.

Republicans in 1994, the Democrats in 2006 were acting in the manner of a responsible opposition party – being steadfast in their resistance to ruling-party programs that they opposed and advancing an alternative vision of the direction of government come election time.

Discussion

The success of the Republicans in 1994 and that of the Democrats in 2006 is unquestioned. The Republicans picked up fifty-four seats in the former election, the Democrats thirty-one seats in the latter (despite a pattern of increasingly gerrymandered Congressional districts to protect incumbents). In this part of the chapter, it was demonstrated that in the years preceding its victory, the party capturing control of the House acted as a unified opponent of the previous ruling party in the legislature and presented something like a national Congressional party platform. I take this to be evidence that party leaders thought when they were formulating their campaign strategies that it was incentive compatible to satisfy the normative ideal of responsible partisanship, at least when confronting the strategic environment surrounding elections such as 1994 and 2006.

In closing this part of the chapter, it is important to address the argument that the party leadership's efforts in 1994 and 2006 did not contribute much to their organization's electoral success. In 1994, for example, some House Republicans groused that they had been campaigning on key elements of the *Contract with America* long before the event Gingrich organized in Washington, and public opinion polls showed that many people had never heard of the *Contract with America*. Similarly, in 2006, the Democratic National Committee Chairman, Howard Dean, was given much of the credit for his party's victories by the media because of his success in recruiting viable candidates to compete in conservative districts.[14] In response to this line of reasoning, it is important to begin

---

[14] One issue to address regarding Dean's efforts to recruit Democrats able to compete in more conservative districts is whether his actions were detrimental to his party's brand name over the long term. At the time I am writing this chapter, the freshman class of the 110th Congress has served in the House for one full year, which is enough time to at least tentatively assess the strength of Dean's "conservative" recruits' commitment to Democratic party principles. If my account is correct that party leaders do not want to disappoint party loyalists in the electorate by allowing too many of its party members in government to be seen as being *worse* than a Republican chosen at random from the set of all Republicans, then a minimum standard for my theory would be that there should be no freshman Democrats to the right of the center of the Republican Party. A stricter test of the theory would

by reiterating that my point here has been to demonstrate, contrary to the conventional wisdom, that it may be *incentive compatible* for an opposition party to behave responsibly. To demonstrate that it was incentive compatible for them to act as a responsible party, it need only be shown that the organization did not harm its electoral prospects and could possibly have advanced its interests by acting in this way. The evidence presented previously shows definitively that party leaders in 1994 and 2006 did not believe they were doing their candidates any harm and may have done them some benefit. Furthermore, it is noteworthy that although these were resounding triumphs for the out-party nationwide, the margin of victory for its challengers in many Congressional districts was quite small. Consequently, even if there were a relatively small number of voters who were moved by the efforts of the national party organization to present itself as a unified team in opposition to the ruling party, then those efforts had a potentially large effect in deciding majority status in Congress.[15]

THE OPTIMAL LEVEL OF PARTY DISCIPLINE

A recurring theme in this book has been that an American political party receives benefits from working together as a unified team because doing so strengthens partisan loyalties in the electorate and reinforces its brand name. It might be natural to conclude from this that more party unity would always be more beneficial to the organization as a whole – even if it meant that some members might occasionally be forced to cast very tough votes that jeopardize relationships with key constituents. It would then seem to follow that party elites would develop formal organizations

be to find that there were no freshman Democrats with voting records placing them to the political right of the most liberal Republican.

To demonstrate that party leaders do in fact value their brand name sufficiently to police their members, I use estimates of the ranking of members of Congress from most liberal to most conservative using Poole's (2005) non-parametric optimal classification tool based on their roll call through December 31, 2007. Based on these rankings, thirteen of the twenty-five most conservative Democrats were freshman MCs; however, there was not a single freshman Democrat who was more conservative than the most liberal Republican, which is consistent with the strict test of the theory just proposed.

[15] For example, 22 of the 30 seats picked up by Democrats in 2006 were won by less than 10 percent of the vote; 13 of the 30 were won by less than 5 percent of the vote. Author's calculations based on election returns reported at: http://www.cnn.com/ELECTION/2006/pages/results/bop/. Link active March 26, 2008.

with sufficient control over group members that the level of party discipline in the U.S. House would be on par with that observed in other parts of the world. To the extent that we do not observe these strong formal organizations in the United States and in fact have observed highly fractured parties in this country at some points in American history, one might therefore be skeptical about the claim that the majority party recognizes the benefits of being perceived as highly unified – a claim that is crucially important for my argument about why parties maintain their brand names.

The argument in this part of the chapter is that although party unity strengthens voter loyalties and reaffirms the organization's shared brand name, it is not necessarily the case that the national party has especially strong incentives to impose high levels of party discipline on organization members. As noted in Chapter 5, the majority party's exercise of agenda control is itself sufficient to achieve the high levels of party unity needed on floor votes. Consequently, the incumbent-party members who, as a group, choose the institutional arrangements and the leaders responsible for imposing party discipline are essentially making a decision about their relative preferences for stronger party attachments in the electorate and the ability to allow candidates to cater to local tastes.

When making assessments about the resources to grant their party's leaders, incumbent politicians take two sets of considerations into account. First, these individuals desire to retain office and will therefore not support institutions that they expect will be used to coerce them into voting against constituent interests on salient issues regardless of whether party discipline has some other desirable consequences. Second, incumbents prefer to belong to the majority party, which means that they will not support institutions that promote party discipline if they expect that these institutions will result in the party losing a substantial number of seats.

Thus, the key question that a party faces when deciding what types of institutions to adopt to regulate members' behavior in government is whether they expect either themselves or a large number of their copartisans to confront issues where their districts' preferences are not well aligned with the positions of the national party. In a manner reminiscent of Rohde's (1991; see also Aldrich and Rohde 1999) theory of conditional party government, if party members are generally well matched with their districts such that they will rarely confront situations where their constituents prefer the issue positions of the challenger's party to that of the incumbent, then they will favor stronger institutions to regulate the behavior of all organization members in order to deliver on campaign promises and to capture the benefits of stronger partisan loyalties in the electorate. On the other hand, the greater the number of organization members who expect to be confronted with issues where the position of the national party is not viewed favorably back home, the weaker the powers granted to party leaders to discipline rank-and-file members so that legislators can better cater to local tastes.

As a general rule in American politics, it seems reasonable to expect that the former situation will prevail, with incumbent House members tending to be members of the national party preferred by their constituents. This follows from the simple observation that candidates who belong to the party preferred locally are substantially more likely to win elections there, especially when that party has an incumbent running for reelection, or in open-seat contests where the onus is on the other party's candidate to find some mechanism of credibly committing to a set of values not supported by her own party. The most important exception to this general rule will occur in political settings where public sentiments are slowly realigning from preferences for one party to preferences for the other party.[16] In this situation, incumbent politicians may find themselves at mid-career to be members of a party that is ideologically mismatched with local constituents. To the extent that it is possible for the incumbent to anticipate this long-term change, she should try to differentiate herself from her party through her roll-call record. Furthermore, if party elites see these preference realignments as part of a process that is not isolated to a few House districts, they should see it as in their party's best interest to weaken the levers of party discipline to retain these seats.

Since the early twentieth century when members of Congress began to have sufficiently long tenures in office to develop private brand names that they could use to contest local elections, the most important slow-moving change in public opinion for voters' party preferences has been the ideological realignment of the American South. My goal here is to show that the response of party elites to realignment in this region can usefully be understood as a balancing act between maintaining a party brand name that provides a credible signal of a candidate's political values and the

---

[16] This could occur because the preferences on an issue are shifting because national opinion is on the move (thereby leaving incumbents whose districts have not changed opinions in the lurch) or because district opinion is on the move.

need to accommodate incumbent-party members who had to adjust their voting behavior in response to changes in their constituents' preferences so that the national party can maintain majority status.

The Strategic Setting

The defining features of Southern life for the half-century following Reconstruction were the segregationist policies of the Jim Crow era and widespread poverty (cf. Wright 1986; Woodward 1974). For much of this period in history, the South was also the foundation for Democratic Party strength in American elections. The basis for Democratic strength in the region was, in part, the party's willingness to look the other way on Southern states' treatment of African-Americans and its advocacy of populist economic policies that were popular among the white Southern farmers who provided the bulk of the region's votes. Perhaps more important was the shared understanding among Southern whites that the creation of a two-party system would inevitably lead to the end of segregation, as both parties would have incentives to enfranchise and court black voters in their quest for office (cf. Key 1949). Without a viable second party to encourage Southern Representatives to moderate their voting behavior, for the first three decades of the twentieth century Congressmen from the region consistently had more liberal voting records (save for the issue of civil rights) than those elected from any other part of the country (Poole 2005).

Over time, changes in the region's economy threatened to undermine Southern whites' unified support for the Democratic Party. After decades of exceptionally poor macroeconomic performance in the aftermath of the Civil War and Reconstruction, the South finally began to catch up with the rest of the country, with growth rates and incomes rising faster than in any other region of the country (Barro and Sala-I-Martin 1991).[17] To document these changes in Southern incomes, Table 6.1 reports Easterlin's (1960) estimates of the per capita incomes in the South Atlantic,

---

[17] Gavin Wright's (1986) observation that real wages for Southern unskilled (read: farm) workers did not rise relative to Northern unskilled workers is not inconsistent with this claim (notably, Wright provides evidence of rising real incomes for farm labor in the South) because there was a marked change in the composition of the Southern economy, with yeoman and tenant farms becoming less important over time and commercial and industrial work becoming more important – a phenomena (documented by Wright) driven in part by out-migration in the South of black workers and in part by urbanization and industrialization in the region.

Table 6.1. *Southern Income Growth, 1900–1950*

	South Atlantic	East South Central	West South Central
1900	45	49	61
1920	59	52	72
1930	56	48	61
1940	69	55	70
1950	74	62	80

Cell values are the percentage of national per capita income earned by residents of three Southern regions as estimated by Barro and Sala-I-Martin (1991).

East South Central, and West South Central states as a percentage of per capita income nationally from 1900 through 1950. As evidence of growing urbanization in the South, Table 6.2 reports Weiher (1977)'s estimates of the number of urban places in the South over the same period of time. One consequence of this economic development was the emergence of a large group of urban and middle- and upper-income white voters whose interests were not advanced by the populist policies traditionally supported by Southern politicians (Shafer and Johnston 2006; McCarty et al. 2005).

Some Southern Democrats serving in the House responded to the growing conservatism of their constituents in precisely the way one might expect from office-motivated politicians – they changed their issue positions to reflect the interests of their districts. Evidence of this shift is provided by Poole (2005) who estimates the mean ideology of Southern Democrats in the House (as measured by their DW-Nominate Scores), of Democrats outside the South, and of Republicans. His data analysis

Table 6.2. *Southern Urbanization, 1900–1950*

	Number of Urban Places in the South	Percent of U.S. Urban Places in the South	Percent of all U.S. Urban Places in South (>10,000 inhabitants)
1900	1737	18.4	15.2
1910	2262	21.2	16.8
1920	2722	23.6	18.1
1930	3165	25.0	19.1
1940	3464	26.6	20.7
1950	4284	28.4	26.1

Cell values are estimates of the level of urbanization in the South as reported by Weiher (1977).

clearly reveals that, on average, Southern Democrats began the twentieth century as the most liberal wing of their party; that by the late 1920s the Southern Democrats had become almost indistinguishable ideologically from party members elsewhere in the country; and that by the late 1930s Southern Democrats had clearly become quite conservative compared to other party members.

From the perspective of my theory, the ideological convergence of Northern and Southern Democrats from 1910 through 1930 was potentially a positive development for the national party in two respects. First, because party members were allowed to adopt issue positions that appealed locally, Democratic candidates continued to dominate Congressional elections in the South during a period when the region's white voters were moving solidly to the political right. Perhaps the most telling evidence of the importance of granting candidates this flexibility is that in the presidential election of 1928, the Republican presidential candidate, Herbert Hoover, carried five states in the South, but the Republican Party won only eight seats in the House of Representatives (picking up only three seats) from the region. Second, the movement of Southern Democrats toward the center of their Congressional caucus helped to reduce the extent of internal-party conflicts. Thus, this shift to the right may have been of some benefit to the party because greater levels of party unity would facilitate partisan logrolling as well as contribute to stronger partisan attachments nationally.

By the late 1930s, circumstances had changed considerably. Divisions between regional wings of the Democratic Party had become quite severe, with the average Southern House member almost as close ideologically to the center of the Republican Party as to the average non-Southern Democrat. These divisions came to a head in 1937 and 1938. At this juncture, President Franklin Roosevelt watched many of his prized New Deal programs be struck down by the Supreme Court. In response, he tried his court-packing scheme, which received staunch resistance from conservative Southern Democrats. Meanwhile, a substantial number of Representatives from the region also opposed the United States Housing Act, the Fair Labor Standards Act, and Roosevelt's plan to reorganize the executive branch (Polenberg 2000). In each case, a coalition of Republicans and conservative Southern Democrats either blocked Roosevelt's policy initiatives or forced FDR to accept much more conservative policies than he might otherwise have preferred (cf. Patterson 1967). The thing that made the success of these conservatives remarkable is that the Democrats held an overwhelming 334 to 88 advantage in the House and a 76 to 16 advantage in the Senate (third-party politicians held the remaining seats).

The emergence of conservative Southern Democrats as a reasonably unified bloc opposed to key elements of the New Deal was potentially problematic for their party for two crucial reasons. First, because of the Democrats' control over the Presidency and their large seat margins in the House and Senate, party members loyal to Roosevelt believed that they were liable to face electoral setbacks in the 1938 Congressional elections. Southern opposition to relief measures resulted in watered-down legislation, which prevented the national Democrats from taking credit for various measures that may have improved the circumstances of ordinary citizens. Second, party leaders believed that their ability to use the Democratic Party brand name as a signal in future elections about a candidate's attributes was in jeopardy – a serious problem for the long-term health of the party. In light of the arguments presented earlier, under these circumstances the national Democrats should have tried to restore higher levels of party discipline in government if they believed that they could do so and still retain majority control of the chamber.

The "Purge" of the Southern Democrats

Generally speaking, there are three techniques that the national parties might employ to limit the scope of intra-party conflict: parties could deny politicians unwilling to play nicely with other members of the organization access to the ballot; they could employ a reward system to encourage party members to cooperate; or they could manipulate the legislative agenda to prevent divisive items from coming to the floor for a vote. Because a party's candidates for Congress are typically chosen by ordinary citizens in primary elections rather than by party elites, efforts to instill party unity will typically take one of the latter two forms. By the late 1930s, however, it had become apparent that the reward structure available to the national party was not sufficient to induce conservative Democrats to cast votes in support of certain aspects of the New Deal.[18] Further, negative agenda control was still being exercised in the sense that the majority party was not getting "rolled" by the minority party (liberal Democrats were upset because they wanted to pass more extreme

---

[18] Further, there were sufficient numbers of conservative Democrats that they could, if allied with Republicans, veto any institutional reforms that empowered party leaders to impose discipline.

legislation, not because Republicans were successful in passing conservative legislation). Therefore, with the goals of instilling higher levels of party unity in the organization's ranks and realizing the liberal policies he favored, Franklin Roosevelt took the unusual step of intervening in the 1938 primary elections on behalf of candidates supportive of the New Deal in an effort to control the nomination process.

The premise behind Franklin Roosevelt's intervention in the primaries that year was that he had won an electoral landslide in 1936 and carried virtually all parts of the country by wide margins. He took his success in the South to be evidence that conservative Southern Democrats did not have political views that were consistent with those of their constituents. Consequently, administration officials thought they could cleanse the party of its unwelcome elements by denying conservative politicians their party's nomination. In the subsequent general election contest, the expectation was that the alternative liberal candidates would have no problems winning the general election, so they would not lose the Southern seats (while improving the long-term prospects for Northern Congressmen). To get the most bang for his buck, Roosevelt's main targets were high-profile Senators, not House members.[19] The focus on Senators was motivated by the belief that by demonstrating his willingness to intervene against a handful of high-profile recalcitrant party members, and to intervene on behalf of incumbent New Dealers facing conservative primary election challengers, Roosevelt could make the rest of the party more obedient, much as the Supreme Court ultimately caved in to pressure created by the threat of court packing even though judicial reorganization never made it through Congress (McKenna 2002). In short, Democratic Party leaders believed that it was possible in 1938 to reconstitute the Southern wing of their party with members who were strong supporters of the New Deal at little cost, thereby improving the likelihood that liberal measures would receive the required support in Congress, while also reaffirming the organization's brand name.

The Roosevelt administration pursued a two-pronged strategy in its intervention in the primary. First, it redirected patronage positions from supporters of the conservative incumbents, so as to deny them access to political resources they could use to solidify their support in the primary

[19] The were ten main incumbent targets of Roosevelt's efforts to purge his party of conservative members – Senators Adams of Colorado, Clark of Missouri, George of Georgia, Gillette of Iowa, Lonergan of Connecticut, McCarran of Nevada, Smith of South Carolina, Tydings of Maryland, and Van Nuys of Indiana, plus the Chairman of the House Rules Committee from New York City, Congressman John O'Connor.

election (Patterson 1967). It was sufficiently vigorous in its manipulation of patronage, especially on behalf of Majority Leader Alben Barkley in Kentucky, that it sparked Senate Committee hearings which confirmed that relief funds were used inappropriately, ultimately resulting in the passage of the Hatch Act in 1939 (e.g., Milkis 1985). Second, to provide credible evidence of the identity of his faction's supporters within the Democratic Party (and to differentiate these individuals from conservative candidates contesting the primary), Franklin Roosevelt campaigned across the country during the primary election season in support of candidates he believed were loyal New Dealers (Shannon 1939).

Roosevelt's attempted "purge" of the Southern Democrats has been well documented by presidential historians. They have variously characterized it as a quixotic attempt to build a pro–New Deal majority (as opposed to merely a Democratic majority) in the Senate or as an irrational intervention on the part of an increasingly megalomaniacal FDR, who was convinced by the Supreme Court's buckling under the pressure of public opinion that he could dominate the policy-making process by the force of his personality. Perhaps there is some validity to both of these interpretations; however, I think that Roosevelt's intervention on behalf of liberal candidates should also be understood as a rational attempt by a party leader to protect his organization's valuable brand name as a signal that "unknown" Democrats seeking federal office would further the New Deal. In advancing this argument, my approach will be to provide a detailed account of FDR's public statements during his purge campaign as evidence that he was concerned about the impact that conservative Democrats were having on his party's brand name.

The Call for Party Unity

The beginning of FDR's public campaign against conservative Democrats was a "Fireside Chat" he gave on June 24, 1938. Roosevelt began this radio address with a scorecard marking the successes and failures of the Democratic Congress, using as his benchmark of success the passage of legislation appearing on the "uncompromisingly liberal" 1936 party platform. He then proceeded to explain that he intended to intervene in Democratic Party primary elections that summer on behalf of "liberal" candidates.

The publicly stated rationale offered by FDR for what historians now call his attempted "purge" of conservative Democrats proceeds in four parts, and it is worth sketching his justification in some detail because it strongly substantiates my interpretation of his motivations. First, he reminded voters that it was up to them, not party leaders, to choose their party's nominee in House and Senate races:

Fifty years ago party nominations were generally made in conventions – a system typified in the public imagination by a little group in a smoke-filled room who made out the party slates.

The direct primary was invented to make the nomination process a more direct one – to give the party voters themselves a chance to pick their party candidates.[20]

Thus, in a one-party state such as South Carolina or Georgia, voters who wanted to elect politicians who supported (or opposed) the Democratic Party's New Deal agenda were responsible for slating that kind of candidate come November – they could not depend on party leaders to make that choice for them.

Second, he made the case that voters should choose the candidate who best reflects the principles of their party, arguing, in a manner consistent with the model of responsible-party government, that democracy works best when the two parties take distinct issue positions:

It is my hope that everybody affiliated with any party will vote in the primaries, and that every such voter will consider the fundamental principles for which his or her party is on record. That makes for a healthy choice between the candidates of the opposing parties on election day in November.

An election cannot give a country a firm sense of direction if it has two or more national parties which merely have different names but are as alike in their principles and aims as peas in the same pod. [21]

Third, Roosevelt observes that there are liberals and conservatives contesting primaries in both parties and draws a sharp distinction between these competing schools of thought, which he believes are the fundamental principles of the Democratic and Republican Parties:

In the coming primaries in all parties, there will be many clashes between two schools of thought, generally classified as liberal and conservative. Roughly speaking, the liberal school of thought recognizes that the new conditions throughout the world call for new remedies....

The opposing or conservative school of thought, as a general proposition, does not recognize the need for government itself to step in and take action to meet

[20] Franklin Roosevelt. Fireside Chat June 24, 1938. http://www.presidency.ucsb .edu/ws/index.php?pid=15662. Link active March 17, 2008.
[21] Franklin Roosevelt. Fireside Chat June 24, 1938. http://www.presidency.ucsb .edu/ws/index.php?pid=15662. Link active March 17, 2008.

these new problems. It believes that individual initiative and private philanthropy will solve them – that we ought to repeal many of the things we have done and go back, for example, to the old gold standard, or stop all this business of old age pensions and unemployment insurance, or repeal the Securities and Exchange Act, or let monopolies thrive unchecked – return, in effect, to the kind of government that we had in the 1920s.[22]

Given that it is the responsibility of primary election voters to select their party's nominees, it becomes apparent from this passage that Roosevelt wanted to convince Democratic voters to stand firmly in favor of liberal candidates and to deny conservative Democrats who opposed Social Security, unemployment insurance, and so on the ability to benefit from their party's label at the ballot box.

Finally, Roosevelt informed the public that he intended to intervene in the primary elections that summer on behalf of liberals who were seeking the Democratic Party's nomination because it was his obligation as a party leader to do so:

As the head of the Democratic party, however, charged with the responsibility of carrying out the definitely liberal declaration of principles set form in the 1936 Democratic platform, I feel that I have every right to speak in those few instances where there may be a clear-cut issue between candidates for a Democratic nomination involving these principles, or involving a clear misuse of my own name.[23]

By making it clear that he would communicate to voters in their home states which candidates he thought were of sound Democratic ideals, Roosevelt was attempting to use his personal prestige as a vehicle to achieve the kind of national party control over nominations exerted by political parties elsewhere in the world. The only catch, of course, is that he had to convince primary voters to cast out incumbent politicians who, if office-motivated, had gone to some lengths to develop a legislative record that appealed to local voters.

Roosevelt on the Campaign Trail

The Fireside Chat was not mere cheap talk. Two weeks later Roosevelt launched his campaign against conservative politicians. His first stops were in Ohio, Kentucky, Arkansas, and Oklahoma to signal his support

[22] Franklin Roosevelt. Fireside Chat June 24, 1938. http://www.presidency.ucsb.edu/ws/index.php?pid=15662. Link active March 17, 2008.
[23] Franklin Roosevelt. Fireside Chat June 24, 1938. http://www.presidency.ucsb.edu/ws/index.php?pid=15662. Link active March 17, 2008.

for incumbent supporters of the New Deal (including Alben Barkley, the Senate Majority Leader and important FDR ally) who were facing serious conservative primary challenges.[24] He continued south through Texas, throwing his support in primary contests to incumbent House member Maury Maverick and a future President, Lyndon Johnson. Roosevelt then turned west, traveling through Colorado, Nevada, and California – at the former two stops making a point of *not* providing conservative incumbents within his party with a coveted photo-op on the rear of the President's train (Shannon 1939a). Then, after a month-long vacation cruise along the Mexican coast, Roosevelt took the fight onto conservative turf more assertively.

In Georgia, the first of his "purge" stops where he actively campaigned against a conservative incumbent, FDR backed the candidacy of Lawrence Camp, a federal district attorney, in a three-way contest that also included former Governor Eugene Talmadge, a famed populist demagogue, and the incumbent Senator, Walter F. George. In a campaign stop in Barnesville, Georgia, Franklin Roosevelt made his case to an audience that included Senator George himself. Having first observed that Senator George's voting record was comparable to that of many Republicans, Roosevelt reiterated a theme from his Fireside Chat – that party discipline was desirable as a means of realizing the goals of the New Deal and as a way of improving democratic processes by connecting the public's vote choices with government action in the manner of a responsible party:

I speak seriously and in the most friendly way in terms of liberal and conservative for the very simple fact that on my shoulders rests a responsibility to the people of the United States. In 1932 and again in 1936 I was chosen Chief Executive with the mandate to seek by definite action to correct many evils of the past and of the present....

To carry out my responsibility as President it is clear that there should be cooperation between members of my own party and myself. That is one of the essentials of a party form of government.... The test is not measured, in the case of any individual, by his every vote on every bill. The test lies rather in two questions: First, has the record of the candidate shown, while differing perhaps in details, a constant active fighting attitude in favor of the broad objectives of the party and of the government as they are constituted today, and secondly, does the candidate really, in his heart, believe in the objectives? I regret that in the case of my friend Senator George, I cannot answer either of these questions in the affirmative.

---

[24] Roosevelt also made a stop in Tennessee, where he choose to remain neutral in a nasty internal party battle among candidates supportive of the New Deal.

Having identified George as a poor match with the ideals of the Democratic Party, Roosevelt continued on to explain why he favored Camp over Talmadge:

In the case of another candidate in the State of Georgia for the United States Senate – former Governor Talmadge...I have read so many of his proposals, so many of his promises, so many of his panaceas, that I am very certain in my own mind that his election would contribute very little to practical progress in government. That is all I can say about him.

The third candidate that I would speak of, United States Attorney Lawrence Camp...I regard him not only as a public servant with successful experience but as a man who honestly believes that many things must be done and done now to improve the economic and social conditions of the country, a man who is willing to fight for these objectives. Fighting ability is of the utmost importance.

Therefore, answering the requests that have come to me from many leading citizens of Georgia that I make my position clear, I have no hesitation in saying that if I were able to vote in the September primaries in this State, I most assuredly should cast my ballot for Lawrence Camp.[25]

As remarkable as it might seem today given the modern norm of Presidential neutrality in primary elections, Roosevelt stood on stage with an incumbent Senator of his own party and endorsed his opponent on the grounds that it would foster higher levels of party unity in government.

The second stop of the "purge train" was South Carolina, where Governor Olin Johnston was contesting the primary against the conservative incumbent Senator "Cotton Ed" Smith, the chairman of the Agricultural Committee, who was described by one observer as "an almost unbelievable throwback to the days of the confederacy" (Phillips 2000). Johnston had announced his candidacy at the White House months before, after meeting with the President (presumably having just received Roosevelt's encouragement to run, and taking advantage of the opportunity to communicate that to the public even if FDR himself was not ready to do so). He stated at the time: "My campaign for the Senate will be based on a record of constant, unshakable loyalty to the Democratic Platform and the head of our party, President Roosevelt" (quoted in Shannon 1939, Part II). When Roosevelt arrived in South Carolina months later, he did not openly condemn Senator Smith for his conservative record, perhaps because he was so famously reactionary that no critique was necessary.

---

[25] Franklin Roosevelt. Address at Barnesville, GA. August 11, 1938. http://www.presidency.ucsb.edu/ws/index.php?pid=15520&st=&st1=. Link active March 17, 2008.

Nor, to Johnston's dismay, did FDR openly endorse his challenge. However, in a very brief statement given in Greenville, he does reiterate the
argument for why primary voters in the South should aid his efforts to
purge the Democratic Party of its conservative members:

As you people probably know, I have made two speeches today and there was
not time nor opportunity to prepare a third speech. Some of you may have heard
what I said down in Georgia, at Barnesville. Those of you who did not hear me,
I hope will read in the newspapers what I said of some of the economic and
social problems of the South and of the necessity of meeting those problems by a
consolidation of the interests of all the southern states, and then by consolidating
those interests with the interests of the whole Nation.

That, my friends, cannot be done without legislation. As President, I cannot do it
alone. The Congress of the United States must pass the laws.

That is why, in any selection of candidates for members of the Senate or members
of the House of Representatives – if you believe in the principles for which we are
striving... I hope you will send representatives to the national legislature who
will work toward those ends.[26]

Roosevelt then alluded to his encouragement of Johnston's candidacy
earlier in the year and took a swipe at the ground's for Smith's opposition
to the Fair Labor Standards Act:

Before I stop – and I believe the train is pulling out in a minute or two – I want
to suggest two things to you.

The first is that a long time ago I promised Governor Johnston that I would come
down some time this year to visit the capital of the State of South Carolina. I have
never been there but I am coming.

The other thing is that I don't believe any family or man can live on fifty cents a
day.[27]

When a third candidate who also proclaimed support for the New Deal
dropped out of the primary contest shortly before the election in August,
Roosevelt was finally fully forthcoming in his support of Johnson, taking
the opportunity to announce that:

---

[26] Franklin Roosevelt. Remarks at Greenville, GA August 11, 1938. http://www
.presidency.ucsb.edu/ws/index.php?pid=15522&st=&st1=. Link active March
17, 2008.
[27] Franklin Roosevelt. Remarks at Greenville, GA August 11, 1938. http://www
.presidency.ucsb.edu/ws/index.php?pid=15522&stamp;=&st1=. Link active
March 17, 2008.

In my opinion, the unexpected withdrawal of State Senator Edgar A. Brown from the senatorial race almost on the eve of the primary elections in South Carolina clarifies the issue. The voters of the state now have their choice between two candidates representing entirely different political schools of thought.

One of these candidates thinks in terms of the past and governs his actions accordingly.

The other thinks in terms of 1938, 1948, and 1958 as well.

On Tuesday the electorate of South Carolina will make this choice. On them rests the responsibility of selecting a representative in the United States Senate to play a part in the framing of legislation to carry out the objectives of the administration's program; legislation to improve the lot of the average American and give him security; to give fair play to the farmer, the laborer, the storekeeper and the great rank and file of our citizens.[28]

The fact that FDR maintained a position of neutrality among Smith's two challengers until this late stage of the campaign was certainly damaging to Johnston's prospects in the election. It makes sense in retrospect only if Roosevelt was holding to the conviction that he should not intervene in a primary election to play kingmaker among politicians loyal to Democratic Party principles.

Roosevelt's third purge stop was in Maryland later that summer, where the incumbent Senator, Millard Tydings, had opposed virtually all aspects of the New Deal. In the primary, FDR threw his support to Davey John Lewis, a member of the House of Representatives and loyal New Dealer. FDR's initial interjection into the race was to read aloud to reporters, and to endorse, an editorial from the *New York Post* condemning Senator Tydings (and Representative O'Connor). It read:

The idea is that the President should be aloof from such sordid considerations as who wins the primaries in his own party. But actually these primaries will determine to a large extent the makeup of the next Congress. And that, in turn, will determine whether or not the President can keep his campaign promises to the people.

Campaign promises are supposed to be the responsibility of the whole party. At least that's the theory. But in practice the head of the party alone is held responsible for them.

In American politics any one can attach himself to a political party whether he believes in its program or not. . . .

---

[28] Quoted by Shannon 1939, Part II, p. 289.

In those circumstances there is nothing for the President to do – as the responsible head of the New Deal – but to publicly repudiate those who have betrayed the New Deal in the past and will again.

If men like Senator Tydings of Maryland said frankly: "I no longer believe in the platform of the Democratic Party as expressed in the New Deal; I'm running for re-election as a member of the Republican opposition to the New Deal," then there would be no reason and no excuse for President Roosevelt to intervene against them.

The issue would be clear. The voter could take his choice between the New Deal and Tydings' record of consistent opposition to it. But Tydings tells the voters he supports the "bone and sinew" of the New Deal. He wants to run with the Roosevelt prestige and the money of his conservative Republican friends both on his side.

In that case it becomes the President's right and duty to tell the people what he thinks of Millard Tydings.[29]

Shortly thereafter, Roosevelt gave a Labor Day speech in Denton, Maryland, on behalf of Lewis. Echoing themes from earlier in the year, he stated:

For a dozen years or more prior to 1933, the Federal Government had not moved forward at all. Life was out of balance and Government had failed completely to recognize that important social needs call for action. In a nation-wide effort to catch up with lost time, to bring a distant past up to the present, a whole series of new undertakings had to be launched in 1933....

During this process there were of course many people both in private and public life who did not like to do the things that had to be done.... They admitted the existence of certain abuses. But in their hearts they wishfully believed that improvement should come from individual initiative or local initiative without the help of Government....

People who feel and think like that I call "conservatives," and even "reactionaries." And people who feel that the past should be brought up to the present by using every legitimate instrument to do the job, including Government, I call "liberals" or "progressives."

Any man – any political party – has a right to be honestly one or the other. But the Nation cannot stand for the confusion of having him pretend to be one and act like the other....

[29] Franklin Roosevelt. "Excerpts from the Press Conference." August 16, 1938. http://www.presidency.ucsb.edu/ws/index.php?pid=15524&st=&st1=. Link active March 17, 2008. Note that Roosevelt also read sections of the article that also condemned Representative O'Connor.

As the leader of [the Democratic] party, I propose to keep it liberal. As President of the United States, I conceive that course to be in the best interest not only of Democrats but also of those millions of American men and women who are affiliated with other parties or with no party at all. And I have the right, in sincerity and honesty, to make that statement in any state, in any county and in any community of the United States of America.[30]

After giving Lewis credit for the first Workmen's Compensation Act to be passed in the United States during his days in the state legislature and for pioneering federal efforts on old-age pensions and unemployment insurance, Roosevelt asked the voters in Maryland to elect someone who would support the New Deal:

[Continuing] progress, I need hardly remind you, comes ultimately from the rank and file of our citizens, and through the representatives of their free choice – representatives willing to cooperate, to get things done in the true spirit of "give and take" – not representatives who seek every plausible excuse for blocking action.

Thus, echoing the sentiments voiced in his Fireside Chat and his Barnesville Address, Roosevelt was calling on the primary voters in Maryland to vote for Jones because he was a loyal Democrat.

The Consequences of FDR's Intervention

Readers of earlier chapters of this book have probably already inferred that Roosevelt's efforts to purge the Democratic party of its conservative elements failed. Of the ten primary election races that Roosevelt targeted, he was successful in defeating just one incumbent in the 1938 primaries – Representative John O'Connor of New York City. Meanwhile, conservative Democrats managed to pick up a Senate seat in Idaho. Rather than sending a clear signal that they should return to the party fold if they were concerned about their prospects for a long career in the House, conservative Democrats were instead emboldened to remain steadfast in their opposition to the liberal policy program favored by the Northern wing of their party – the voters in their states had clearly conveyed a preference for conservative policies.

Congressional Democrats were then confronted with a choice between trying to strengthen institutions inside the House to encourage higher

---

[30] Franklin Roosevelt speech, September 5th, 1938. Denton, MD. http://www.presidency.ucsb.edu/ws/index.php?pid=15534&st=&st1=. Link active March 17, 2008.

levels of party discipline, or modifying the organization of the House to accommodate policy disagreement in the chamber. Given the strategic logic presented earlier, it would only have been rational for the national Democrats to continue to pursue costly efforts to discipline the party's conservative members if doing so contributed to the goal of winning a legislative majority. This was not to come to pass. In November 1938, the Republicans won big in House races, almost doubling their seat share from 88 seats in the 75th Congress to 169 seats in the 76th. In contrast to the circumstances confronting the Democrats just two years before, when they could have thrown every Southerner out of the party and retained control of the House and Senate, as of 1939 the Democrats could not afford to lose even half of the Southern House seats (limiting the analysis to just former Confederate states, not including states with large numbers of other conservative Democrats such as Maryland, Kentucky, Oklahoma, and Missouri) to the Republicans or a sectionally based third party and still maintain majority status.[31] Because the Democrats knew that they needed large numbers of Southern seats, and that the primary elections of 1938 demonstrated the conservatism of Southern voters, the national party conceded defeat in its effort to substantially rein in its members from the region. As Cooper and Brady (1981) note, the election of Sam Rayburn as Speaker during the 76th Congress represented a regime change in the organization of the House, with party leaders now expected to broker agreements among factions within the chamber that could receive widespread support, rather than being placed in command of an army of party loyalists.

Discussion

Viewed from the vantage of the 1960s, when the Democratic Party took an accommodative stance toward its conservative members, it is easy to understand why astute observers of Congress such as Richard Fenno and David Mayhew might conclude that American political parties are not organized to protect shared brand names and promote common policy goals. If the converse were true, then the Congressional Democrats should have provided party leaders with greater resources to discipline their members.

[31] Author's calculations based on Congressional seat apportionments as reported at: http://clerk.house.gov/art_history/house_history/congApp.html as of March 13, 2008.

Viewed from the vantage of the late 1930s, however, it becomes apparent that the Democrats were not nearly as nonchalant about the prospects that they might forfeit a previously strong brand name. FDR's intervention in the 1938 primaries on behalf of liberal Democrats provides prima facie evidence that party leaders were deeply concerned about the consequences of allowing conservative Democrats to become entrenched in Congress. That Roosevelt justified his actions, in part, by arguing that it was desirable to have party labels convey accurate information about candidates' issue positions, and that having conservative Democrats on the ballot in November prevented that information from being accurately communicated, speaks to the fact that he was concerned about the consequences of internal conflicts for his party's reputation.

That FDR's purge campaign failed so miserably also provides insight into why the national Democrats ultimately decided to accommodate their conservative members. When a popular sitting Governor such as Olin Johnston could not unseat a reactionary such as Cotton Ed Smith in the Democratic primary, that signaled to the party that they had to choose between conservative Southern Democrats and conservative Southern Republicans. Given that this was tantamount to choosing between majority- and minority-party status, it is little wonder that the incumbent party members in Washington were willing to place their ability to use their brand name to signal information about future Democrats in jeopardy. Tellingly, it was not until the influx of large numbers of liberal Democrats in 1974, the so-called Watergate Babies, where the 147-seat Democratic majority was of sufficient size that they did not need to keep all 75 remaining Southern Democrats in the fold to retain procedural control of the House, that the Democratic Caucus finally began to reapply strong party pressures on their members (Rohde 1991; Sinclair 2006).

CONCLUSIONS

Over the past two decades, political scientists have accumulated a substantial body of evidence that Congressional parties have an important influence on the legislative process and the voting behavior of individual legislators. Previous work has variously argued that members of Congress agree to the establishment of rules and norms that grant party leaders the power to influence the behavior of rank-and-file party members to further their policy goals (Rohde 1991) or electoral ambitions (Cox and McCubbins 1993, 2005; Kiewiet and McCubbins 1991). I share the view advocated by Smith (2007) that these two considerations are not mutually exclusive, with legislators valuing partisan institutions for both policy-making and electoral credit-claiming purposes, and argue in this book that a third incentive to form institutions able to promote intra-party cooperation is the desire to solve the adverse selection problem in elections.

In this chapter, a series of case studies were presented that provide support for the claim that political elites recognize and place some value on political parties performing the role of a surety that solves adverse selection problems in elections. First, using the case of the Bucktail party in New York, it was shown that if a party brand name does not exist, then politicians who are unable on their own to provide a credible signal about their own policy preferences may form a political party, complete with a set of rules and norms able to regulate the behavior of its members, in order to compete against rivals with strong private brand names. The persistent weakness of independent and third-party candidates in American elections strongly suggests that politicians' need to belong to a party that is able to perform this function may be ubiquitous.

Second, a case study of the Congressional elections of 1994 and 2006 showed that when the ruling party is perceived to be electorally vulnerable, it may be rational for the opposition party to act in a manner consistent with the classic responsible-party model. These incentives exist because electoral challengers (against candidates of both parties) rely on party brand names to provide credible signals of their political commitments, which provides out-party candidates a tremendous advantage when the ruling party is receiving unfavorable reviews. By behaving in the manner of a responsible opposition party, the out-party enhances the credibility of the signal from their party leaders about the direction of government in the event that its candidates defeat incumbent members of the majority party.

Third, a study of the Democratic Party's response to the emergence of sectional cleavages during the 1930s demonstrated that politicians value their party brand name as a solution to adverse selection problems only to the extent that it contributes to their prospects for winning legislative majorities. When maintaining the party brand name requires large numbers of incumbent members to vote contrary to their constituencies' preferences, then the organization should choose to weaken party control institutions. Thus, the incentives for behaving in the manner of a responsible party are contingent upon incumbents belonging to a party that is ideologically well matched with the preferences of their constituents.

7

Conclusions

Early democratic theorists were primarily concerned with the question of whether the people had the right and the competence to govern themselves. Little thought was given to the question of how public opinion would translate into successful government outcomes (cf. Schattschneider 1942). That changed in 1879 when Woodrow Wilson published "Cabinet Government in the United States," an essay written in response to the widespread condemnation of universal suffrage among American intellectuals during the Industrial Revolution. Wilson contended that universal suffrage was being made the "scapegoat" for an unresponsive government, producing an incoherent set of policies regulating the nation's economic and foreign policies, when the real problem with the American political system was inferior institutions, especially inside Congress. In the decades that ensued, Wilson and others argued in favor of a system of responsible-party government, modeled after the British Westminster system, which allowed for accountable government in a representative democracy despite the fact that few voters meet idealized notions of the independent, informed democratic citizen.

Its proponents trumpet three main benefits from a system of responsible-party government. First, responsible-party government reduces the complex set of questions regarding how best to govern a complex society to a simple choice for voters between the policies of the incumbent ruling party in government and those advocated by the opposition. Nicely, by observing current conditions and the identity of the ruling party (and their memories of the past performance of the opposition party), voters have all the information they need to cast their ballots, despite the complexity of modern societies. Second, because of the strength of formal party organizations in the Westminster system that bind individual politicians to their party, voters can rationally treat the ruling party as the agent it has chosen to govern. As a result, it is straightforward for the electorate to hold the ruling party accountable for its performance in office through its votes for individual politicians who belong to the organization. (One might usefully think of rank-and-file politicians as being their party's agent in their district rather than being their district's agent in government.) Third, parties have strong incentives to maintain consistency between the promises they make to the public and the policies they pursue once in office. To do otherwise would lead voters to conclude that the party could not be trusted to keep its promises in the future (see also Downs 1957).

In this book, it was argued that political parties do not need the control apparatus of a hierarchical, West European-style political party to facilitate accountable governance, any more than representative democracies require the participation of some idealized democratic citizenry. The central insight of the book was that political parties facilitate accountable governance by performing the role of a surety in the principal-agent relationship between voters and their representatives in government. That is, a political party (or perhaps more accurately its leadership) is an actor "hired" by politicians, who voters fear are ideologues whose actions in government may be inconsistent with the interests of constituents, to warrant how votes for themselves might translate into policy outcomes. Specifically, party leaders "guarantee" that if they become the head of the ruling party, (1) ideologues in their organization will not be allowed the opportunity to pull policy too far from the political center and (2) the government will only produce policies that shift policy in the direction of the party's program. Party leaders perform this function because they value both their position of power in the chamber and their ability to pursue policies that are consistent with their personal preferences. Party leaders are trusted to follow through on their commitments because they post as "bond" their organization's reputation for effectively serving as a third-party guarantor of their back-benchers' performance (i.e., legislative outputs).

By way of conclusion, I intend to argue that by performing the functions of a surety, American political parties convey many of the benefits to the electorate of a system of responsible-party government.

THE SIMPLIFICATION OF THE ALTERNATIVES

One of the central arguments in support of the responsible-party model is that voters benefit from having two parties announce competing policy programs. This book argued that political parties ultimately perform this function and offer the electorate competing policy programs because their members are motivated by ideological considerations. The argument proceeded from the assumption that the individuals who are willing to incur the greatest costs (and who are therefore most likely to be successful) to win elected office will have stronger, more extreme policy views than ordinary citizens. Parties form because politicians with similar policy preferences recognize that they will be able to more effectively contest office and move public policy in their preferred direction by working together as teams. Given that the United States' electoral institutions encourage two-party competition, the natural tendency is for the groups of like-minded politicians to consolidate around their support for, or their opposition to, the decisions of the government.

To be sure, because one cannot implement policy without first winning office, there are strong electoral pressures encouraging the two parties to converge toward the political center, even with policy-motivated politicians; however, there are important countervailing forces that prevent them from doing so. First, as long as the two parties are on opposite sides of the political center, but are not too extreme, they are able to deter serious third-party challenges (see also Palfrey 1984). The incumbent parties are able to deter third-party candidates because it is not possible for a new entrant to stake out a position in the policy space that will attract sufficient electoral support. However, if a party converges to the middle, then it creates opportunities on her flank for the entry of a serious third-party challenge.

Second, as demonstrated in Chapter 3, party reputations are long-lived. As a result, it would take quite some time for a party that changes its policy positions to be perceived by the public as being more centrist. In the interim, the organization would jeopardize the support of its strong partisans who would see smaller differences between the two parties and who would become more uncertain about the types of politicians who belong to this party because of the change in party positions. Over the longer term, changing policy positions in this way might even prove detrimental because voter preferences change over time – parties trying to change their image for short-term gains therefore risk losing their ability in the long run to take full advantage of a favorable partisan tide.

Third, a party that chases the median voter nationally jeopardizes the support of its activist base. As developed in Chapter 4, the strength of a person's support for a political party varies with their preferences for that party verses the alternative. As a result, if a party converges to the political center, it might attract some votes, but it weakens the incentives for its supporters in the general electorate to contribute to its cause, especially if the opposition party also moves to the middle. To the extent that parties rely on their activist base to effectively contest elections, they must stake out positions that differentiate themselves from each other (see also Aldrich 1995).

PARTIES AS COLLECTIVE ENTITIES

A critical element of the argument for responsible parties is that they make it rational for the public to hold the ruling party accountable as a *team* for its performance in office. Political scientists, traditionally, have not viewed legislative elections in the United States as being contested between two "parties." The emphasis in the literature is on the local nature of Congressional elections. Individual politicians, motivated by the desire to capture office, have strong incentives in standard accounts to adopt issue positions that appeal most to the constituents in their district. There may exist forces that encourage politicians to diverge from the political center (e.g., their own policy preferences or the need to win primary elections), but the election is still about the candidates competing locally.

This book argued that the focus on the characteristics of the candidates competing locally is misguided, at least up to a point. Its main insight on this subject is that in legislative elections, the election of a candidate to office affects the policy choices of the legislature through two very different channels. First, it affects the policy choices of the legislature through the votes cast by the winner, so her policy preferences, her commitment to district interests, and so on matter to voters. Second, the election affects which party has control over the legislative agenda, as suggested by the theory of conditional party government and procedural cartel theory. If the majority party uses its agenda-setting power to control what legislation gets put forward for a vote, then a candidate's party affiliation therefore also matters to voters.

In many instances, it is clear that the choice of whether the Democrats or the Republicans become the ruling party is more consequential than the expected voting record of candidates for office because the choice of the agenda-setting agent is the more important decision. For example, a left-leaning district might be confronted with the choice between a Republican its residents believe would vote in accord with district tastes on all final-passage votes and a Democrat who they believe would vote for extremely liberal public policies if given the opportunity. Taking into account the attributes of the individual legislator and her party membership, the majority of voters in that district would be far better off if they elected the ideologue. The district is insulated from her extremism by the fact that she is just one voter in a large legislature and the leadership of her party has incentives to use its agenda-setting powers to prevent the consideration of extreme public policies. So, the ideologue's election might shift the government's policy choices by a small amount to the left; however, if the Republicans became the ruling party, there would be no policies enacted on issues where the two parties disagree where her constituents would be made better off.

There are a number of well-established empirical regularities in American politics that are consistent with the argument that legislative elections are largely about parties rather than individual candidates. To name a few:

- Voters seem to know very little about candidates running for office.
- Americans draw upon partisan cues when they make inferences about candidates' issue positions.
- People may use information about candidate partisanship to guide their behavior, even when confronted with evidence to the contrary.
- Partisanship is an important predictor of voting behavior.
- Members of Congress are concerned about their party's reputation.
- Partisan electoral tides suggest that parties are held accountable as political teams for their actions.

Of course, past researchers have tried to explain each of these observations through the lens of the classic model of boundedly rational decision making, with voters drawing upon partisan cues at the ballot box as a low-cost decision-making cue to reduce uncertainty about candidate attributes. It seems hard to argue with the proposition that party labels reduce voter uncertainty, but Chapter 2 demonstrated that a voter's desire to reduce her uncertainty about candidate attributes is an insufficient explanation for why she uses partisan cues at the ballot box. In legislative elections, if there is even a small chance that a candidate will pursue issue positions spatially between those advocated by the two major parties, voters actually prefer that candidate in most instances, even with tremendous uncertainty about her anticipated behavior in office. (As noted in

Chapter 2, that explains why a system of party government requires institutions to limit the entry of independent and third-party candidates).

THE CREDIBILITY OF A PARTY'S POLICY COMMITMENTS

A final argument for a system of responsible-party government is that it creates incentives for politicians to keep their campaign promises. According to the theory of responsible-party government, the hierarchal structure of a responsible party greatly limits the opportunities for politicians to do anything other than obey their leadership. Party leaders, in turn, have strong incentives to develop a reputation for keeping their campaign promises once in office because that reputation helps a party's candidate win elections. Party labels therefore provide a kind of brand name that provide credible signals about how votes for a particular party's candidates will shape the government's decisions.

American political parties, in contrast, are often said to not have brand names that provide credible information about candidates' political attributes. A Republican elected from New York or Massachusetts is likely to have a very different voting record than one from Kansas or South Carolina. Party labels in the United States, therefore, do not convey the same quality of information as that provided by the label of a responsible party.

Conceding that there is much more variation in the behavior of politicians within an American political party than observed in other political systems, this book argued that the major parties in the United States can still maintain brand names that convey credible information about how votes for a candidate affect the decisions of government. This argument was based on the observation that one does not need a homogenous product line or a hierarchal management structure to use a brand name to "sell" a product. All that is required to maintain a brand name is that an organization has a reputation that it values; that it places its reputation in jeopardy if someone carrying its brand name causes a bad outcome for a decision maker who trusted the brand; and that the decision maker believes that there exists some mechanism(s) by which an organization is able to prevent the decision maker from realizing a bad outcome. This explains why it is possible for firms to signal product quality through the process of brand extension, franchising, and even brand licensing agreements with other firms, and why political parties might be able to use their label to provide credible information about the consequences of electing a Democratic or Republican candidate.

Much of this book has focused on the question of how voters relate to parties as brands. Some of the key arguments and findings in support of this idea follow.

Party Reputations Are Long-Lived

The reason that people trust product brand names is that they believe that there exists a firm that values its reputation so much that it will not sell a low-quality product. The key mechanism driving this behavior is the inference made by consumers that if the firm acts opportunistically, then they will remember that they were duped into paying too much for the brand-name product, and the firm's reputation for selling high-quality products is lost. The reputations for brand-name products are therefore long-lived because people want to remember whether they were sold high- or low-quality products.

For voters to trust party brand names as signals about how candidates will act, it must similarly be true that party reputations are long-lived. The reason that voters have confidence in the information provided by party labels is that they believe that the party organization (i.e., the incumbent party members in government) forfeit the benefits of their brand name if they fail to enforce party discipline. If parties behave opportunistically in the sense that they do not prevent their members in government from betraying their party's principles, voters infer that party leaders lack the capacity and/or the incentives to discipline their members, and the party's reputation for affiliating with certain types of candidates is lost. Party reputations are therefore long-lived because voters value past information about the frequency of opportunistic behavior on the party's behalf. If voter beliefs about parties are instead based on only the most recent events, then voters lose important information that helps them to judge whether the party places sufficient value on its brand name to incur the costs of policing organization members.

One of the key pieces of evidence in support of the theory articulated in this book is therefore the evidence presented in Chapter 3 that voter beliefs about political parties are based on a lifetime of experience, not just current events. In that chapter, it was shown that voters update their beliefs about the scope of conflict between the two parties as a function of the level of ideological conflicts between Democrats and Republicans in government and that people's uncertainty about a party varies systematically with the level of conflict within its Congressional caucus. More to the point is the finding, which turns on its head the conventional notion that people gain political knowledge and sophistication as they age, that younger people's beliefs are more consistent with the behavior of political parties today, whereas older people's beliefs appear to be shaped in important ways by the behavior of party elites in the more distant past.

Party Reputations Suffer from Breakdowns in Party Discipline

It would only be rational for someone to find party affiliations to provide credible information about candidates if the party suffers in the event that party discipline fails and its members betray the organization's principles in office. Chapters 3 and 4 identified the mechanism by which parties suffer negative consequences from a breakdown in party unity. In Chapter 3, it was shown that when party unity is high, people see parties as teams working together on a set of common issues; however, when party unity breaks down, people become uncertain about the attributes that party members hold in common. The key evidence in support of this claim was the original finding that Americans became more uncertain about the positions of party members during the 1960s and 1970s when the national parties experienced relatively high levels of intra-party conflict, and that as the party system has polarized, party reputations have once again crystallized in the minds of voters.

Chapter 4 identified the penalty that parties suffer when voters become more uncertain about the attributes of party members. It argued that if voters are risk-averse (and they clearly are if they prefer major-party candidates with brand names to independent and minor-party candidates), then the strength of their partisan loyalties will be linked to their uncertainty about the party, with more certain voters being stronger partisans, and less certain voters being weaker partisans. Because voter uncertainty is a consequence of party unity, parties benefit from party unity because it strengthens partisan attachments (and strong partisans are an important asset for the organization for a multitude of reasons), with the caveat that the level of voter uncertainty about parties will lag changes in elite behavior, especially among older voters for the reasons outlined earlier. To support this claim, the chapter provided individual-level evidence showing that more certain voters had higher expected utility for parties and had stronger partisan attachments toward their more preferred party; aggregate data showing that the strength of partisan identities trends with the level of party unity in government; and time-series data broken down by birth cohort showing that the strength of party attachments varies by generation in a manner consistent with voters granting or withholding support based on a lifetime of evidence about a party's ability to maintain discipline in government. The last evidence is especially important for the theory because it means that if party discipline breaks down, it will be difficult for the party to rebuild its damaged brand name because voters alive today will remember that failure and continue to withhold support from the organization.

Most Politicians Have Weak Private Brand Names

One of the central themes of this book is that the familiar characterization of American elections as being candidate-centered affairs, with Congressional candidates campaigning on the basis of private brand names and voters having little regard for politicians' party affiliations (cf. Fenno 1978; Mayhew 1974a), is incorrect, or at least incomplete. In addition to the empirical regularity that voters depend greatly on partisan cues when evaluating politicians, this book provided three reasons to believe that elections are not contested on the basis of candidates' personal reputations.

First, the standard model of candidate-centered politics posits that voters evaluate each candidate according to her policy positions (as well as her overall fitness for office, etc.) and cast their votes for the individual whom they prefer. Embedded in this model is the assumption that voters actually find politicians' campaign promises to be credible – people are not going to vote based on the ideals a politician espouses on the campaign trail if they believe that she does not intend to follow through on those commitments once in office. Chapter 2 reported that voters do not believe that office-seekers will act on the ideals they espouse during election campaigns. Instead, public opinion data regularly shows that voters believe that politicians are dishonest and will make promises that they do not intend to fill. Furthermore, the public is correct in this belief, with a considerable body of literature demonstrating that politicians regularly do not keep their word once in office. Candidates hoping to run on the basis of personal reputations will have a very difficult time signaling their commitment to their own policy platforms because of the public's distrust.

Second, the early portions of Chapter 5 addressed whether it was possible that incumbent politicians might have private brand names that overcome voter distrust, the logic being that by keeping her campaign promises, a Representative might develop a reputation that she values (and has incentives to protect) because it would help her to secure reelection in the future. It was argued that although this is a theoretical possibility, the empirical evidence shows that most members of Congress are unsuccessful (if they try at all) at creating private brand names. Very few voters are able to recall their Congressperson's name; that many people when told that name are unable to indicate whether they feel warmly or coolly towards her; that only about half of survey respondents are able to even marshal a guess as to whether their Representative is liberal or conservative or about her stances on a broad range of economic or social issues; and that when people do guess her votes on issues where party affiliations provide an unclear signal, they fail to give an accurate answer more often than not.

Third, bucking the standard view that voters' ignorance about candidates is simply a result of their disinterest in politics, the second half of Chapter 5 argued that the explanation for these weak private brand names is that incumbents do not, in general, have strong incentives to cultivate a personal reputation that appeals back home. This argument was based on the insight that it is costly for politicians to develop private brand names and that they might be better served by simply running as the Democratic or Republican Party's candidate and expending their scarce campaign resources on other activities. In particular, an incumbent should only work to differentiate herself from her party if (1) her constituents prefer that she vote contrary to her party's line on important issues and (2) the other party voted in accord with constituent interests so that its candidate could credibly claim that she would have voted differently.

Building from the observation by Cox and McCubbins (2005) that the House leadership exercises its agenda-setting powers to prevent measures that badly divide the majority party from coming to the floor for a vote, some formal results were provided which proved that relatively few incumbents will be forced to choose between a party-line vote and a vote to satisfy constituency concerns on any given issue. Extending this analysis, it was argued that the only group with strong incentives to develop private brand names are incumbents who find themselves in more centrist districts, who support the majority party on some issues and the minority party on others: these actors are motivated to cast votes that differentiate themselves from their party on key issues back home (which results in their developing a centrist voting record) and to inform their constituents about this behavior. To support this claim, evidence was provided that incumbents with centrist voting records are more likely to differentiate themselves from the actions of their party in their messages to the public; that incumbents with centrist voting records are more likely to spend campaign resources on developing a private brand name by making contact with their constituents; and that centrist incumbents have much higher name recognition than other legislators (unless there is a quality challenger who is trying to brand an incumbent with an extreme voting record as out of step with her district).

Parties Organize to Solve the Adverse Selection Problem in Elections

The validity of my theory ultimately rests on the claim that political elites (1) recognize that party brand names provide a solution to the adverse selection problem in elections and (2) understand that party unity in government contributes to establishing the credibility of their brand names as a signal of candidate quality. Chapter 6 reported the findings from case studies of three distinct historical eras that substantiate this claim. First, based on an examination of party formation during the American antebellum period, it was established that the newly emergent group of middle-class politicians in the United States formed political organizations with the institutional capacity to discipline group members because they needed a brand name to compete against social and economic elites. The first mass parties were therefore created with the express purpose of solving the adverse selection problem in elections. Second, it was shown that during the midterm elections of 1938, Franklin Roosevelt attempted to purge his party of its newly emergent group of conservative Southern Democrats partially out of concern that these individuals would jeopardize his party's ability to use its brand name to signal in the future that Democratic candidates were liberals. FDR backed down only after it became apparent that he needed to tolerate conservative Democrats in order for his party to retain majority status in Congress. Third, looking at the parties' campaign tactics over the past two decades, it was demonstrated that on both occasions when the ruling party was defeated in November, the minority party in Congress acted in the manner of a responsible opposition party (voting in a united front against the majority, issuing an election-year platform) with the intent of signaling to the public the policies its members who did not hold office at the time would pursue if they were elected. All three of the cases studies demonstrated a willingness on the part of party leaders to discipline organization members in order to develop and/or maintain a brand that they valued for electoral purposes.

SUBJECTS BRACKETED FOR PARSIMONY

One of the greatest strengths and greatest weaknesses of this book was its narrow focus on how Congressional parties in the United States maintain their brand names. The strength of this approach is that it allowed me to hone in with great precision on the question of how one set of actors governed by one set of institutions react to the possibility of partisan brand names. The weakness of adopting such a narrow focus is that it required bracketing a discussion of how interaction between parties in the House of Representatives and other facets of the American political system might affect the analysis. In closing this book, it is therefore worthwhile to take a step back and address how some of the features that have not been considered in detail – in particular the Senate and the Presidency – might affect its conclusions.

The Senate

The argument that a legislative party could develop a brand name that it uses as a signal could apply equally well to House and Senate elections, yet nary a word was said about the latter. There are several reasons for this, perhaps the most important of which is that the scholarly understanding of the role of parties in the organization of the Senate trails far beyond that of the House (Smith 2007). The crux of the problem is that the majority party in the Senate does not monopolize the legislative agenda in the same way it does in the House and rules and norms in the chamber emphasize universalism over partisanship. Therefore, although party affiliations do appear to exert a meaningful effect on members' voting behavior controlling for their ideological preferences (e.g., McCarty et al. 2001), and the majority party rarely gets "rolled" on final passage votes (Gailmard and Jenkins 2007) so it seems that the kind of negative agenda control that protects party brand names in the House also operates in the Senate, absent a better understanding of the procedures that Senate parties use to maintain their reputations I withhold judgment about the applicability of my theory to that chamber.[1]

One possible explanation for why the Senate appears to have weaker partisan institutions is that candidates for office in that chamber have

---

[1] I conjecture that the key institutional lever wielded by party leaders on Capitol Hill to regulate Senators' behavior is the threat by the House leadership to prevent measures from reaching a Conference Committee unless they have assurances from the Senate that their party will be satisfied with the final outcome.

stronger private brand names than House candidates. Incumbent members of the Senate, most of whom have had long careers on Capitol Hill, have noticeably higher public profiles and therefore stronger private brand names than rank-and-file members of the House (Jacobson 2004). This is also true of the overwhelming number of Senate challengers, the vast number of whom are quality candidates who have previously held elected office and therefore have the ability to compete on the basis of a hard-earned personal reputation (Squire 1992; Lublin 1994). To the extent that most Senate candidates (incumbents and challengers alike) compete on the basis of private brand names, it is harder to make a persuasive case that the maintenance of a shared party brand name motivates the partisan organization of the Senate.

If Senators are less concerned about maintaining their party's brand name than House members because it has less relevance to their career prospects, then it is possible that they might take actions that damage their party's brand name. In particular, if Senate Democrats (Republicans) were noticeably more (less) conservative than their House counterparts or had noticeably different party unity scores, then it is possible that the behavior of Senators would affect their party's reputation as being liberal or conservative or as being unified. Fortunately for the purposes of this book, previous analyses of roll-call behavior in the House and Senate find that this is not a serious concern for the period under investigation. Instead, it appears that the distribution of legislators' ideology (based on their roll-call votes) are similar across the two chambers when sorted by party and session of Congress (e.g., McCarty et al. 2005).

The Presidency

A potentially more troubling omission from this book was the limited attention given to the role of the presidency, which clearly complicates the discussion of party brand names. Most importantly, the President is widely perceived to be the head of her party and as such would seem to have an important influence on her party's reputation. After all, when thinking about a party's policy accomplishments at different moments in history, it is common to think in terms of the programs such as the Square Deal, the New Deal, or the Great Society that have been advanced by sitting Presidents. However, when thinking about the President's impact on her party's brand name, it is important to take into account a few factors which suggest that her effect on party brand names is endogenous to the decisions made by other members of her party.

First, when the President is first nominated to the post, she is chosen by her party to be its agent. Once in office, she may no longer think of herself as such, but her party placed her in a position of power (with the consent of the American people) because she demonstrated herself over the course of her political career to be a faithful supporter of the broad principles supported by her party. The lengthy process that American political parties undergo when nominating their candidates for the presidency can be usefully thought of as being designed to vet candidates to ensure that they have preferences closely aligned with the party faithful (so that the party does not need to impose a set of institutions to regulate the behavior of its President). As a result, it might look like the President has an important effect on her party's reputation, but that is only because the party placed her in a position of trust to act in its interest.

Second, the best way to think about the President's influence on her party's brand name may be in the role as her party's chief bargaining agent in negotiations with the legislature. Without intending to wade deeply into debates over legislative-executive relations (e.g., Cameron 2000; Groseclose and McCarty 2000), it is useful to accept that the President typically represents the public face of her party on matters of public policy; that she is able to marshal public support for initiatives favored by her legislative party when she is politically popular (making it harder for the other party to oppose the President), improving their prospects for passage; and that on issues where it believes it has a popular advantage, the opposition party has incentives to develop a coordinated "message strategy" along the lines described by Evans, Sellers, and others, to overcome the advantages attendant on the bully pulpit. By using the her office's high profile to her party's benefit, and by opening the doors to having the opposition party frame the debate on key issues in terms of being opposed to the President's policies, it is little wonder that we tend to think of the chief executive as having a disproportionate impact on her party's brand name.

Third, the key evidence in support of my interpretation of the role of the President is the observation that the influence she has on her party's reputation is ultimately conditional on the support of its members. In situations where the President pushes an issue agenda that is out of step with the broader set of principles receiving widespread support of her party, and her party's members refuse to support one of her programs, then the party will not be associated with being a supporter of her policy. One recent example of this phenomenon occurred when President Bush pushed for comprehensive immigration reform in 2007. In that year, the resistance of large numbers of Republicans in Congress doomed the plan, and it is quite clear that his party is not associated in the public's mind with a liberalization of immigration policy: if anything, the Republican Party is perceived by the American public as opposed to immigration policies that do not require the deportation of illegal immigrants (something Bush strongly opposed) and that do improve border security. Another example presented in Chapter 6 of this book was the case of Franklin Roosevelt and the newly emergent class of conservative Democrats in the late 1930s. In that chapter, it was shown that FDR attempted to purge his party of its conservative elements because he was concerned that the Democrats would not be able to take credit for the successes of the New Deal despite strong Presidential support for the program. Echoing my earlier comments about the Senate, however, any conclusions about the President's influence on the legislative parties' brand names can only be tentative for the time being because we do not know enough about how the national parties manage the relationship between the two branches of government.

IMPLICATIONS FOR COMPARATIVE THEORIES OF PARTY POLITICS

Perhaps the most interesting thing that I learned in writing this book was that classic party theorists believed that the institutions that party organizations choose to regulate member behavior was a function of whether party leaders had the constitutional power to dissolve the government and call an election (Schattschneider 1942; Wilson 1900). In cases where party leaders have this power, members of Parliament gladly cede the authority needed to discipline back-benchers out of fear that a handful of renegades might expose party loyalists to a new round of elections. (Notably, that threat is sufficient to hold together not just a single political party, but also multiparty coalitions.) Before reading Schattschneider and the rest, I had always taken for granted that the hierarchical control apparatus of a West European–style political party was a cause of party discipline in government, not a consequence of the fact that MPs live in terror that a party split will place their jobs in jeopardy.

This observation by the responsible-party theorists leaves unanswered the question as to what makes a party leader's threat to dissolve the government credible. Presumably, the leader of a ruling party would prefer to retain power as the head of a divided party than to dissolve the government, an action that would place her job and position of power in Parliament in jeopardy. Knowing this, party back-benchers should limit the ability of party leaders to impose discipline because they would not be concerned that a faction of recalcitrant MPs would expose all party members to a reelection campaign that placed their jobs at risk. Thus, without the threat to dissolve the government, the incentives to grant party leaders the ability to impose party discipline are very similar to those observed in the United States.

Although this book was intended to only explain how American political parties might encourage accountable governance through the development of brand names that comes close to those achievable in an idealized Westminster system, my theory also explains why party leaders' threat to dissolve the government in parliamentary systems is credible. The logic is as follows: Suppose that it is universally true that voters distrust politicians, that where possible politicians rely on party brand names to make their campaign promises credible, and that a parliamentary party with a history of maintaining party discipline develops such a brand name in precisely the manner described in this book. To the extent that this is true, a party values this brand name because it helps its candidates to win elections, thereby improving its prospects for becoming the ruling party. If the party leader fails to dissolve the government after a significant party fissure emerges, she could retain her position of power over the short term (assuming she is not unseated by her back-benchers); however, her failure to dissolve the government would seriously damage her party's ability to use its brand name to signal candidate quality. As a result, its long-term prospects for obtaining majority status are badly weakened. A ruling-party leader concerned about her party's long-term interests will therefore dissolve the government, and if she fails to act in this way, perhaps because she values her office in the short run, then it is in her party's interest to depose her as leader and replace her with someone who will act to the party's long-run benefit.

Thus, the reason that the threat to dissolve the government is credible stems from the fact that parliamentary parties have brand names they value that they are only able to maintain through party discipline in government. If a party fractures over key issues and the government is not dissolved so that the ruling party can slate a set of candidates who it believes will be loyal to the organization in the subsequent session of parliament, then its ability to use its brand name will be badly damaged.

References

Abramowitz, Alan and Kyle L. Saunders. 2006. "Exploring the Bases of Partisanship in the American Electorate: Social Identity vs. Ideology." *Political Research Quarterly* 59: 175–87.

Abramson, Paul. 1976. "Generational Change and the Decline of Party Identification in America: 1952–1974." *American Political Science Review* 70: 469–78.

Abramson, Paul. 1979. "Developing Party Identification: A Further Examination of Life-Cycle, Generational, and Period Effects." *American Journal of Political Science* 23: 78–96.

Achen, Christopher H. 1975. "Mass Political Attitudes and the Survey Response." *American Political Science Review* 69: 1218–31.

Achen, Christopher H. 1992. "Social Psychology, Demographic Variables, and Linear Regression: Breaking the Iron Triangle in Voting Research." *Political Behavior* 14: 195–211.

Achen, Christopher H. 2002. "Parental Socialization and Rational Party Identification." *Political Behavior* 24: 151–70.

Achen, Christopher. 2005. "Two-Step Hierarchical Estimation: Beyond Regression Analysis." *Political Analysis* 13: 447–56.

Adams, James, Samuel Merrill III, and Bernard Grofman. 2005. *A Unified Theory of Party Competition*. New York: Cambridge University Press.

Agranoff, Robert. 1976. *The Management of Electoral Campaigns*. Boston: Holbrook Press.

Akerlof, George. 1970. "The Market for 'Lemons': Quality Uncertainty and the Market Mechanism." *Quarterly Journal of Economics* 84: 488–500.

Aldrich, John H. 1995. *Why Parties?* Chicago: University of Chicago Press.

Aldrich, John and Jeffrey Grynaviski. ND. "Theories of Political Parties." *Forthcoming in the Oxford Handbook of Political Science*.

Aldrich, John and David Rohde. 1994. "Conditional Party Government Revisited: The House GOP and the Committee System in the 104th Congress, Extensions of Remarks." APSA Legislative Section Newsletter: 19: 5–7.

Aldrich, John and David Rohde. 1999. "The Consequences of Party Organization in the House: Theory and Evidence on Conditional Party Government." *Unpublished Manuscript*.

Alesina, Alberto. 1988. "Credibility and Policy Convergence in a Two-Party System with Rational Voters." *American Economic Review* 78: 796–806.

Alesina, Alberto and Stephen Spear. 1988. "An Overlapping Generations Model of Electoral Competition." *Journal of Public Economics* 37: 359–79.

Alvarez, Michael. 1998. *Information and Elections*. Ann Arbor: University of Michigan Press.

Alvarez, Michael and Charles Franklin. 1994. "Uncertainty and Political Perceptions." *Journal of Politics* 56: 671–88.

American Political Science Association. 1950. *Toward a More Responsible Party System, a Report*. New York: Rinehart.

Ansolabehere, Stephen and Phil Jones. 2007. "Constituents' Policy Perceptions and Approval of their Members of Congress." Paper presented at the Workshop in Political Economy at the University of Chicago.

Ansolabehere, Stephen, Jonathan Rodden and James M. Snyder, Jr. 2008. "The Strength of Issues: Using Multiple Measures to Gauge Preference Stability, Ideological Constraint, and Issue Voting." *American Political Science Review* 102: 215–32.

Ansolabehere, Stephen, James M. Snyder, Jr., and Charles Stewart III. 2001. "Candidate Positioning in U.S. House Elections." *American Journal of Political Science* 45: 136–59.

Aranson, Paul and Peter Ordeshook. 1972. "Spatial Strategies for Sequential Elections." In Richard Niemi and Herbert Weisberg, eds. *Probability Models of Collective Decision-Making*. Columbus, OH: Merrill.

Armey, Richard. 1995. *The Freedom Revolution*. Washington, DC: Regnery.

Arnold, Douglas. 1990. *The Logic of Congressional Action*. New Haven: Yale University Press.

Ashworth, Scott and Ethan Bueno de Mesquita. 2008. "Informative Party Labels with Institutional and Electoral Variation. *Journal of Theoretical Politics* 20: 251–73.

Axelrod, Robert. 1984. *The Evolution of Cooperation*. New York: Basic Books.

Bach, Stanley, and Steven S. Smith. 1988. *Managing Uncertainty in the House of Representatives*. Washington, DC: Brookings.

Baker, Jean. 1998. *Affairs of Party: The political culture of Northern Democrats in the mid-nineteenth century*. New York: Fordham University Press.

Balz, Dan and Ronald Brownstein. 1996. *Storming the Gates: Protest Politics and Republican Renewal*. New York: Little, Brown and Co.

Barro, Robert and Xavier Sala-I-Martin. 1991. "Convergence across States and Regions." *Brookings Papers on Economic Activity*, 107–92.

Bartels, Larry. 1996. "Uninformed Votes: Information Efects in Presidential Elections." *American Journal of Political Science* 40: 194–230.

Bartels, Larry. 2000. "Partisanship and Voting Behavior, 1952–1996." *American Journal of Political Science* 44: 35–50.

Bartels, Larry. 2001. "A Generational Model of Partisan Learning." *A paper presented at the American Political Science Association meetings*, San Francisco.

Bartels, Larry. 2002. "Beyond the Running Tally: Partisan Bias in Political Perceptions." *Political Behavior* 24: 117–50.

Baumer, Donald C. and Howard J. Gold. 1995. "Party Images and the American Electorate." *American Politics Quarterly* 23: 33–61.

Baumeister, R. F., Bratslavsky, E., Finkenauer, C., and Vohs, K. D. (2001). "Bad Is Stronger Than Good." *Review of General Psychology*, 5: 323–70.

Beck, Paul Allen and Kent Jennings. 1991. "Family Traditions, Political Periods, and the Development of Partisan Orientations." *Journal of Politics* 53: 742–63.

Becker, Carl. 1907. *The History of Political Parties in the Province of New York, 1760–1776.* Bulletin of the University of Washington History Series, Vol. 3: 1–290.

Bernhardt, Daniel and Daniel Ingberman. 1985. "Candidate Reputations and the Incumbency Effect." *Journal of Public Economics* 27: 47–67.

Besley, T. and S. Coate (1997). "An Economic Model of Representative Democracy." *Quarterly Journal of Economics* 112(1): 85–106.

Bianco, William. 1994. *Trust: Representatives and Constituents.* Ann Arbor: University of Michigan Press.

Black, Earl and Merle Black. 1987. *Politics and Society in the South.* Cambridge, MA: Harvard University Press.

Black, Earl and Merle Black. 1992. *The Vital South.* Cambridge, MA: Harvard University Press.

Black, Earl and Merle Black. 2002. *The Rise of Southern Republicans.* Cambridge, MA: Belknap Press.

Box-Steffensmeier, Janet, David Kimball, Scott Meinke, and Katherine Tate. 2003. "The Effects of Political Representation on the Electoral Advantages of House Incumbents." *Political Research Quarterly* 56: 259–70.

Brady, David, John Cogan, Brian Gaines, and Douglas Rivers. 1996. "The Perils of Presidential Support: How the Republicans took the House in the 1994 midterm elections." *Poitical Behavior* 18: 345–67.

Brady, David W., Joseph Cooper, and Patricia Hurley. 1979. "The Decline of Party Voting in the U.S. House of Representatives." *Legislative Studies Quarterly* 4: 381–407.

Brady, Henry and Jeremy Pope. 2002. "Down to the Wire." *Hoover Digest*, issue 4.

Burns, James MacGregor. 1949. *Congress on Trial: The Legislative Process and the Administrative State.* Harper.

Cain, Bruce, John Ferejohn, and Morris Fiorina. 1987. *The Personal Vote: Constituency Service and Electoral Independence.* Cambridge, MA: Harvard University Press.

Cameron, Charles. 2000. *Veto Bargaining: Presidents and the Politics of Negative Power.* New York: Cambridge University Press.

Campbell, Angus, Philip Converse, Warren Miller, and Donald Stokes. 1960. *The American Voter.* Chicago: University of Chicago Press.

Canes-Wrone, Brandice, David Brady, and John Cogan. 2002. "Out of Step, out of Office: Electoral Accountability and House Members' Voting." *American Political Science Review* 96: 127–40.

Carmines, Edward G. and James A. Stimson. 1989. *Issue Evolution: Race and the Transformation of American Politics.* Princeton, NJ: Princeton University Press.

References

Choi, Jay Pil. 1998. "Brand Extension as Information Leverage." *The Review of Economic Studies*, 655–69.

Claggett, William, William Flanigan, and Nancy Zingale. 1984. "Nationalization of the American Electorate." *American Political Science Review* 78: 77–91.

Claycamp, H. J. and L. E. Liddy. 1969. "Predictions of New Product Performance: An Analytical Approach. *Journal of Marketing Research* 6: 414–20.

Clinton, Josh, Simon Jackman, and Douglas Rivers. 2004. "The Most Liberal Senator? Analyzing and Interpreting Congressional Roll calls." *PS: Political Science and Politics* 37: 805–12.

Conover, Pamela. 1988. "The Role of Social Groups in Political Thinking." *British Journal of Political Science* 18: 51–76.

Conover, Pamela and Stanley Feldman. 1989. "Candidate Perceptions in an Ambiguous World." *American Journal of Political Science* 33: 912–40.

Converse, Philip. 1962. "Information Flow and the Stability of Partisan Attitudes." *Public Opinion Quarterly* 26: 578–99.

Converse, Philip. 1964. "The Nature of Belief Systems in Mass Publics." In David Aptrer, ed. *Ideology and Discontent*, pp. 219–41. New York: Free Press.

Converse, Philip. 1976. *The Dynamics of Party Support: Cohort Analyzing Party Identification*. Beverly Hills, CA: Sage.

Converse, Philip. 1979. "Rejoinder to Abramson." *American Journal of Political Science* 23: 97–100.

Converse, Philip and Gregory Markus. 1979. "Plus Ca Change: The New CPS Election Study Panel." *American Political Science Review* 73: 32–49.

Cooper, Joseph. 1999. *Congress and the Decline of Public Trust*. New York: Westview.

Cooper, Joseph and David W. Brady. 1981. "Institutional Context and Leadership Style: The House from Cannon to Rayburn." *American Political Science Review*: 411–25.

Cox, Gary and Jonathan Katz. 2002. *Elbridge Gerry's Salamander*. New York: Cambridge University Press.

Cox, Gary W. and Mathew W. McCubbins. 1993. *Legislative Leviathan: Party Government in the House*. Los Angeles: University of California Press.

Cox, Gary W. and Mathew W. McCubbins. 2005. *Setting the Agenda*. Cambridge University Press.

Cox, Gary and Keith Poole. 2002. "On Measuring Partisanship in Roll Call Voting: The U.S. House of Representatives, 1877–1999." *American Journal of Political Science* 46(3):477–89.

Davidson, Roger, Walter Oleszek, and Thomas Kephart. 1988. "One Bill, Multiple Committees: Multiple Referrals in the U.S. House of Representatives." *Legislative Studies Quarterly* 13: 3–28.

Davis, M. L. and Ferrantino M. 1996. "Towards a positive theory of political rhetoric: why do politicians lie?" *Public Choice* 88: 1–13.

Delli Karpini, Michael and Scott Keeter. 1996. *What Americans Know about Politics and Why It Matters*. Yale University Press.

de Marchi, Scott and Christopher Gelpi, and Jeffrey Grynaviski. 2004. "Untangling Neural Nets." *American Political Science Review* 98: 371–78.

References

Demsetz, Harold. 1990. "Amenity Potential, Indivisibilities, and Political Competition." In Kenneth Shepsle and James Alt eds. *Perspectives on Positive Political Economy*. Cambridge, UK: Cambridge University Press.

Desart, Jay. 1995. "Information Processing and Partisan Neutrality." *Journal of Politics* 57: 776–95.

Diermeier, Daniel and Timothy Feddersen. 1998. "Cohesion in Legislatures: The Vote of Confidence Procedure." *American Political Science Review* 92: 611–22.

DiMaggio, Paul, John Evans, and Bethany Bryson. 1996. "Have American's Social Attitudes Become More Polarized?" *American Journal of Sociology* 102: 690–755.

Downs, Anthony. 1957. *An Economic Theory of Democracy*. New York: Harper and Brothers.

Duverger, Maurice. 1954. *Political Parties: Their Organization and Activity in the Modern State*. New York: Wiley.

Easterlin, R. A. 1960. "Interregional Differences in Per-Capita Income, Population, and Total Income, 1840–1950." *Trends in the American Economy in the Nineteenth Century*. Princeton University Press.

Edsall, Thomas Byrne and Mary D. Edsall. 1991. *Chain Reaction*. New York: Norton.

Egan, Patrick. 2007. "Issue Ownership and Representation in the United States: A Theory of Legislative Response to Constituency Opinion." Working Paper.

Enelow, James and Melvin Hinich. 1981. "A New Approach to Voter Uncertainty in the Downsian Spatial Model." *American Journal of Political Science* 25: 483–93.

Enelow, James and Michael Munger. 1993. "The Elements of Candidate Reputation: The Effect of Record and crEdibility on Optimal Spatial Location." *Public Choice* 77: 757–72.

Erikson, Robert, Michael Mackuen, and James Stimson. 2002. *The Macro Polity*. Cambridge: Cambridge Univ. Press.

Erikson, Robert and Gerald Wright. 1997. "Voters, Candidates, and Issues in Congressional Elections." In Lawrence Dodd and Bruce Oppenheimer eds. *Congress Reconsidered*, 6th ed. Washington, DC: CQ Press.

Erikson, Robert and Gerald Wright. 2000. "Voters, Candidates, and Issues in Congressional Elections." In David Brad, John Cogan, and John Ferejohn, eds. *Change and Continuity in Hose Elections*. Stanford: Stanford University Press.

Erikson, Robert, Gerald Wright, and John McIver. 1993. *Statehouse Democracy: Public Opinion and Policy in the American States*. Cambridge, MA: Cambridge University Press.

Evans, Lawrence. 2001. "Committees, Leaders, and Message Politics." In Lawrence Dodd and Bruce Oppenheimer, eds. *Congress Reconsidered*, 6th ed. Washington, DC: Congressional Quarterly Press.

Feldman, Stanley and Pamela Conover. 1983. "Candidates, Issues, and Voters." *Journal of Politics* 45: 810–39.

Fenno, Richard. 1978. *Home Style: House Members in Their Districts*. Harper Collins Publishers.

References

Ferejohn, John, Richard McKelvey, and Edward Packel. 1984. "Limiting Distributions for Continuous State Markov Models." *Social Choice and Welfare* 1: 45–68.

Fiorina, Morris. 1981. *Retrospective Voting in American National Elections.* New Haven, CT: Yale University Press.

Fiorina, Morris. 2006. *Culture War? The Myth of a Polarized America.* New York: Pearson-Longman.

Fishel, Jeff. 1985. *Presidents and Promises: From Campaign Pledge to Presidential Performance.* Washington, DC: Congressional Quarterly Press.

Fiske, Susan T. and Shelley E. Taylor. 1991. *Social Cognition,* 2nd edition. New York: McGraw-Hill.

Frank, Thomas. 2004. *What's the Matter with Kansas.* New York: Metropolitan Books.

Franklin, Charles. 1984. "Issue Preferences, Socialization, and the Evolution of Party Identification." *American Journal of Political Science* 28: 459–78.

Franklin, Charles and John Jackson. 1983. "The Dynamics of Party Identification." *American Political Science Review* 77: 957–73.

Gailmard, Sean and Jeffery Jenkins. 2007. "Negative Agenda Control in the Senate and House: Fingerprints of Majority Party. *Journal of Politics* 69: 689–700.

Gelman, Andrew, John Carlin, Hal Stern, and Donald Rubin. 1995. *Bayesian Data Analysis.* New York: Chapman and Hall.

Gelman, Andrew and Gary King. 1990. "Estimating Incumbency Advantage without Bias." *American Journal of Political Science* 34: 1142–64.

Gerber, Alan and Donald Green. 1999. "Misperceptions about Perceptual Bias." *Annual Review of Political Science* 2: 189–210.

Gerber, Alan and Donald P. Green. 1998. "Rational Learning and Partisan Attitudes," *American Journal of Political Science* 42: 794–818.

Gerring, John. 1998. *Party Ideologies in America, 1828–1996.* Cambridge, MA: Cambridge University Press.

Gimpel, James G. 1996. *Legislative the Revolution: The Contract with America in Its First 100 Days.* Boston: Allyn and Bacon.

Gingrich, Newt. 1998. *Lessons Learned the Hard Way.* HarperCollins.

Goodman, Paul. 1967. "The First American Party System" in Chambers and Burnham eds. *The American Party Systems: Stages of Development.*

Green, Donald. 1988. "On the Dimensionality of Public Sentiment toward Partisan and Ideological Groups." *American Journal of Political Science* 32: 758–80.

Green, Donald and Bradley Palmquist. 1990. "Of Artifacts and Partisan Stability." *American Journal of Political Science* 34: 872–902.

Green, Donald, Bradley Palmquist, and Eric Schickler. 2002. *Partisan Hearts and Minds.* New Haven, CT: Yale University Press.

Green, Donald and Eric Shickler. 1993. "A Multiple Method Approach to the Measurement of Party Identification." *Public Opinion Quarterly* 57: 503–35.

Green, Donald and David Yoon. 2002. "Reconciling Individual and Aggregate Evidence Concerning Partisan Stability." *Political Analysis* 10: 1–24.

References

Grofman, Bernard. 2004. "Downs and Two-Party Convergence." *Annual Review of Political Science* 7: 25–46.

Grofman, Bernard, Samuel Merrill, Thomas Brunell and William Koetzle. 1999. "The Potential Electoral Disadvantages of a Catch-All Party." *Party Politics* 5: 199–210.

Grynaviski, Jeffrey. 2006. "A Bayesian Learning Model with Implications for Party Identification." *Journal of Theoretical Politics.*

Grynaviski, Jeffrey and Bryce Corrigan. 2006. "Specification Issues in Proximity Models of Candidate Evaluation (with Issue Importance). *Political Analysis* 14: 393–420.

Grynaviski, Jeffrey. and Shang Ha. 2003. "Party Polarization and Party Activists." *Unpublished Manuscript.*

Grynaviski, Jeffrey and Melissa Harris-Lacewell. 2004. "Shifting Allegiances? Are Black Voters Ready to Rethink Allegiance to the Democratic Party?" *Paper presented at the American Political Science Association meetings.*

Hamill, Ruth, Milt Lodge, and Frederick Blake. 1985. "The Breadth, Depth, and Utility of Class, Partisan, and Ideological Schemata." *American Journal of Political Science* 29: 850–70.

Harrington, Joseph Jr. 1992. "The Role of Party Reputation in the Formation of Policy." *Journal of Public Economics* 49: 107–21.

Harris, Douglas. 2006. "Legislative Parties and Leadership Choice: Confrontation or Accommodation in the 1989 Gingrich-Madigan Whip Race." *American Politics Research* 34: 189–221.

Hayes, Danny. 2005. "Candidate Qualities through a Partisan Lens: A Theory of Trait Ownership." *American Journal of Political Science* 49: 908–23.

Herrnson, Paul. 1988. *Party Campaigning in the 1980s.* Cambridge, MA: Harvard University Press, 1988.

Herrnson, Paul. 2004. *Congressional Elections: Campaigning at Home and in Washington*, 4th edition. Washington, DC: CQ Press.

Hetherington, Marc. 2001. "Resurgent Mass Partisanship: The Role of Elite Polarization." *American Political Science Review* 95: 619–32.

Hinich, Melvin H., John Ledyard, and Peter Ordeshook. 1972. "Nonvoting and Existence of Equilibrium under Majority Rule." *Journal of Economic Theory* 4: 144–53.

Hinich, Melvin H. and Michael C. Munger. 1997. *Analytical Politics.* Cambridge: Cambridge University Press.

Hinich, Melvin H. and Peter Ordeshook. 1969. "Abstentions and Equilibrium in the Electoral Process." *Public Choice* 7: 81–106.

Hofstadter, Richard. 1969. *The Idea of a Party System.* Berkeley: University of California Press.

Hong, Sung-Tai and Robert Wyer Jr. 1989. "Effects of Country-of-Origin and Product-Attribute Information: An Information Processing Perspective." *Journal of Consumer Research* 16: 175–87.

Huber, John. 1996. "The Vote of Confidence in Parliamentary Democracies." *American Political Science Review* 45: 780–98.

Huckfeldt, Robert, Jeffrey Levine, and William Morgan, and John Sprague. 1999. "Accessibility and the Utility of Partisan and Ideological Orientations." *American Journal of Political Science* 3: 888–911.

Issacharoff, Samuel and Richard H. Pildes. 1998. "Politics as Markets: Partisan Lockups of the Democratic Process." *Stanford Law Review.*

Jackson, John E. 1975. "Issues, Party Choices, and Presidential Votes." *American Journal of Political Science* 19: 161–85.

Jackson, John E. 1983. "The Systematic Beliefs of the Mass Public: Estimating Policy Preferences with Survey Data." *Journal of Politics* 45: 840–65.

Jacobson, Gary. 1996. "The 1994 House Elections in Perspective." *Political Science Quarterly* 111: 203–23.

Jacobson, Gary. 2004. The Politics of Congressional Elections. 6th ed. New York: Longman.

Jennings, Kent and Gregory Markus. 1984. "Partisan Orientations over the Long Haul: Results from the Three-Wave Political Socialization Panel Study." *American Political Science Review* 68: 1000–18.

Jennings, Kent and Richard Niemi. 1978. "The Persistence of Political Orientations: An Over-Time Analysis of Two Generations." *British Journal of Political Science* 8: 333–63.

Jennings, Kent and Richard Niemi. 1981. *Generations and Politics: A Panel Study of Young Adults and Their Parents.* Princeton, NJ: Princeton University Press.

Kahneman, Daniel and Amos Tversky. 1979. "Prospect Theory: An Analysis of Decision under Risk." *Econometrica* 47: 263–92.

Keefer, Philip. 2007. "Clientelism, Credibility, and the Policy Choices of Young Democracies." *American Journal of Political Science* 51: 804–21.

Keith, Bruce, David Magleby, Candice Nelson, Elizabeth Orr, Mark Westlye, and Raymond Wolfinger. 1992. *The Myth of the Independent Voter.* Berkeley, CA: University of California Press.

Keller, Kevin Lane. 2001. *Strategic Brand Management*, 2nd ed. Upper Saddle River, NJ: Prentice Hall.

Key, V. O. 1949. *Southern Politics in State and Nation.* Knoxville: The University of Tennessee Press.

Key, V. O. 1966. *The Responsible Electorate: Rationality in Presidential Voting, 1936–1960.* Cambridge, MA: Harvard University Press.

Kiewiet, D. Roderick and Mathew McCubbins. 1991. *The Logic of Delegation: Congressional Delegation and the Appropriations Process.* Chicago: University of Chicago Press.

Kingdon, John. 1981. *Congressmen's Voting Decisions.* New York: Harper & Row.

Klein, Benjamin and Keith Leffler. 1981. "The Role of Market Forces in Assuring Contractual Performance." *Journal of Political Economy* 89: 615–41.

Koch, Jeffrey. 1994. "Group Identification in Political Context." *Political Psychology* 15: 687–98.

Kolodny, Robin. 1999. *Pursuing Majorities.* Norman: University of Oklahoma Press.

Krehbiel, Keith. 1993. "Where's the Party?" *British Journal of Political Science* 23: 235–66.

Krehbiel, Keith. 1998. *Pivotal Politics: A Theory of U.S. Lawmaking*. Chicago: University of Chicago Press.

Kreps, David. and Robert Wilson. 1982. "Reputation and Imperfect Information." *Journal of Economic Theory* 27: 253–79.

Krosnick, Jon and Matthew Berent. 1993. "Comparisons of Party Identification and Policy Preferences: The Impact of Survey Question Format." *American Journal of Political Science* 37: 941–64.

Ladd, Carll. 1990. "Public Opinion and the Congress Problem." *Public Interest* 100: 57.

Lau, Richard and David P. Redlawsk. 2001. "Advantages and Disadvantages of Cognitive Heuristics in Political Decision Making." *American Journal of Political Science* 45(October): 951–71.

Laymon, Geoffrey and Thomas Carsey. 2002. "Party Polarization and Conflict Extension in the American Electorate." *American Journal of Political Science* 46: 786–802.

Levermore, Charles. 1896. "The Whigs of Colonial New York." *The American Historical Review* 1: 238–50.

Levy, Gilat. 2004. "A Model of Political Parties." *Journal of Economic Theory* 155: 250–77.

Leyden, Kevin and Stephen Borrelli. 1994. "An Investment in Goodwill: Party Contribution and Party Unity Among U.S. House Members in the 1980s." *American Politics Research* 22: 421–52.

Lipinski, Daniel. 2004. *Congressional Communication: Content and Consequences*. Ann Arbor: University of Michigan Press.

Lodge, Milton and Ruth Hamill. 1986. "A Partisan Schema for Political Information Processing." *American Political Science Review* 90: 505–20.

Lott, John R., Jr. 1987. "The Effect of Nontransferable Property Rights on the Efficiency of Political Markets: Some Evidence." *Journal of Public Economics* 32: 231–46.

Lowell, Lawrence. 1913. *Public Opinion and Popular Government*. London: Longmans, Green, and Co.

Lublin, David. 1994. "Quality, Not Quantity: Strategic Politicians in U.S. Senate Elections, 1952–1990." *Journal of Politics* 56: 228–41.

Lupia, Arthur and Matthew McCubbins. 1998. *The Democratic Dilemma*. Cambridge, UK: Cambridge University Press.

Mann, Thomas. 1978. *Unsafe at Any Margin: Interpreting Congressional Elections*. Washington, DC: American Enterprise Institute.

Markus, Gregory. 1983. "Dynamic Modeling of Cohort Change: The Case of Political Partisanship." *American Journal of Political Science* 27: 717–39.

Markus, Gregory and Philip Converse. 1979. "A Dynamic Simultaneous Equation Model of Electoral Choice." *American Political Science Review* 73: 105570.

Masters, Nicholas. 1961. "Committee Assignments in the House of Representatives." *American Political Science Review* 55: 345–57.

Mayhew, David. 1974a. *Congress: The Electoral Connection*. New Haven, CT: Yale University Press.

Mayhew, David. 1974b. "Congressional Elections: The Case of the Vanishing Marginals." *Polity* 6: 295–317.

References

McCarty, Nolan and Timothy Groseclose. 2000. "The Politics of Blame: Bargaining Before an Audience." *American Journal of Political Science* 45: 100–19.

McCarty, Nolan, Keith Poole, and Howard Rosenthal. 2001. "The Hunt for Party Discipline." *American Political Science Review* 95: 673–87.

McCarty, Nolan, Keith Poole, and Howard Rosenthal. 2005. *Polarized America: The Dance of Ideology and Unequal Riches*. Boston: MIT Press.

McCormick, Richard. 1966. *The Second American Party System: Party Formation in the Jacksonian Era*. Chapel Hill: The University of North Carolina Press.

McDermott, Monika L. 1997. "Voting Cues in Low-Information Elections: Candidate Gender as a Social Information Variable in Contemporary United States Elections." *American Journal of Political Science* 41: 270–83.

McKenna, Marian C. 2002. *Franklin Roosevelt and the Great Constitutional War*. New York: Fordham University Press.

McKelvey Richard. 1976. "Intransitivities in multidimensional voting models and some implications for agenda control." *Journal of Economic Theory* 12: 472–82.

McKelvey, Richard. 1979. "General conditions for global intransitivities in formal voting models." *Econometrica* 47: 1085–112.

McKelvey, Richard. 1986. "Covering, dominance, and institution-free properties of social choice." *American Journal of Political Science* 30: 283–315.

Merrill, Samuel, Bernard Grofman, Thomas Brunell, and William Koetzle. 2000. "The Power of Ideologically Concentrated Minorities." *Journal of Theoretical Politics* 11: 57–74.

Milgrom, Paul and John Roberts. 1986. "Price and Advertising Signals of Product Quality." *Journal of Political Economy* 94: 796–821.

Milkis, Sidney. 1985. "Franklin D. Roosevelt and the Transcendence of Partisan Politics." *Political Science Quarterly* 100: 479–504.

Milkis, Sidney. 1999. *Political Parties and Constitutional Government*. Baltimore: Johns Hopkins University Press.

Miller, Arthur H. et al. 1981. "Group Consciousness and Political Participation." *American Journal of Political Science*. 25:491–511.

Miller, Arthur H., Christopher Wlezien, and Ann Hildreth. 1991. "A Reference Group Theory of Partisan Coalitions." *Journal of Politics* 53: 1134–49.

Miller, Warren and Merrill Shanks. 1996. *The New American Voter*. Cambridge, MA: Harvard University Press.

Miller, Warren and Donald Stokes. 1963. "Constituency Inflence in Congress." *American Political Science Review* 57: 45–57.

Mondak, Jeffery and Mary Anderson. 2004. "The Knowledge Gap: A Reexamination of Gender-Based Differences in Political Knowledge." *Journal of Politics* 66: 492–512.

Nelson, Philip. 1970. "Information and Consumer Behavior." *Journal of Political Economy* 78: 311–29.

Nelson, Phillip. 1974. "Advertising as Information." *Journal of Political Economy* 82: 729–54.

Nie, Norman, Sidney Verba, and John Petrocik. 1979. *The Changing American Voter*. Cambridge, MA: Harvard University Press.

Niemi, Richard and Kent Jennings. 1991. "Issues and Inheritance in the Formation of Party Identification." *American Journal of Political Science* 35: 970–88.

Niven, John. 1983. *Martin van Buren: The Romantic Age of American Politics.* New York: Oxford University Press.

Nokken, Timothy. 2000. "Dynamics of Congressional Loyalty: Party Defection and Roll-Call Behavior, 1947–97." *Legislative Studies Quarterly* 25: 417–44.

Nokken, Timothy and Keith Poole. 2004. "Congressional Party Defection in American History." *Legislative Studies Quarterly* 29: 545–68.

Osborne, M. J. and A. Slivinski (1996). "A Model of Competition with Citizen Candidates." *Quarterly Journal of Economics* 111(1): 65–96.

Osborne, M.J. and Rabee Tourky. 2007. "Party formation in single-issue elections." Working Paper.

Page, Benjamin. 1976. "The Theory of Political Ambiguity." *American Political Science Review* 70: 742–52.

Page, Benjamin and Jones. 1979. "Reciprocal Effects of Policy Preferences, Party Loyalties, and the Vote." *American Political Science Review* 73: 1071–90.

Palfrey, Thomas. 1984. "Spatial Equilibrium with Entry." *The Review of Economic Studies* 51: 139–56.

Palmer, Matthew. 1995. "Toward an Economics of Comparative Political Organization: Examining Ministerial Responsibility." *Journal of Law, Economics and Organization* 11: 167–91.

Patterson, James. 1967. *Congressional Conservatism and the New Deal: The Growth of the Conservative Coalition in Congress, 1933–1939.* University of Kentucky Press.

Petrocik, John. 1989. "The Theory of Issue Ownership." *Paper presented at the 1989 American Political Science Association Meetings.*

Phillips, Cabell. 2000. *From the Crash to the Blitz.* New York: Fordham University Press

Polenberg, Richard. 2000. *The Era of Franklin D. Roosevelt 1933–1945.* Macmillan.

Pomper, Gerald. 1972. "From Confusion to Clarity: Issues and American Voters, 1956–1968." *American Political Science Review* 66: 415–28.

Pomper, Gerald and Marc Weiner. 2002. "Toward a More Responsible Two-Party Voter: The Evolving Bases of Partisanship." In John Green and Paul Herrnson eds. *Responsible Partisanship: The Evolution of American Political Parties since 1950.* University of Kansas Press.

Poole, Keith. 1998. "Recovering a Basic Space from a Set of Issue Scales." *American Journal of Political Science* 42: 954–93.

Poole, Keith. 2005. "The Decline and Rise of Party Polarization in Congress During the Twentieth Century." *Extensions*, Fall.

Poole, Keith T. and Howard Rosenthal. 1991. "Patterns of Congressional Voting." *American Journal of Political Science* 35: 228–78.

Poole, Keith and Howard Rosenthal. 1997. *Congress: A Political-Economic History of Roll Call Voting.* New York: Oxford University Press.

Pope, Jeremy and Jonathan Woon. 2008. "Made in Congress? Testing the Electoral Implications of Party Ideological Brand Names." *Journal of Politics,* 823–36.

Popkin, Samuel L. 1994. *The Reasoning Voter: Communication and Persuasion in Presidential Campaigns.* Chicago: University of Chicago Press.

Prendergast, William B. 1999. *The Catholic Voter in American Politics.* Washington, DC: Georgetown University Press.

Price, Charles and Joseph Boskin. 1966. "The Roosevelt 'Purge': A Reappraisal." *Journal of Politics* 28: 660–70.

Rae, Nicol C. 1998. *Conservative Reformers: The Republican Freshmen and the Lessons of the 104th Congress.* New York: M. E. Sharpe.

Rahn, Wendy M. 1993. "The Role of Partisan Stereotypes in Information Processing about Political Candidates." *American Journal of Political Science* 37: 472–96.

Ranney, Austin. 1954. *The Doctrine of Responsible Party Government.* Urbana: University of Illinois Press.

Reeves, Keith. 1997. *Voting Hopes or Fears?* New York: Oxford University Press.

Remini, Robert. 1959. *Martin van Buren and the Democratic Party.* New York: Columbia University Press.

Ringquist, Evan and Carl Dasse. 2004. "Lies, Damned Lies, and Campaign Promises?" *Social Science Quarterly* 85: 400–19.

Ringquist, Evan and Milena Neshkova. 2006. "Campaign Promises and Environmental Policy Choices in the U.S. Senate." *Paper presented at the April, 2006, Midwest Political Science Association Meetings.*

Roberts, Jason and Steven Smith. 2003. "Procedural Contexts, Party Strategy, and Conditional Party Voting in the U.S. House of Representatives, 1971–2000." *American Journal of Political Science* 47: 305–17.

Roemer, John. 2001. *Political Competition.* Cambridge, MA: Harvard University Press.

Rohde, David. 1991. *Parties and Leaders in the Postreform House.* Chicago: University of Chicago Press.

Rohde, David and Kenneth Shepsle. 1973. "Democratic Committee Assignments in the House of Representatives: Strategic Aspects of a Social Choice Process." *American Political Science Review* 67: 889–905.

Rusk, Jerrold. 1970. "The Effect of the Australian Ballot Reform on Split Ticket Voting: 1876–1908." *American Political Science Review* 1220–38.

Sanders, Arthur. 1988. "The Meaning of Party Images." *Western Political Quarterly* 41: 583–99.

Schattschneider, E. E. 1942. *Party Government.* New York: Farrar and Rinehart, Inc.

Schickler, Eric and Donald Green. 1995. "Issue Preferences and the Dynamics of Party Identification." In John Freeman ed. *Political Analysis*, Vol. 5. Ann Arbor: University of Michigan Press.

Schofield, Norman. 1978. "Instability of Simple Dynamic Games." *Review of Economic Studies* 45: 575–94.

Schofield, Norman. 1983. "Generic Instability of Majority Rule." *Review of Economic Studies* 50: 695–704.

Schofield, Norman. 1985. *Social Choice and Democracy.* Springer, Berlin.

Schwartz, Thomas. 1977. "Collective Choice, Separation of Issues, and Vote Trading." *American Political Science Review* 71: 999–1010.

Sellers, Patrick. 2000. "Manipulating the Message in the U.S. Congress." *Harvard International Journal of Press/Politics.* 5: 22–31.

Shafer, Byron and Richard Johnston. 2006. *The End of Southern Exceptionalism.* Cambridge, MA: Harvard University Press.

Shannon, J. B. 1939. "Presidential Politics in the South: 1938, I." *Journal of Politics* 1: 146–70.

Shapiro, Carl. 1983. "Premiums for High Quality Products as Returns to Reputations." *Quarterly Journal of Economics* 9: 659–79.

Shepsle, Kenneth. 1979. "Institutional Arrangements and Equilibrium in Multidimensional Voting Models." *American Journal of Political Science* 23: 27–59.

Shepsle, Kenneth. 1987. "The Institutional Foundations of Committee Power." *American Political Science Review* 81: 85–104.

Silbey, Joel. 1967. *The Shrine of Party: Congressional Voting Behavior, 1841–1852.* Pittsburgh: University of Pittsburgh Press.

Sinclair, Barbara. 1999. "Transformation Agent or Faithful Leader? Principal-Agent Theory and House Majority Party Leadership." *Legislative Studies Quarterly* 24: 421–49.

Sinclair, Barbara. 2006. *Party Wars.* Norman: University of Oklahoma Press.

Smith, Steven and Bruce Ray. 1983. "The Impact of Congressional Reform: House Democratic Committee Assignments. *Congress and the Presidency* 10: 219–40.

Smith, Steven. 2007. *Party Influence in Congress.* New York: Cambridge University Press.

Snyder, James and Tim Groseclose. 2000. "Estimating Party Influence in Congressional Roll-Call Voting." *American Journal of Political Science* 44: 193–211.

Snyder, James and Tim Groseclose. 2001. "Estimating Party Influence on Congressional Roll Call Voting: Regression Coefficients vs. Classification Success." *American Political Science Review* 95: 689–98.

Snyder, James M. and Michael Ting. 2002. "An Informational Rationale for Political Parties." *American Journal of Political Science* 46: 90–110.

Snyder, James and Michael Ting. 2003. "Roll Calls, Party Labels, and Elections." *Political Analysis* 11: 419–44.

Squire, Peverill. 1992. "Challenger Quality and Voting Behavior in U.S. Senate Elections." *Legislative Studies Quarterly* 17: 247–64.

Steely, Mel. 2000. *The Gentleman from Georgia: The Biography of Newt Gingrich.* Macon, GA: Mercer University Press.

Stokes, Donald. 1965. "A Variance Components Model of Political Effects." In John Claunch ed. *Mathematical Applications in Political Science.* Dallas: Southern Methodist University Press.

Stokes, Donald and Warren Miller. 1962. "Party Government and the Salience of Congress." *The Public Opinion Quarterly* 26: 159–71.

Tirole, Jean. 1996. "A Theory of Collective Reputations, with Applications to the Persistence of Corruption and to Firm Quality." *Review of Economic Studies* 63: 1–22.

Trilling, Richard. 1976. *Party Image and Electoral Behavior.* New York: Wiley.

Tufte, Edward. 1978. *Political Control of the Economy.* Princeton, NJ: Princeton University Press.

Tversky, Amos and Daniel Kahneman. 1974. "Judgment under Uncertainty: Heuristics and Biases." *Science* 185: 1124–31.

Tversky, Amos and Daniel Kahneman. 1983. "Extensional versus Intuitive Reasoning: The Conjunction Fallacy in Probability Judgment." *Psychological Review* 90: 293–315.

Wallace, Michael. 1969. "Changing Concepts of Party in the United States: New York, 1815–1828." *American Historical Review* 74: 453–91.

Wattenberg, Martin. 1981. "The Decline of American Party Politics: Negativity or Neutrality?" *American Political Science Review* 75: 941–50.

Wattenberg, Martin P. 1982. "From Parties to Candidates: Examining the Role of the Media." *Public Opinion Quarterly* 46: 216–27.

Wattenberg, Martin P. 1991. *The Rise of Candidate-Centered Politics: Presidential Elections of the 1980s*. Cambridge: Harvard University Press.

Wattenberg, Martin P. 1994. *The Decline of American Political Parties 1952–1992*. Cambridge, MA: Harvard University Press.

Weiher, Kenneth. 1977. "The Cotton Industry and Southern Industrialization, 1880–1930." *Explorations in Economic History* 14: 120–40.

Weisberg, Herbert. 2002. "The Party in the Electorate as a Basis for More Responsible Parties." In John Green and Paul Herrnson eds. *Responsible Partisanship: The Evolution of American Political Parties since 1950*. University of Kansas Press.

Weisberg, Herbert. 1980. "A Multidimensional Conceptualization of Party Identification." *Political Behavior* 2: 33–60.

Wernerfelt, Birger. 1988. "Umbrella Branding as a Signal of New Product Quality: An Example of Signaling by Posting a Bond." *RAND Journal of Economics* 19: 458–66.

Wilson, Woodrow. 1900. [2002]. *Congressional Government*, 15th ed. New Brunswick, NJ: Transaction Publishers. Originally published by Houghton-Mifflin.

Wittman, Donald. 1983. "Candidate Motivation: A Synthesis of Alternative Theories." *American Political Science Review* 77: 142–57.

Wolinsky, Asher. 1983. "Prices as Signals of Product Quality." *The Review of Economic Studies* 50: 647–58.

Woodward, C. Vann. 1974. *The Strange Career of Jim Crow*. New York: Oxford University Press.

Wright, Gavin. 1986. "Old South, New South: Revolutions in the Southern Economy since the Civil War." Baton Rouge: Louisiana State University Press.

Zaller, John. 1992. *The Nature and Origins of Mass Opinion*. New York: Cambridge University Press.

Index

abortion, 85, 115, 124, 183, 185
Abramowitz, Alan, 100
Abramson, Paul, 131
Achen, Christopher H., 10, 61–68, 83, 96, 112
Adams, Alva B., 194
Adams, John Quincy, 174–175
adverse selection problem, 7, 25, 27, 32, 38, 206, 217
  welfare implications, 28
African-Americans, as evidence for unstable party attachments, 85–87, 97
  See also perceptions of party differences, Southern realignment
agency relationships
  party leaders as agents of caucus, 142, 148–150
agenda control. See negative agenda control, positive agenda control
Agricultural Committee, 199
Aldrich, John H., 2, 6, 7, 15, 28, 58, 166, 167, 188
Alesina, Alberto, 26
Alvarez, R. Michael, 102
ambition. See political ambition
American National Election Studies, 54, 77, 102–104
Ansolabehere, Stephen, 24, 96, 138, 139
antebellum period, 169, 174, 217
Appropriations Committee, 45
Armey, Richard, 179, 183
Arnold, Douglas, 26
Ashworth, Scott, 2
assignments. See committee assignments

Bach, Stanley, 143
balanced-budget amendment, 183–184
Balz, Dan, 182, 183
Barkley, Alben, 195, 198
Barro, Robert, 190
Bartels, Larry, 4, 52, 67, 114, 164
Baumeister, R.F., 109
Bayesian learning model, 64–76
  about the mean, 66–68
  about the variance, 68–70
  and party unity, 79–80
  empirical expectations, 76
  rate of learning, 67, 68–69
Beck, Paul Allen, 99
Becker, Carl, 169
Berent, Matthew, 96
Black, Earl, 97
Black, Merle, 97
Borelli, Stephen, 46
Box-Steffensmeier, Janet, 158, 159, 162
Brady, David W., 204
Brady, Henry, 178
brand names
  candidate brand names, 134–139, 215
  party brand names, 51, 134–139, 156, 168–169, 175–177, 213
  social psychological models of, 3–4
Brown, Edgar A., 201
Brownstein, Ronald, 182, 183
Bucktail Party, 169, 172–175, 206
Budget Committee, 45
Bueno de Mesquita, Ethan, 2
Burns, James MacGregor, 2

Other Books in the Series (*continued from page iii*)

Gary W. Cox and Jonathan N. Katz, *Elbridge Gerry's Salamander:
The Electoral Consequences of the Reapportionment Revolution*
Raymond M. Duch and Randolph T. Stevenson, *The Economic Vote: How
Political and Economic Institutions Condition Election Results*
Jean Ensminger, *Making a Market: The Institutional Transformation of an
African Society*
David Epstein and Sharyn O'Halloran, *Delegating Powers: A Transaction Cost
Politics Approach to Policy Making under Separate Powers*
Kathryn Firmin-Sellers, *The Transformation of Property Rights in the Gold
Coast: An Empirical Study Applying Rational Choice Theory*
Clark C. Gibson, *Politicians and Poachers: The Political Economy of Wildlife
Policy in Africa*
Avner Greif, *Institutions and the Path to the Modern Economy: Lessons from
Medieval Trade*
Stephen Haber, Armando Razo, and Noel Maurer, *The Politics of Property
Rights: Political Instability, Credible Commitments, and Economic Growth in
Mexico, 1876–1929*
Ron Harris, *Industrializing English Law: Entrepreneurship and Business
Organization, 1720–1844*
Anna L. Harvey, *Votes Without Leverage: Women in American Electoral
Politics, 1920–1970*
Murray Horn, *The Political Economy of Public Administration: Institutional
Choice in the Public Sector*
John D. Huber, *Rationalizing Parliament: Legislative Institutions and Party
Politics in France*
John E. Jackson, Jacek Klich, and Krystyna Poznanska, *The Political Economy
of Poland's Transition: New Firms and Reform Governments*
Jack Knight, *Institutions and Social Conflict*
Michael Laver and Kenneth Shepsle, eds., *Cabinet Ministers and Parliamentary
Government*
Michael Laver and Kenneth Shepsle, eds., *Making and Breaking Governments:
Cabinets and Legislatures in Parliamentary Democracies*
Margaret Levi, *Consent, Dissent, and Patriotism*
Brian Levy and Pablo T. Spiller, eds., *Regulations, Institutions, and
Commitment: Comparative Studies of Telecommunications*
Leif Lewin, *Ideology and Strategy: A Century of Swedish Politics*,
English edition
Gary Libecap, *Contracting for Property Rights*
John Londregan, *Legislative Institutions and Ideology in Chile*
Arthur Lupia and Mathew D. McCubbins, *The Democratic Dilemma:
Can Citizens Learn What They Need to Know?*
C. Mantzavinos, *Individuals, Institutions, and Markets*

For EU product safety concerns, contact us at Calle de José Abascal, 56–1°,
28003 Madrid, Spain or eugpsr@cambridge.org.

www.ingramcontent.com/pod-product-compliance
Ingram Content Group UK Ltd.
Pitfield, Milton Keynes, MK11 3LW, UK
UKHW010038140625
459647UK00012BA/1472